Object Lesson

I0709735

ON THE
INFLUENCE OF

Richard Benson

Table of Contents

Contributions

Preface

The many eminent contributors included in this book speak to the
lasting influence of Richard Benson—also known familiarly as "Chip."
They have added their recollections of him via written anecdotes
but also, critically, through a selection of concrete visual works. These
selections most often reference specific moments of mentorship,
encouragement, and teaching—they are a distillation of lessons learned
in image and text. The writings that accompany the visual works are
at turns funny and irreverent, serious and thoughtful. Together they
assemble a vivid sense of Benson as teacher and artist and of the
importance of his family, most notably his wife Barbara Benson, in his
guidance of young artists.

These anecdotal contributions can also be seen as an informal
mapping of a singular tributary within the larger story of American
photography. This history is written via the transmission of images into
the future—either as physical prints or through their reproduction in
books, magazines, and other printed matter. Even as the tools of
making change, and the history of the medium itself continues to
expand and make room for the recovery of stories passed over in their
own time, it is thanks to the lasting record of physical objects, or
reproductions of those objects, that we can continue to learn and
evolve. Benson contributed directly to our changing understanding of
how to faithfully render an image on paper. He did this simultaneously
as a master printer, professor of photography (and later, dean of the
Yale School of Art from 1996 to 2006), consultant for Adobe—and as
someone who helped others make beautiful illustrated books. The
publications included in this volume, while not offering nearly a
complete bibliography of Benson's technical and artistic work in the
field of photobooks, highlight the major moments in his career as a

printer, separator, and someone who cared deeply about the physical reflection of the world through images.

Photographic history is also carried forward and transformed by the individual experiences of those who care enough about the medium to dedicate their life to the field—as image makers, as artisans, and as educators. The genealogy of American photography is a family tree recorded, in part, by the branches of educators such as László Moholy-Nagy, Harry Callahan and Aaron Siskind, Nathan Lyons, Ansel Adams, and Minor White. The Benson branch as mapped in these pages extends itself broadly to include photo departments run and nurtured under former students and colleagues of Richard Benson. It begins with Walker Evans and Tod Papageorge, among others at Yale University, and is extended by educators like Dawoud Bey at Columbia College Chicago; Arthur Ou and Ka-Man Tse at Parsons the New School for Design; Shannon Ebner at Pratt Institute; Sarah Stolfa at TILT Institute in Philadelphia; printers and workshop educators Sal Lopes and Jon Goodman; as well as those who carry forward a deep understanding of the processes and technologies of the printed image, such as Robert Hennessey, Sue Medlicott, Thomas Palmer, and so many more.

The lasting imprint of Richard Benson is found in their voices—and in the work as it continues, making books and photography, curating exhibitions, printing, creating in the digital photographic space, and teaching in art schools. This book aims to trace and render as crisply as possible the continuation—and evolution—of these legacies.

Introduction

While a vast repository of historical and technical knowledge, Richard Benson was also an artist and educator committed to the present tense. He regularly drew attention to the fact that artists rarely know enough about their chosen medium, while their intellectual lives often distract from the wellspring of discovery and "ideas" that come with technical fluency and hands-on problem-solving. In an academic field where position-taking and theorizing frequently steer clear of the compositional language and poetic structures of photography, Benson's relentless interrogation of how a photograph generates meaning or fails to achieve eloquence exploded convenient and gross generalizations such as "straight photography"—or whatever the alternative labels du jour were at any given moment. The "intellectuals" among his students were challenged to address the problems *in* their photographs rather than the conversations surrounding them. Regardless of your practice or path, it was hard to argue with his frequent refrain: "An artist is a person who tends to be really good at one thing but spends most of their time trying to do something else." In the reading *or* the making of photographs, the revelations and the ideas were in the details, the unsentimental specificity, or what his friend Garry Winogrand referred to as the mystery of "a fact clearly described."

Benson's work (and attention) ranged across a variety of mediums and technologies beyond photography, including but not limited to clockworks, poetry, steam engines, interactive digital programming, painting, bluegrass banjo, and the restoration of Ford Model As. But it was his early engagement with the offset printing press, and later, his revolutionary innovations in expanding the expressive palette and fidelities of photographic reproductions that remained at the core of his pursuits. Images, like ideas or perception itself, could always be improved upon and refined. The ever-present mix of technical fluency

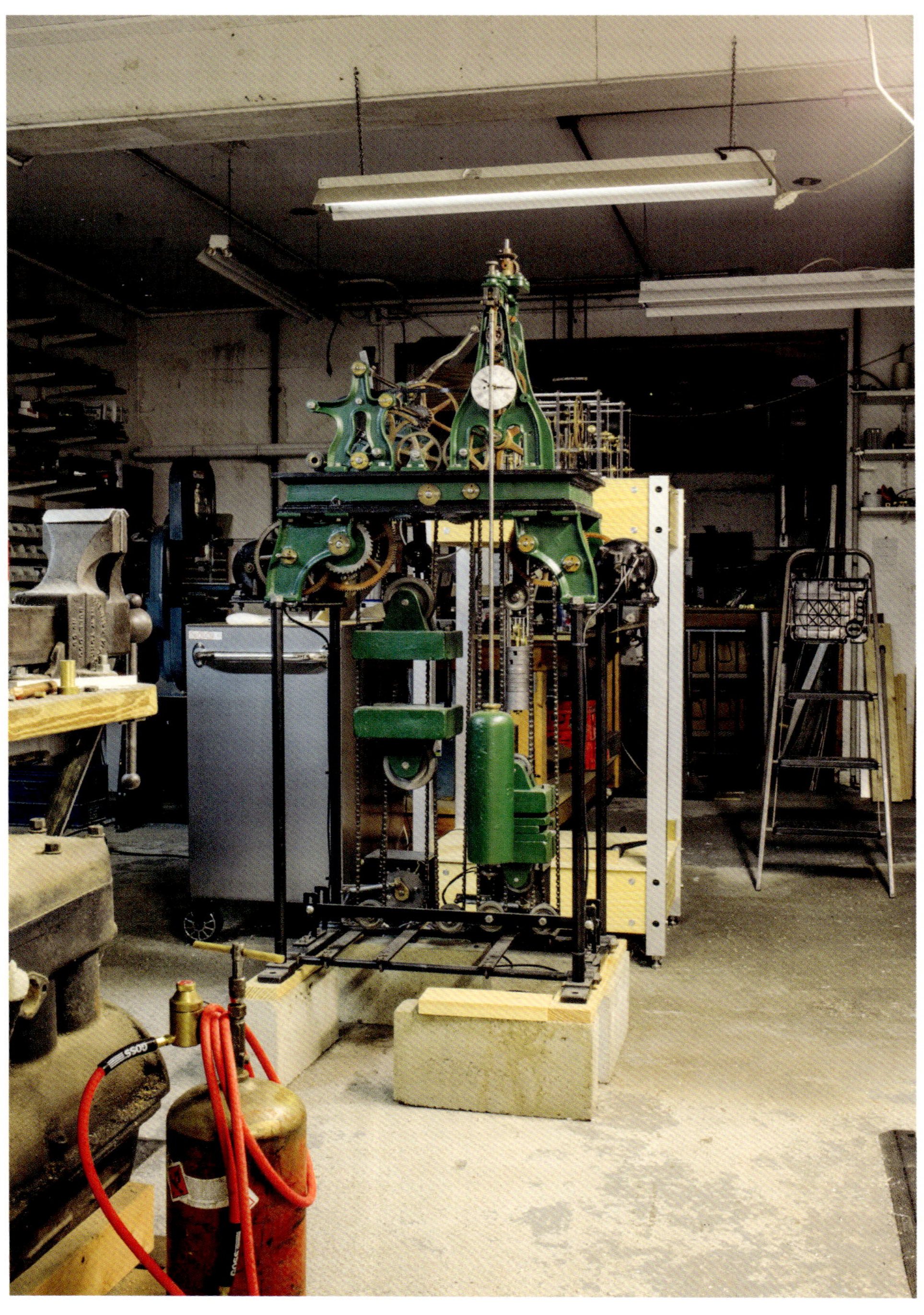

and artist's intuition inscribed in his own work, and in the many books that he produced for other photographers, continues to invite equal parts scrutiny and wonder. In many ways, the importance of Benson's influence and example is historically more familiar within the realms of music and recording. The symbiotic and bar-raising role that music producers and musicians such as George Martin, Rudy Van Gelder, or more recently, Nigel Godrich, have played in showing artists who they are, who they might be, is the more productive comparison. As with the great producers, Benson sought to expand the artist's understanding of possibility and discovery within the evolving spheres of production and post-production, while all efforts remain geared toward getting it together, getting it right, and finally, getting out of the way so that others might experience the work for themselves.

In a certain respect, Benson's engagement with photography was only part of what was arguably his probing of the entire nineteenth century as both a traceable history of interrelated inventions and radically new aesthetic expressions. The simultaneous engagement with the possibilities and limitations of the photographic medium combined with a restless and speculative approach to "subject"— an anonymous photograph of tall ships in a turn-of-the-century port city or the sprawling bodies of work by Timothy H. O'Sullivan or Eugène Atget—in Benson's ethos, argued for themselves as art, all the more so for having been made outside the imprimatur of High Art. That Benson kept the question of "progress" open while viewing certain projects begun in the nineteenth century as ongoing meant that sentimentality, or worse, nostalgia, would raise his critical hackles especially when detected in his students.

Tools had a life and significance that he felt were too often obscured by technical fetish or self-congratulatory artisanal shtick. The value of a lens or camera, paper or printer, could only be understood within an individual artist's effort to translate their perception of the visible world into a mute rectangle.

Richard Benson's work speaks for itself. A Benson photograph or hand-lathed clockwork engages a viewer with or without prior knowledge or backstory. The sum total of his work resides in the precarious relationship between virtuosic technique and humble attention to

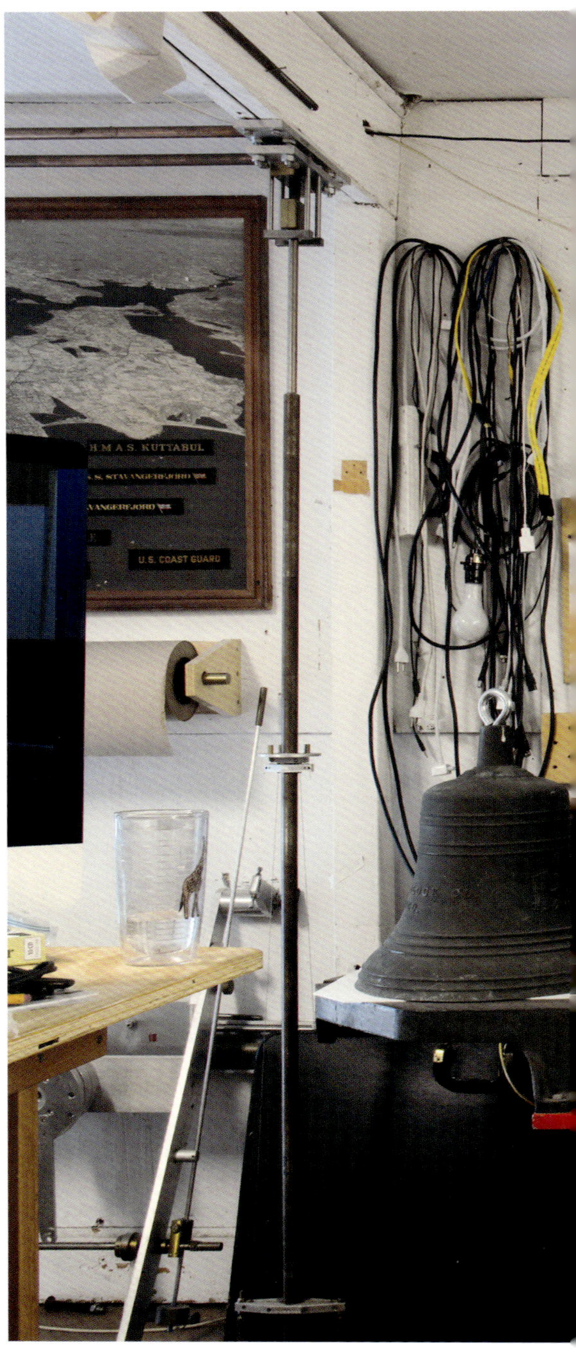
H M A S. KUTTABUL
S. STAVANGERFJORD
VANGERFJORD
U. S. COAST GUARD

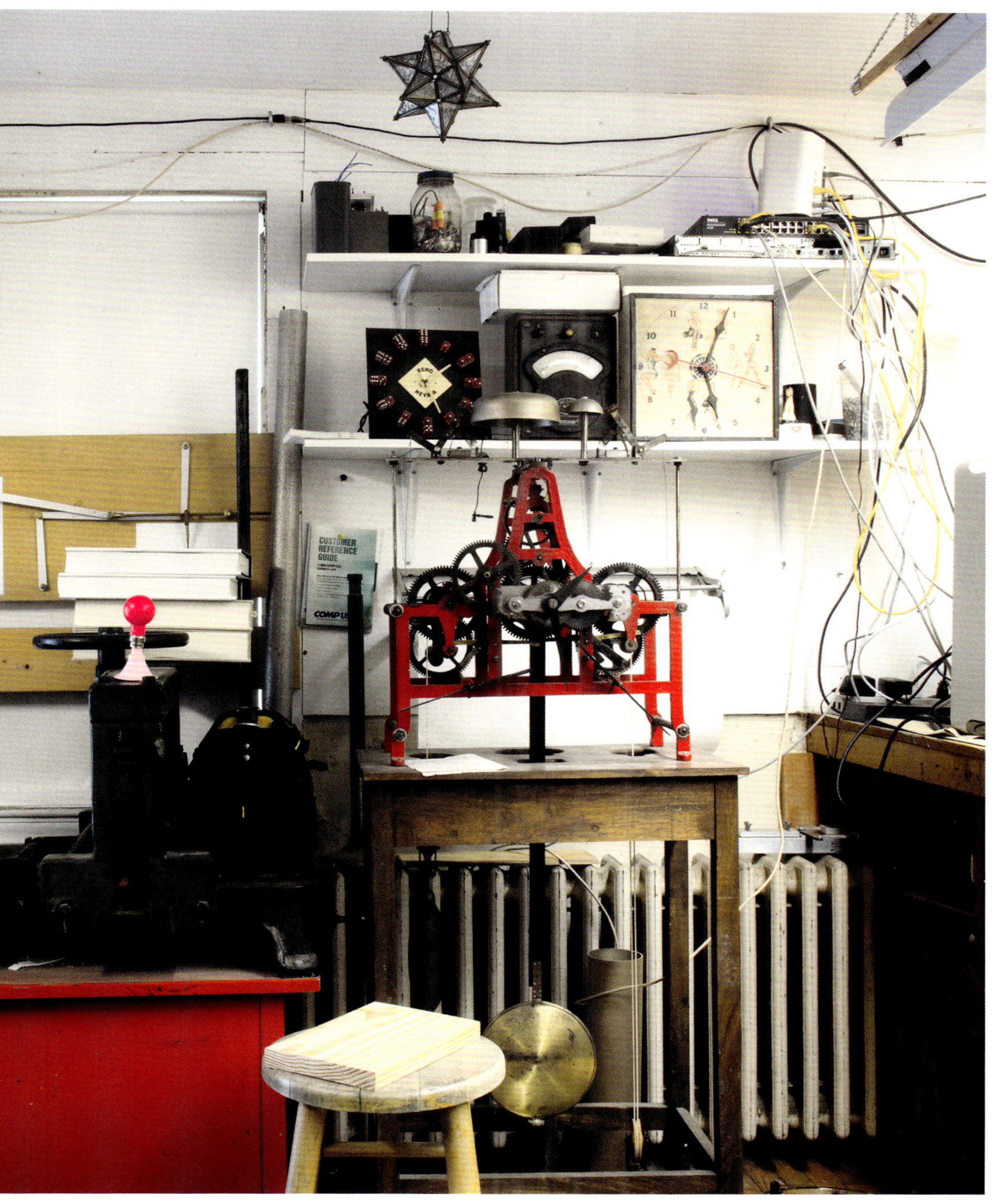

Clocks, Gauges, and Routers, Benson Home and Workshop, Newport, Rhode Island, 2017
Inkjet print
13 × 19 in. (33 × 48.3 cm)

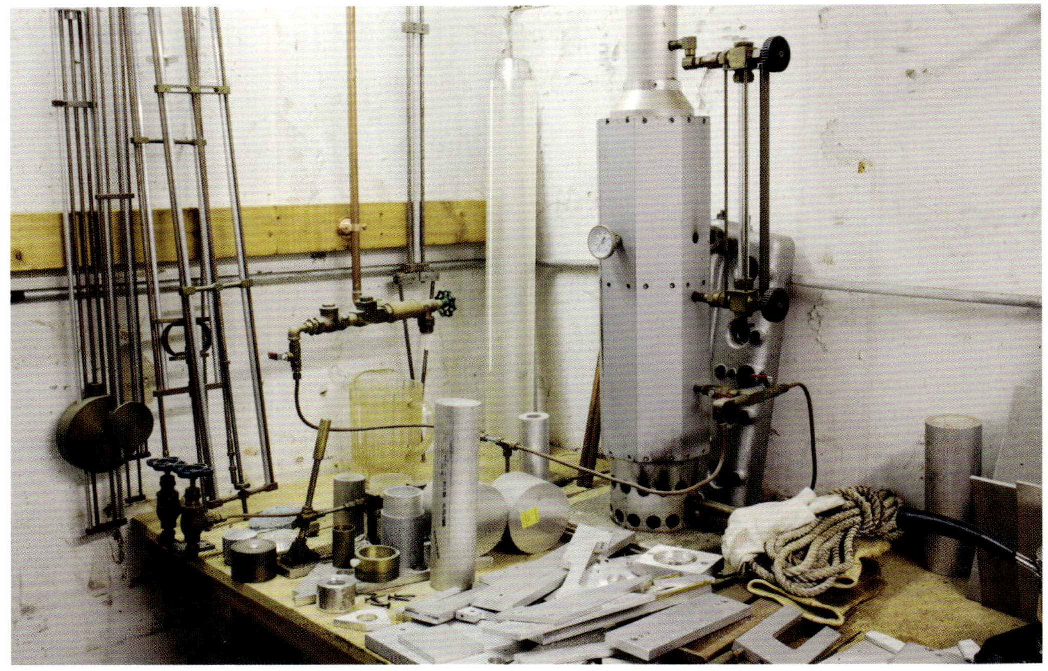

detail or something akin to what William Carlos Williams espoused as: "No ideas but in things." The challenge of responding to Richard Benson's legacy in any form is daunting. Nobody had a finer nose for pretention or derived more pleasure in pointing it out than Richard Benson. This book has been created by reaching out to individuals who accepted the challenge of addressing aspects of Richard's work and the role that his influence may have played in their own work and thought. As much as possible, the format we have followed is one that Richard admired, namely John Szarkowski's *Looking at Photographs*, i.e. a single photograph on one page and a text related to that photograph on the facing page. It is a format that is designed to explore the sheer amount of thought that a photograph can inspire. It allows for a photograph to be reproduced unburdened by design considerations, providing ample room for accompanying text to be printed at generous type sizes and creating a taut relationship between an author's words and the reproduction of the *object* they have chosen to contemplate. Pushing the relationship between an infinitely reproducible image and the reproduction itself, of course, never being far from Richard's thought and lessons, this book also echoes Benson's *The Printed Image* exhibition and catalogue by presenting an eclectic and diverse group of images with unique backstories which, combined, present a vibrant current of connections and surprises.

Shed with Ropes and Steam Engine, Benson Home and Workshop, Newport, Rhode Island, 2017
Inkjet print
13 × 19 in. (33 × 48.3 cm)

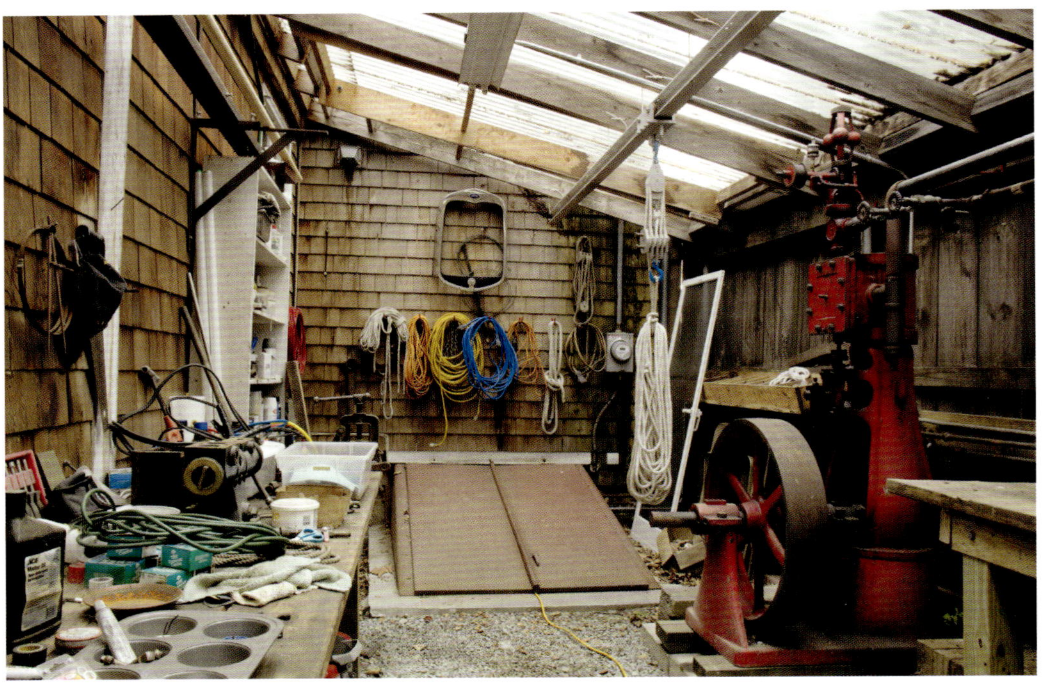

Contributions

I began my studies at Yale in 2005, a moment that I now consider the last gasp before the department began to incorporate digital technology alongside the analog. This was a familiar feeling, as a similar technological shift had unfolded in 1995, the year I began my undergraduate studies. Back then, I was assigned my first email address, which I used to log into the library; its staff had begun to digitize documents while phasing out reproductions printed on microfiche.

Like most other photography departments, Yale's would soon have to choose between opting in or out of digital printing processes. No one knew how the digital toolkit would impact photography, both conceptually and in application. But Chip was enthusiastically embracing these technological changes while transitioning out of his tenure as dean.

As time goes on, I continue to understand how fortunate I was to have studied with Chip, particularly during that pivotal moment. Chip was nimble. While a number of practitioners protested this shift in photography, Chip was someone of an older generation who didn't miss a beat. He continued to be curious, to thrive and evolve with the medium. He embraced the unknown. Chip shared his knowledge in a way that it could be received as mutable, something that a student could interpret and make their own. The world became an open-ended field of potential. Larger instead of smaller.

5641, 2016
Archival pigment print
42 × 29½ in. (106.7 × 74.9 cm)

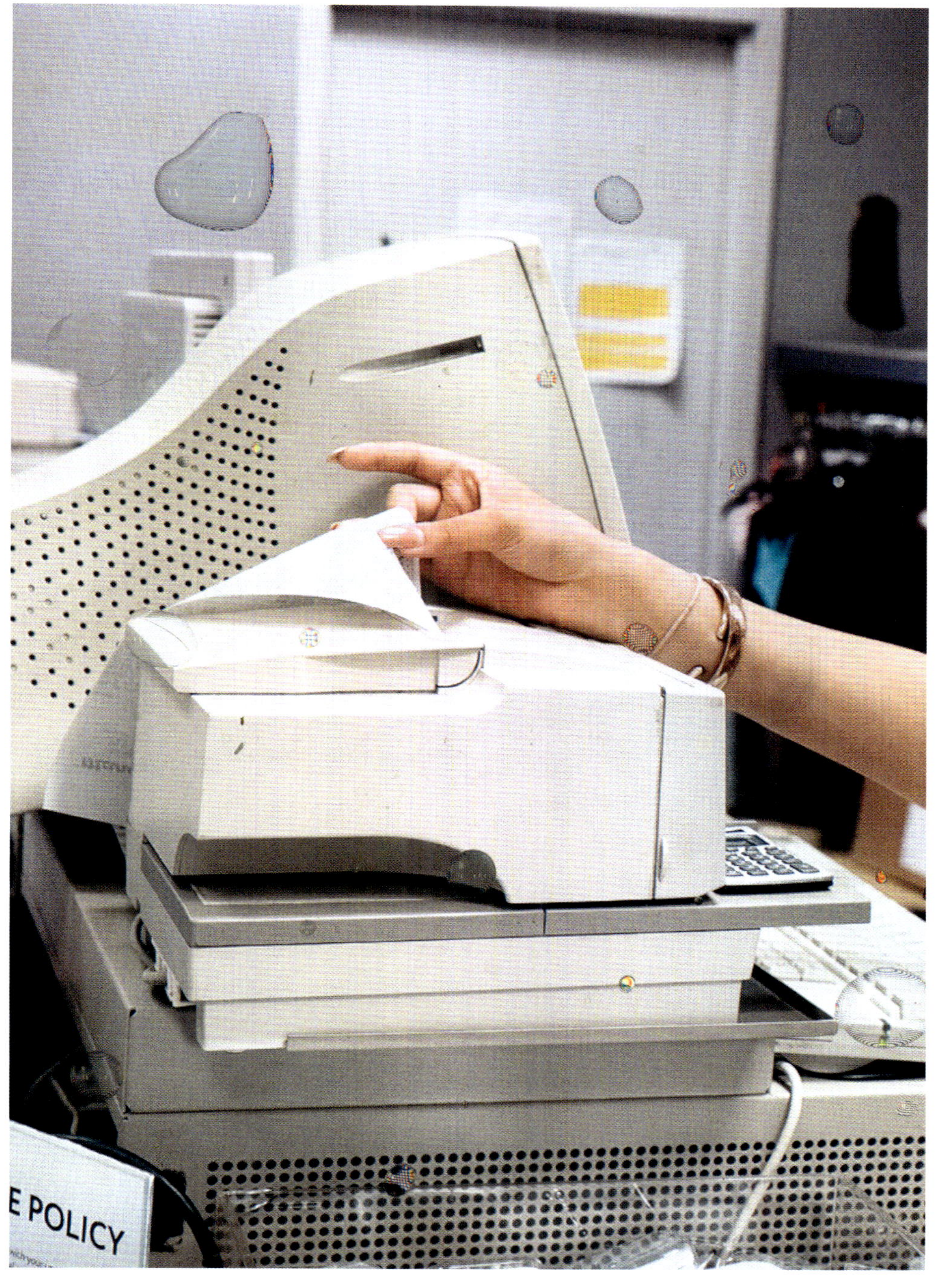

"You should go outside, learn from the world."

My daughter was eight years old when I enrolled at Yale in 1988. I was slightly older than the other students and was constantly striving to balance parenting with the demands of the program. I had already devised a schedule of photographing at night, often using flash, when I was living in New Orleans, as night was when I had uninterrupted time to work; I photographed and printed while my baby slept. At Yale, Richard told me to take my camera outside during daylight hours. He said my visual engagement with natural light would expand my relationship with photography. He was right. I began to photograph the postindustrial landscape of the Naugatuck River Valley, not far from New Haven. I knew this scarred landscape well: I had grown up in the scrappy town of Naugatuck. After a century of industrial pollution, the waters of the Naugatuck River were devoid of life and literally foamed with colorful streaks. The photo I've included here depicts the river's edge. The frame encloses debris but also foliage, weeds, a railroad trestle, and a peek of the river. And then there is the sunlight. The radiance touches most everything, and beyond the river, details disappear into luminous space. This is a neglected landscape where the vestiges of manufacturing lay abandoned. It is foul and toxic. Yet the light and the weedy growth suggest a hint of renewal.

Richard always said, "The world is smarter than you." I understood this to mean that curiosity is sparked by encounters in the world. For me, the magic of photography is its referent, whisper of the real. I know that those early wanderings through the polluted, yet luminous landscape of my hometown impacted my photography. My encounters with an earth in flux, from the drained Florida Everglades to the shifting tectonic plates of Iceland, have continued to ground my work. And my palette has forever shifted to silvery grays and soft, muted colors.

Naugatuck River, 1998
Gelatin-silver print
20 × 24 in. (50.8 × 61 cm)

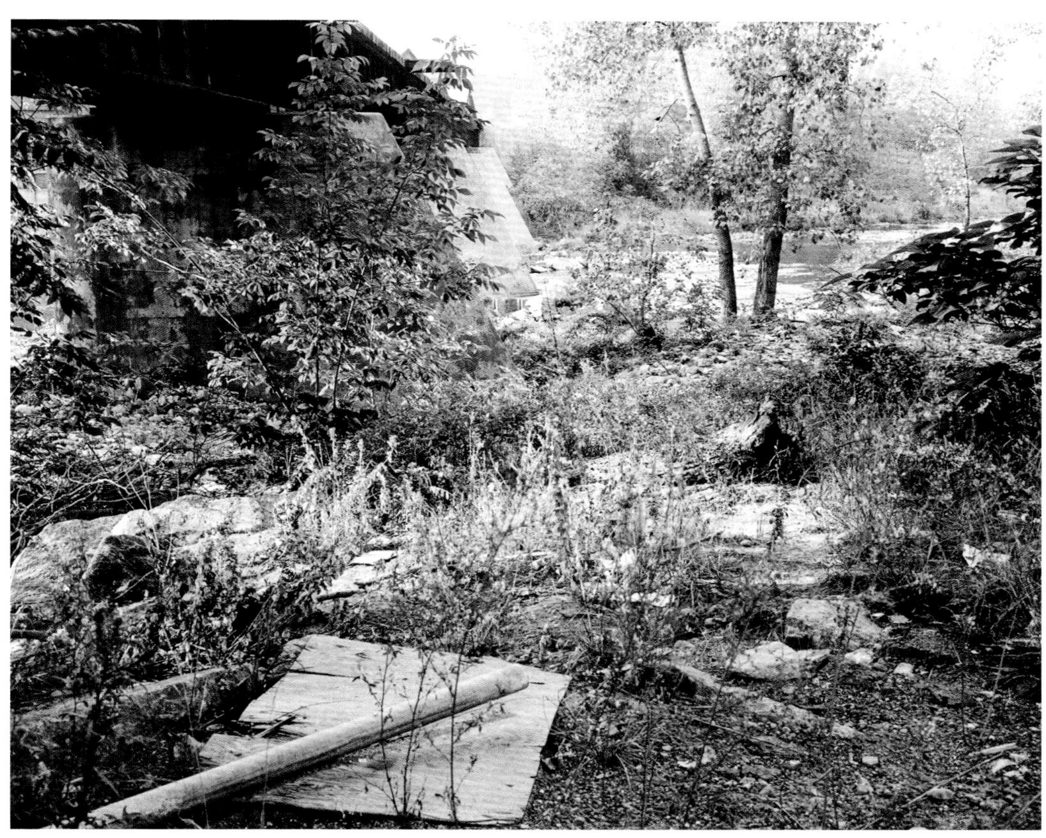

I probably first became aware of the name Richard Benson early in my budding career, when I heard about a portfolio of eighteen photographs by James Van Der Zee. The portfolio had been published by Washington, DC, art dealer (and, it was whispered, former CIA agent) Harry Lunn in 1974. The prints, I was told, had been made by a man named Richard Benson. I had encountered Van Der Zee's photographs in 1969 at the Metropolitan Museum of Art in the controversial exhibition *Harlem on My Mind*, which had been the first museum exhibition I ever attended on my own. My grandmother had gifted me my first camera the year before, and I carried it with me. Van Der Zee's photographs, and the experience of seeing photographs of Black people in a museum, left an indelible impression. For several years, James Van Der Zee was the only name I could conjure when trying to imagine a Black photographer, which I was in the midst of deciding I would become. Slowly, the names and the photographs of Roy DeCarava and Gordon Parks were added to the list. But Van Der Zee was the first. And the "Lunn portfolio" remained for me an unseen holy grail. For a long time, that was all I knew of Richard Benson: that he had printed what I then considered to be the legendary James Van Der Zee portfolio.

It was only in 2008, while doing a residency project at the Walters Art Museum in Baltimore, that I finally laid eyes on the portfolio. By then, I had met, studied with, and become friends with Chip. In the intervening years since becoming aware of his name, I had kept track of him, quickly learning that the highest quality photography books, by the likes of Lee Friedlander, Eugène Atget, and Paul Strand, bore the imprint of his technical brilliance in reproducing photographs in ink. Later, I read the extensive profile of Benson that Calvin Tomkins had written for the *New Yorker* in 1990. By the time I read that article, I was myself but a year away from applying to and being accepted into the MFA photography program at Yale, where Benson had been teaching since 1979.

I had heard about Chip from photographer friends like Michael Spano and Abe Morell, who had gone through the programs decades before me. When I became seriously interested in studying photography, the field hadn't yet become professionalized; the wealth of BFA and MFA programs of today didn't exist yet. I came up through an informal kind of apprenticeship, finding photographers who appeared

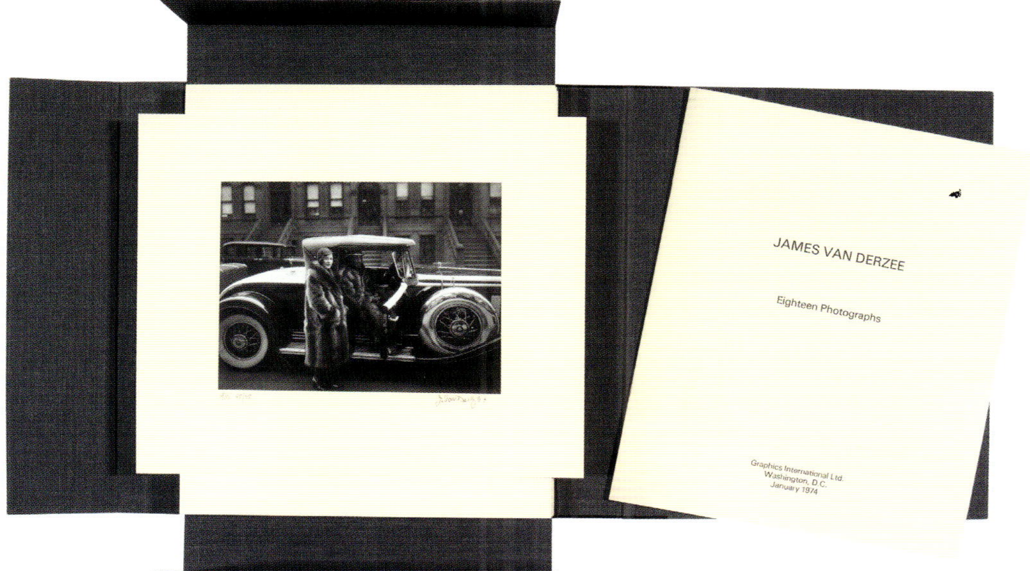
JAMES VAN DERZEE

Eighteen Photographs

Graphics International Ltd.
Washington, D.C.
January 1974

to know more and have more experience than I did and then attaching myself to them. The circle of Black photographers who were a generation ahead of me became my first mentors and then friends, particularly Louis Draper and other members of the Kamoinge collective. Lou would invite me to show him what I was working on and give me his feedback, encouraging me to apply for fellowships when he thought I was ready. Closer to my own age were Jules Allen and Frank Stewart, who became important cohorts, along with Carrie Mae Weems. Together, we formed a critical community of support for each other, sharing our work when there was really no one else to share it with. Jules had spent time with Garry Winogrand in California, and Frank had studied with Roy DeCarava at Cooper Union, and the rigor of those engagements showed in their work. Eventually, Carrie went off to grad school at UC San Diego, encouraging me to think seriously about applying to graduate school as well. And so I applied to Yale, which seemed to be the graduate program that privileged making over theorizing.

At the admission interview, I met Richard Benson for the first time. I was an older applicant, just two years shy of forty years old, with a wife and a new baby. The process felt more like a conversation than a formal interview. Chip had a serious but easygoing manner throughout. An open and gregarious man, he was not at all intimidating, and I took an immediate liking to him. This feeling seemed mutual. I got my acceptance letter sometime after and moved with the family from Brooklyn to New Haven to begin the program in September 1991.

I had already been alerted to the more intense aspects of the program—the sometimes extremely grueling critiques—so those didn't faze me. What did impress me were the brilliant observations that regularly issued forth from the mind of Richard "Chip" Benson during those crits. He had the uncanny ability to embrace your intentions while making just the right critical observations. He asked you the kinds of pointed questions that burrow deep into your intentions and made you either reconsider them or confirm that they are, in fact, seriously rooted. He brought you into a conversation with yourself and your work that you would not have had otherwise. And he did this week after week, often leaving me amazed at the pearls of observational wisdom that sprang from his mouth.

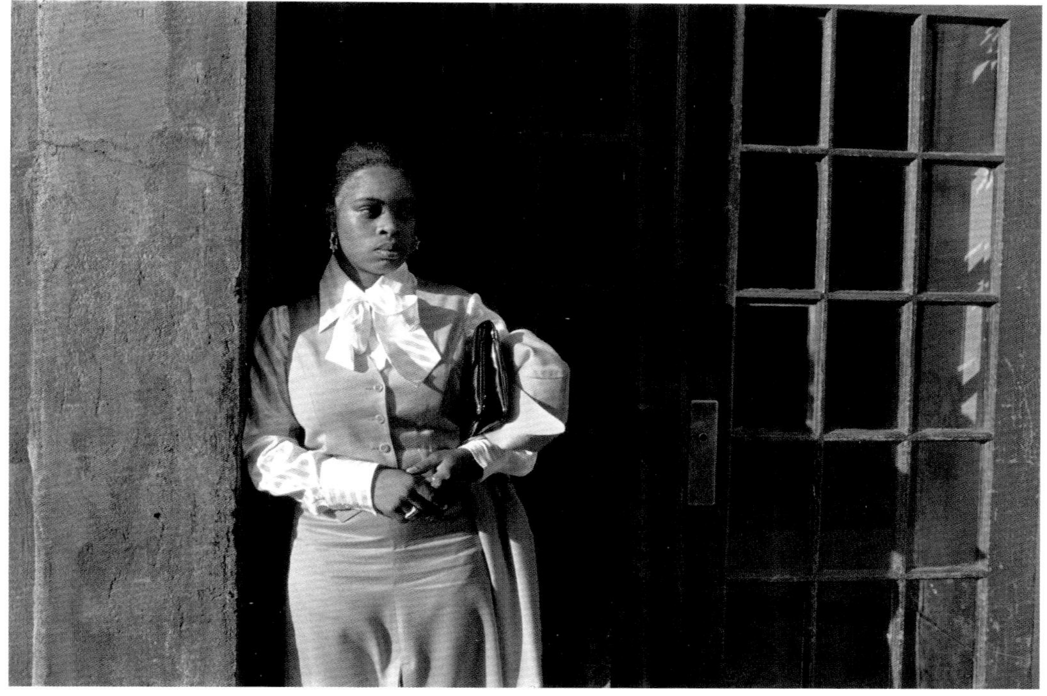

A Woman Waiting in the Doorway, Harlem, 1976
Gelatin-silver print

I was a pretty mature artist when I entered the graduate program. I had mounted several exhibitions—my first solo exhibition was in 1979 at the Studio Museum in Harlem—and I had received several fellowships and grants. But as a printer, I was pretty much self-taught, other than my early undergrad encounters with master printer Sid Kaplan at the School of Visual Arts. Kaplan had famously printed for Robert Frank for decades. But I guess I was too young a photographer then to take full advantage of Kaplan's lessons in the darkroom. My results were often good but not always consistent. Having started out under the sway of Roy DeCarava's dark prints and worked my way back into the light, I had a firm grasp of what mattered to me as a photographer when I showed up at Yale, but a less than certain sense of myself as a printer. I had every reason to believe that I could put that uncertainty to rest if I spent time with Richard Benson.

It didn't take long to realize that Chip would give you extensive advice and suggestions when responding to your prints. The one thing he didn't do was to go into your darkroom and demonstrate what you might do. I became quietly determined to get Chip into my student darkroom to do just that, to get him to actually make a print from one of my negatives while I watched.

At the time, I was still making black-and-white portraits in the streets with a 4-by-5 camera, much in the way I had been doing in the years prior to Yale. I was showing Chip a print of one of the street portraits that I had just made. It was still wet, coming straight from the darkroom. He began to give me a detailed technical critique of the print: how I could make it sing a bit more, how I could change the exposure just slightly, burning in this area and holding back that area. He went on for a while, until I finally asked him, "Chip, why don't you come into my darkroom and show me?" He thought about it for a minute and finally relented, giving me a look that let me know that he was onto me.

He took a look at my enlarger timer, changed it slightly, took one final look at my print, then turned the room light off. I handed him a sheet of paper and stood to the side to watch. He began working once he hit the timer on the enlarger. Moving his hands ever so slightly and quickly over the paper, he performed all the necessary burning and dodging with his hands—no printing tools. He then handed me the sheet of exposed paper and asked me to develop it. We then turned on the room light and brought the print out of the darkroom. The print, of course, sparkled. Full of life, it showed clearly defined highlights and plenty of detail in the darker areas. If you asked me what exactly he did, I wouldn't be able to tell you. But he did something only Richard Benson could do. With seemingly little effort and a deep understanding of the materials at hand, he made an exquisitely rendered print. I tell people that I'd been making photographs for a long time before going to Yale, but that I didn't really know how to print until I met Richard Benson.

Studying with Richard left me with a profound respect for books and craftsmanship that has been central to my life as a photographer, teacher, and director of a university press. Perhaps the most valuable lesson I learned was that the only way to ensure that a task was accomplished to the highest possible standard was to do it yourself. By figuring out how something works, you gain an understanding of its possibilities and limitations, which allows you to find ways to control and improve the process. To this day, I do everything myself, whether it's developing my own film, making my own prints, or even matting and framing my own work for exhibitions.

For the last assignment in Richard's graduate class, we had to publish a collective book of our own photographs. I was very pleased that the other students picked one of my pictures for the book's cover—even if it was not chosen for its superior merit, but rather for the content. Our classwork included selecting and sequencing the images, designing the book's layout, and taking a field trip to Meriden Gravure, where our book was to be printed. There, we also watched Richard supervise the printing of Lee Friedlander's *Factory Valleys.*

The final step of production involved a trip to Richard's studio in Newport, Rhode Island, where we learned how to expose and develop the film used to engrave images on halftone printing plates. I'll never forget Richard's demonstration of his technique for developing the litho film: he grasped the developer tray with both hands and vigorously jerked it back and forth while chemicals splashed all over the assembled students. As Richard explained: "You have to shake it like a son of a bitch!"

Graduate Photography at Yale 1981–82
(New Haven, CT: Yale School of Art, 1982)

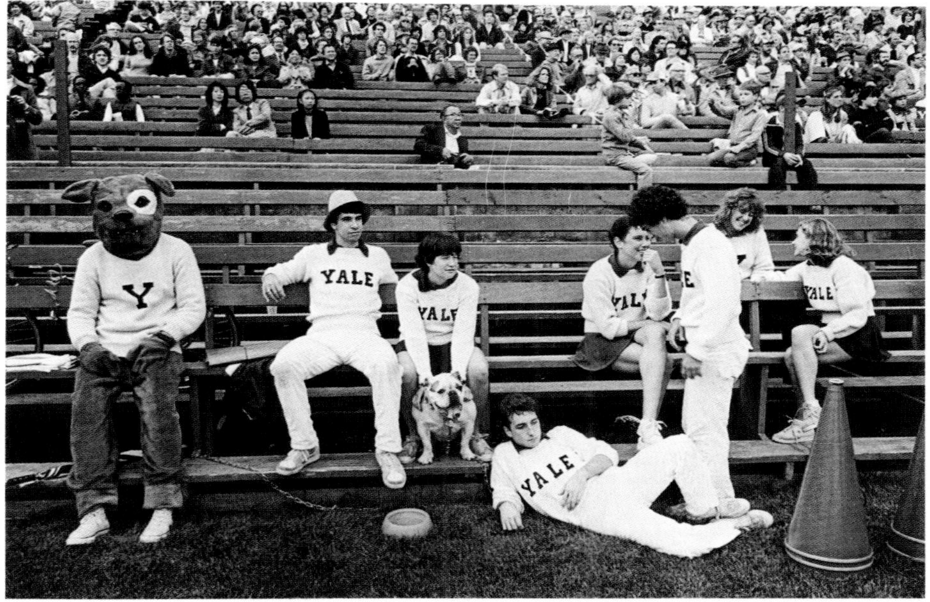

GRADUATE PHOTOGRAPHY AT YALE 1981–82

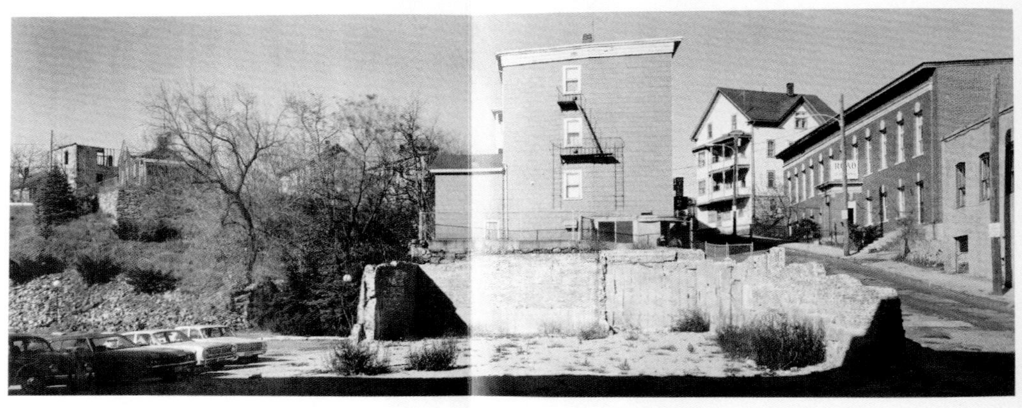

Graduate Photography at Yale 1981–82
(New Haven, CT: Yale School of Art, 1982)

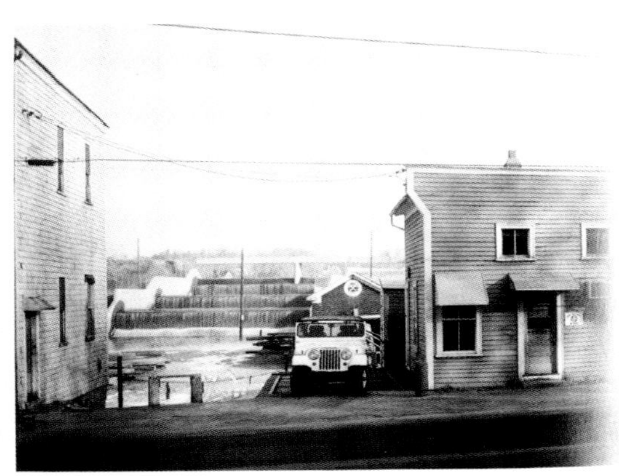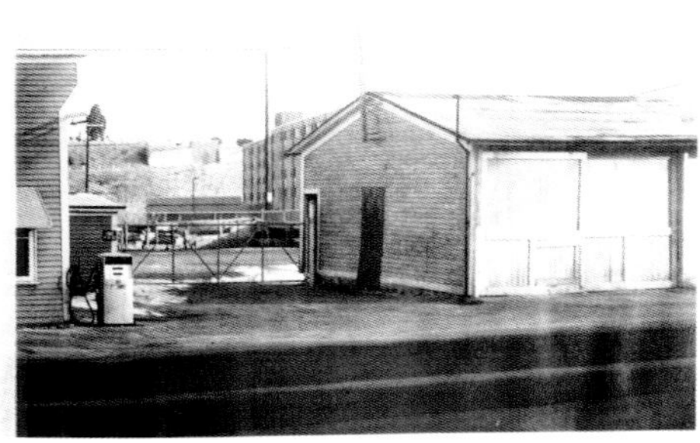

In 1977, I went to see the Tina Modotti exhibition at MoMA and was dazzled by the quality of these new platinum prints, which the press release identified as having been made by Richard Benson. I thought I knew what a good platinum print was, from four years of making prints myself and from my time studying the prints of Frederick H. Evans, Peter Henry Emerson, Edward Weston, Clarence H. White, Paul Strand, and Gertrude Käsebier at MoMA under the watchful eye of John Szarkowski (who would sometimes wander out and ask me what I was looking at). I wrote Richard Benson a letter, and he responded through his assistant Salvatore Lopes, inviting me to come up for a visit to Newport on his return from France. He was working on the Paul Strand portfolio at the time and was adamant that his focus was on his work but that after dark, we could talk about printing and exchange ideas. Two years after we met, I applied to Yale's graduate school and was accepted. At the time, I didn't know Richard would be there, so I was surprised and thrilled to become his student.

Richard's knowledge of the history of the photographic image, printmaking, and photographic reproduction was encyclopedic. He had worked on what I considered most of the great photographic books of his era. He began working on the four-volume set of Atget books with Szarkowski at MoMA during my time as a graduate student (the first was published in 1981), so we heard a lot of stories and learned about Atget by looking at the proofs Richard would bring down from Newport. He was always collecting examples of prints from the flea market, from friends and students, and later online. He was very excited about every acquisition, as each one showed him (and he showed us) how the history and magic of photography fit together. One day, he excitedly pulled me aside to show me a silk Mao weaving from the Cultural Revolution that he got on eBay. "Look," he noted as he turned it over, "the image appears in negative on the other side."

Richard taught our graduate class the very exacting process of dust-pulled photogravure, from how to make the positive film to etching the plates. It involved numerous steps over many days and weeks. He built an elaborate box with a handle to stir up the "dust." This fine layer of rosin dust would later act as a wiping guide for the ink. First, the dust has to be seared into the plate, heated from below with a gas torch. All of these steps were full of hazards and potential

The Museum of Modern Art

11 West 53 Street, New York, N.Y. 10019 Tel. 956-6100 Cable: Modernart

NO. 2
FOR RELEASE: JAN. 10, 1977

TINA MODOTTI

An exhibition of 40 photographs by Tina Modotti, an Italian-born actress
and political activist as well as a photographer, will be on view at The Museum
of Modern Art from January 10 through April 3. The exhibition, believed to
be the most extensive showing of Modotti's work since her death in 1942, includes original prints as well as new prints (in palladium and silver) made
from Modotti's negatives by Richard Benson. The exhibition has been selected
and installed by John Szarkowski, Director of the Department of Photography.

Tina Modotti was born in Udine, Italy, in 1896, and emigrated to San
Francisco in 1913. After working as a seamstress and acting in silent films
(where she usually played the role of the exotic vamp), Modotti in 1921 met
Edward Weston, now recognized as one of the masters of modern photography,
and became his lover. There is no evidence, however, that Modotti became
actively interested in photography until 1923, when she and Weston went to
Mexico to live and work together. Many of the photographs included in the
exhibition were made during the time Modotti and Weston were in Mexico, a
period that ended with Weston's return to his family in California at the end
of 1926.

Tina Modotti was not a prolific photographer. Her significant work was
done within a six- or seven-year period, and from these years perhaps no more
than 100 pictures survive. Although the dating of many of her pictures is
problematic, it would seem Modotti's work might be divided into two periods:
most of the pictures made during her association with Weston reflect a dis-
interested pleasure in the exploration of basic photographic form. They are,
if anything, rather more abstract, intellectual, and ethereal than Weston's
work. After 1926 Modotti became increasingly devoted to Communism, and during
the next three years she attempted to combine the rigorous standards of visual

(more)

for failure, and though Richard explained each carefully, most of my classmates were trepidatious. Most had never held a torch before. When we got to the acid etching steps, it was especially scary. It's then that he told us how each minute of exposure to these particular acids would eat our brain cells and make us stupid (his words). Because I wanted to learn, I took elaborate notes and, using great precaution, followed everything through for eight plates.

To create something is to take a piece of the world that intrigues you and find a way to share it with someone else—that's what being an artist is. During the COVID-19 pandemic, I felt an urgency to observe the landscape closely and through a different shape—not a rectangle but a circle, which I had been obsessed with, including collecting other kinds of circular art—as a way to learn. I wanted to reinvent the way I photographed in order to understand what was going on in the world. I began working with both circular and oval masks that I had my brother make for me, with Richard's voice in my head, encouraging me to keep experimenting.

Part of the intrinsic and central character of Richard was his ability to encourage you to take that leap of faith. "Why not?" the voice asks. Making a commitment is central to seeing things through. You may fail, but there are things that happen that you wouldn't have found other-wise. Richard taught me that it is important to look at those failures and to learn from them.

I feel like I carry a little bit of Richard with me every day. Influence is like that. It's an ongoing conversation with someone that continues long after that person is gone. It's up to you to further that legacy.

Apple Store, Fifth Avenue, 2020
Archival pigment print from an 8×10 film negative
23 × 28 in. (58.4 × 71.1 cm)

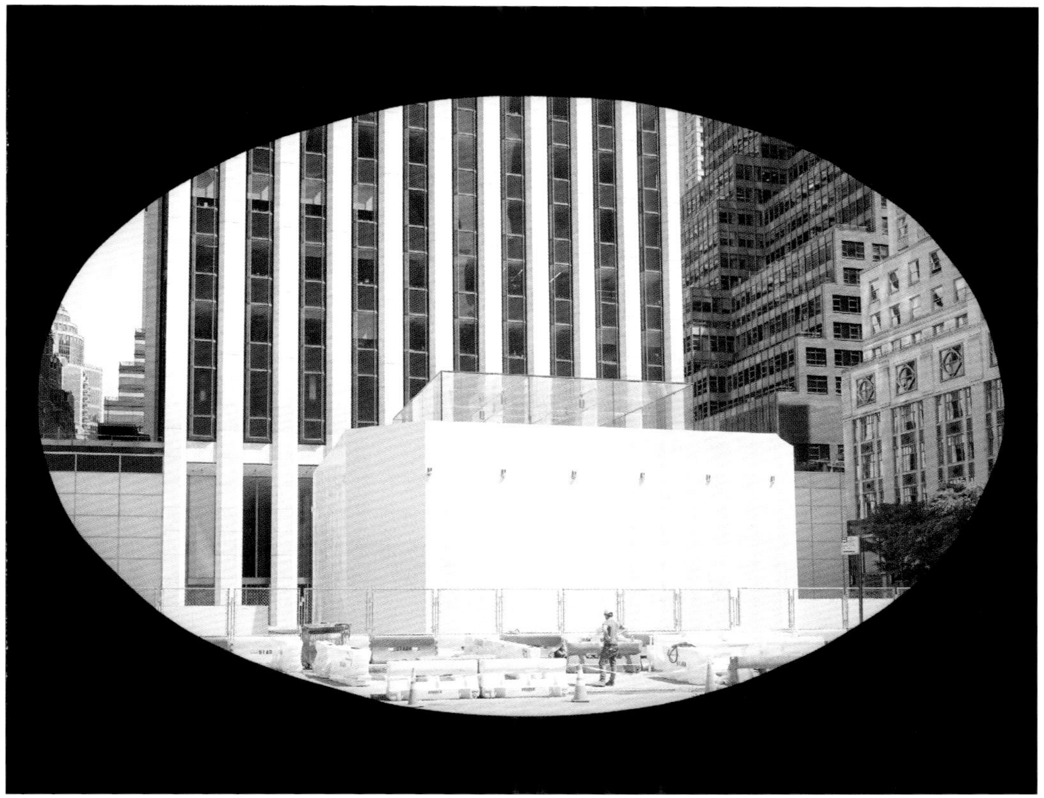

I was one of Chip's students during a transitional moment in the history of photography. We were just a few years into the twenty-first century and only beginning to contend with the shifts that digital technologies were ushering into the medium. In hindsight, it is difficult to conjure the atmosphere of skepticism that prevailed among art photographers about these changes. Our devotion to analog processes was so deeply ingrained that many viewed the inevitable computed alternatives with the same foreboding as we would an approaching extinction event.

Chip had little patience for these attitudes. He saw clearly through the haze of fetishistic regard for C-print surfaces and denials about their inherent instability. Rather, he taught us to see photography clearly for what it is: a continual evolution of technologies that would supplant one another. For him, new processes had characteristics inextricably linked to—and best able to address—the historical moment in which they emerged.

The era of chemical prints was passing. In their stead, Chip was prophetic about inkjet printers. As someone who committed considerable energy to mastering the reproduction of photographs through offset lithography, he saw these clunky beige machines serving up the holy grail he had been pursuing most of his life: photographs reproduced in continuous tones of ink on an array of papers.

His enthusiasm was infectious, and he encouraged me to experiment with these tools. In turn, they destabilized my assumptions about photography's relationship to what it indexed. The picture I include here is an early composite street photograph I made as a student. It was a crude experiment cobbled together from several negatives, but one that intrigued Chip enough to include in his *Printed Picture* exhibition.

I was never quite happy with this image, but I suspect Chip would approve of that feeling. He often relished in rough-handling prints that were given the white-glove treatment by his students. In doing so, he was trying to impart a more important lesson. For Chip, grappling with the problems of how to make something was almost always more interesting than the results. He wanted us to see photographs the way he did: less as precious products served up for judgment and consumption and more as outcomes of a life feverishly engaged in inquiry.

New York City, 2004
Archival pigment print
35 × 50 in. (88.9 × 127 cm)

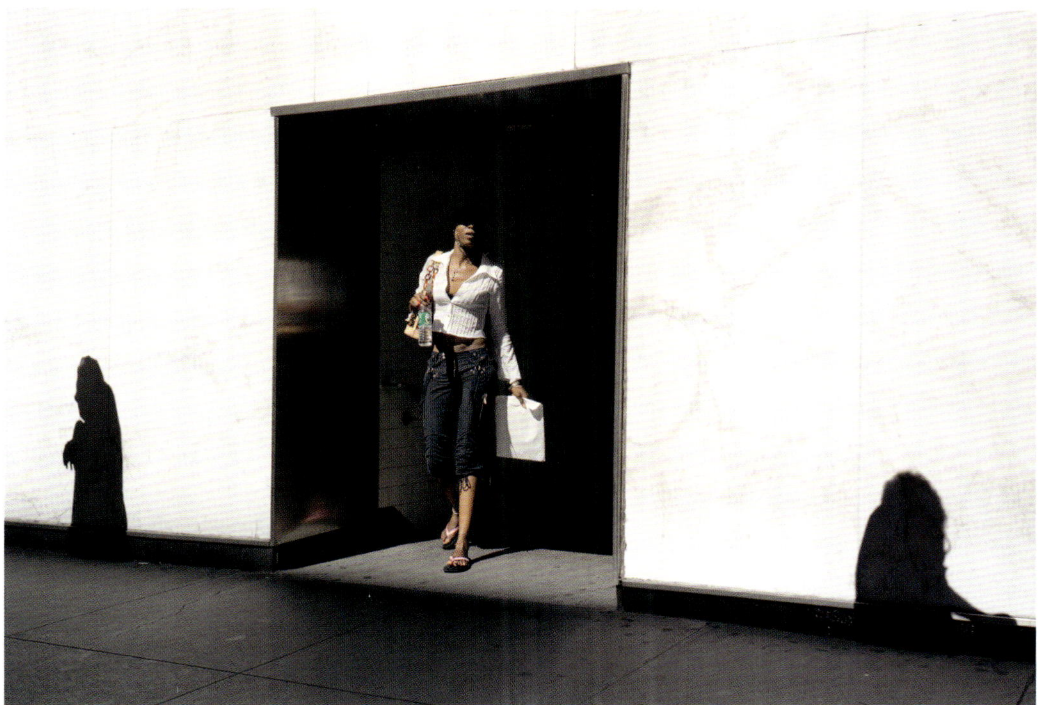

There used to be an image library attached to Yale's Department of the History of Art: three flatbed-sized oak cabinets in a Gothic atrium, each cradling lantern slides. One was labeled "Sculpture," another "Painting," and the third "Minor Arts." All of photography was contained in the last.

My laughter ricocheted around the quiet hall on Election Day, 2000, when I discovered this logjam of codification. Richard Benson was dean of the Yale School of Art at that time. Chip rarely spoke of "art" without a disdainful smirk, as if he were discussing food poisoning—something dire but inevitable. He had come of age as a practitioner in a time when photography had found itself as an art form in the Szarkowskian warrens of the Museum of Modern Art. Back then, photography was taken seriously not because it was suddenly conversant with painting and sculpture, but because of how it spoke in a language all its own. Art forms were what they were because of how they emphasized and accentuated, stretched and stylized their own inherent properties: for painting, paint and brushes; for photography, lenses and chemistry. The segregation of the medium preserved its uniqueness and autonomy.

A few weeks later, my fellow Yalies headed to MoMA to attend the opening of the Andreas Gursky show. It was the first time a photographer had mounted a solo show outside of the suburb of the photography department, and it felt like a coming-of-age, the arrival of the medium on the sacred shores of art proper. Everyone was there. I remember looking around and thinking that the images didn't hold up on the enormous scale he'd printed them. I was a little embarrassed. Maybe we weren't ready.

The blessings and curses of acceptance into the art world proper fell upon my education with biblical whiplash. On some days, Yale felt like an NFL Combine for the Art World, with celebrities perusing our chops as though flipping through a fashion magazine. Then Richard Benson would bluster in, grab that same magazine, and describe exactly how it was printed, with what inks and what enormous machines. He didn't see art; he saw made things, things that were reproduceable, changeable, and whose material birth into the world was more interesting than either their subjects or what was in the hearts of their makers. When I showed him the initial images in my series *Retail*, of long nighttime exposures of houses whose windows showed reflections of adjacent stores, we had a disagreement about the reciprocity factor of tungsten-balanced film. When I asked what he thought of the images themselves, Richard gave me his fox-in-the-henhouse grin and said: "You're too smart for your own good."

Students throughout the school were agitating for interdisciplinary critiques, to burst out from our stalls in Sculpture, Painting, Photography, and Graphic Design, and comingle. When they finally happened, the photography students slunk back to their darkrooms after, looking bereft. No one knows how to talk about our work, they acknowledged. Photographers have an occult, innate language that almost no one on the outside speaks. Using it, Chip was a shaman. And like a shaman, he had some interest in keeping out the uninitiated. He famously made a clock, machining each cog and gear, that he claimed was more accurate than any timepiece on earth. But it had no hands; it kept the time instead of telling it. I loved Chip because I could sense he was a confidence man, lulling us with gruff Yankee cussedness into thinking he was a salty relic, when he was secretly teaching us the occult incantations of our coven, the Minor Artists who press a button on a machine and then alchemically transmogrify nothing into silver that somehow sings the soul of the world.

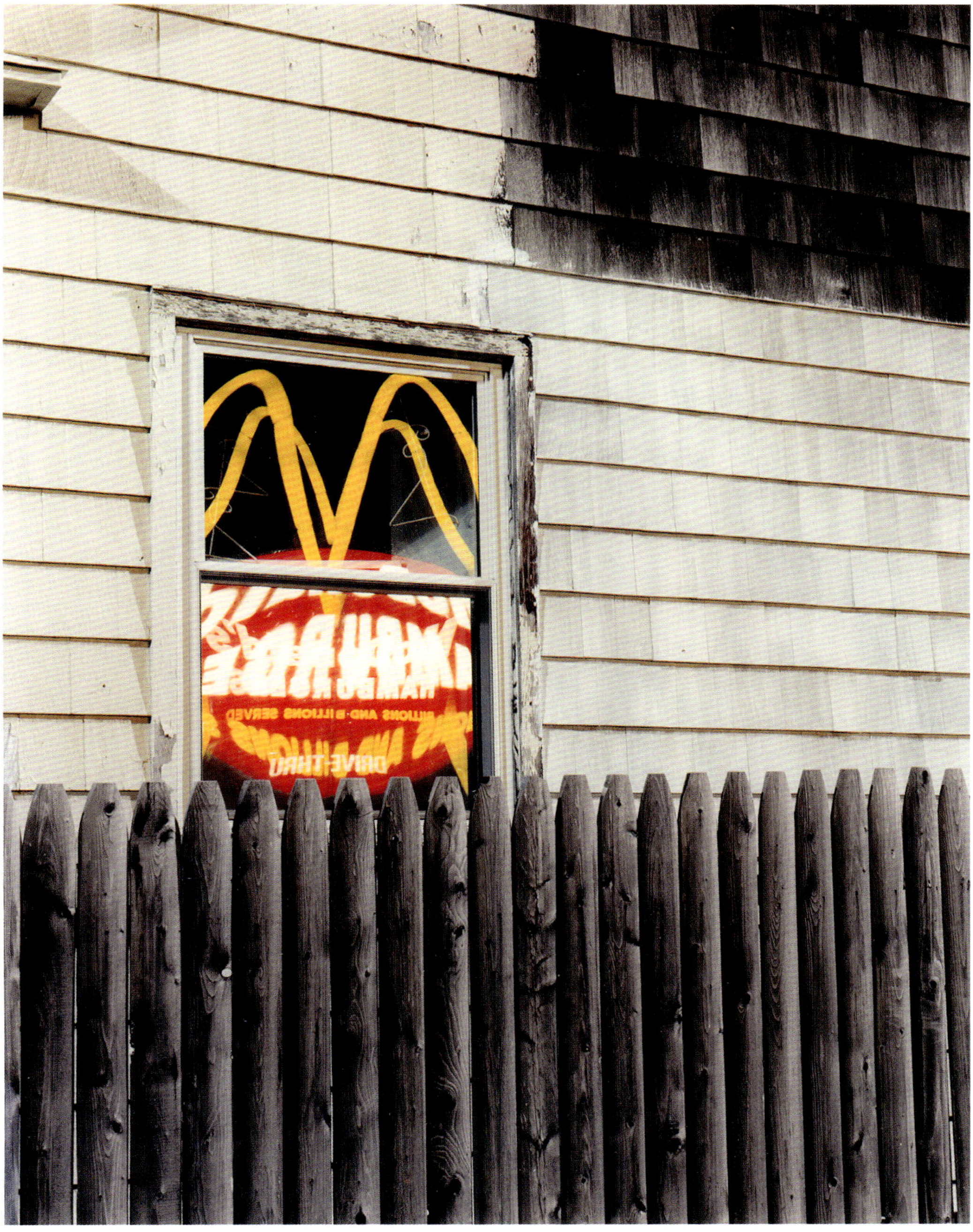

McDonald's 2, 2001
C-print
60 × 48 in. (152.4 × 121.9 cm)

Chip was always surrounded by tools. These were everywhere he might possibly be rooted, even momentarily. Anything he made or adapted was characteristic of his particular hand; they were always useful things of some beauty. I recognized similarities to the creations of my grandfather—a fellow product of Quakers, a gentleman who always had projects to work on. Chip's sparse but cluttered studio was a glimpse of familiar spaces from different phases of my life. These were fun places to be.

This atmosphere was true of both his work and home life, but most of us experienced this in his office during meetings. I knew two of Chip's offices during different Yale eras while he was dean. These were absolute hives of people coming and going from various doors, all being seen and helped.

Chip's office in the 1990s was in the "old," Paul Rudolph–designed Art and Architecture Building—a Brutalist, concrete-walled warren of rooms. I remember Chip at a circular table with our cohort of nine students around him. He was a person always at work, always open to finding ways to keep making things.

There was a button-down shirt hanging from one door, at the ready for the dean's work not involving ink or chemicals. A tool in its own right for navigating the bureaucratic world of academia.

Chip was still dean when I returned to Yale to teach. We were relocated to a newly renovated building (formally the Jewish Community Center of Greater New Haven), and his new office was filled with windows. It was open, often sunny from memory, and contained any number of tools. We would look at Photoshop (then in its early days), then swing chairs around so he could enthusiastically show some multiprinting technique that had solved a problem—even though he may have created another. The problems could be worked out on the spot if necessary. That was clearly a way to live and to work: surrounded by students, scanners, and printers.

These many discussions were not hypothetical: we could see the results of an idea before our eyes by experimenting to test the theory. The notion that we might not fully understand an idea until it has a physical manifestation was, for me, key to the draw of Yale's photography department, and I found a hero in Chip. Where to be simple, and where to be complex? These questions often come down to the act of making—how an object's form and content are measured and impact each other.

There were also books in his office. His own books—all well-worn copies—were there to serve as illustrations of possibility and demonstrate the importance of thinking about how ink inundates paper to make something that holds a mirror to reality. There were also printers, the latest computer, a new type of digital camera, all things ready for the curious to test an idea.

One bookend—a piece of stone carved by Chip's brother Nick—was etched with the directive "Remember Death." This was and is the propellant we have to create something that may last beyond our existence. The message has become heavier with time, but I also enjoy the teasing nature of it, which offers a glimmer of humor in the intensity of life. I bear that in mind and try to live my life always ready to make things.

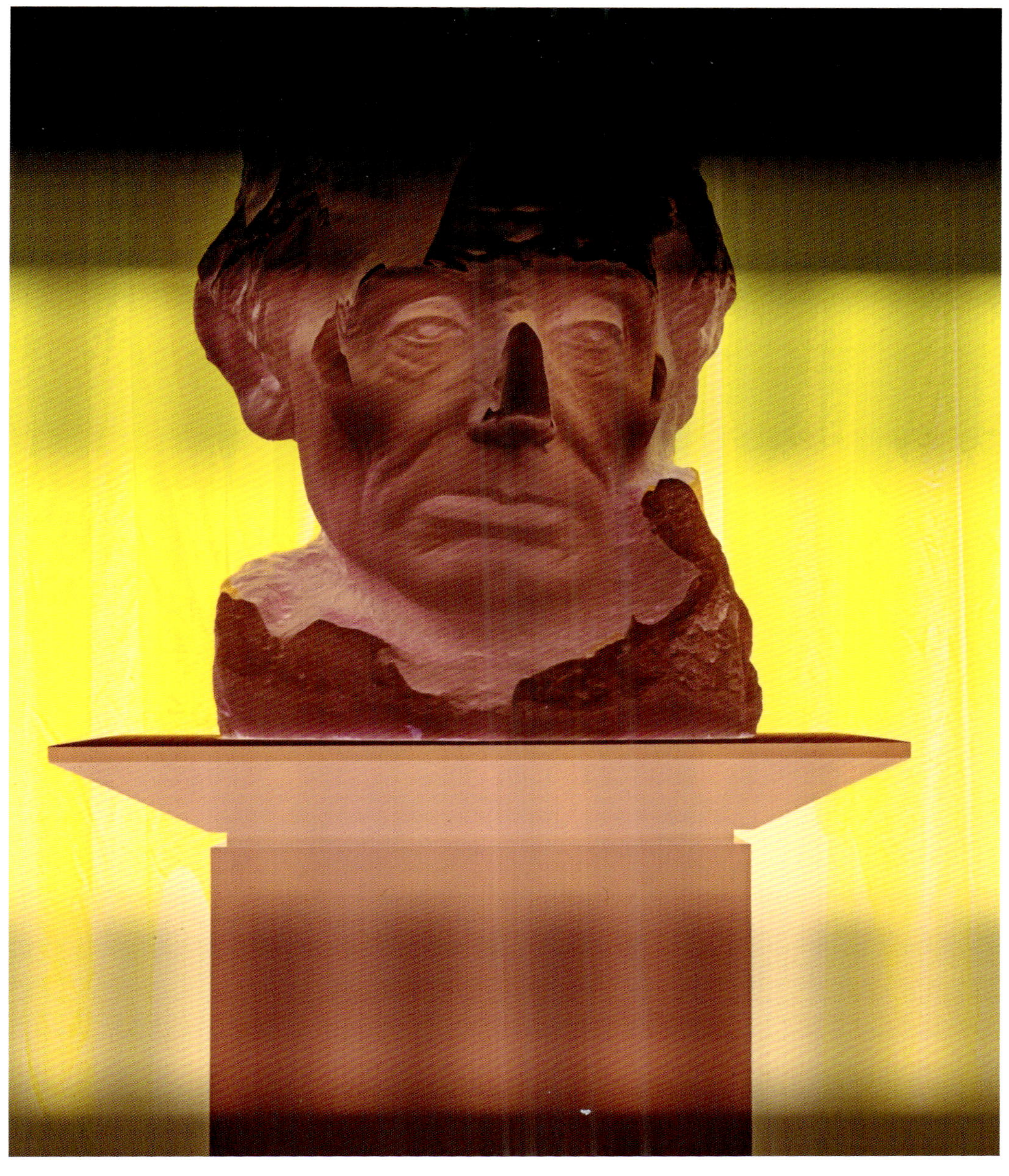

Scan Line, 2021
Archival inkjet print
24 × 20 in. (61 × 50.8 cm)

My students don't know this, but I am often having a conversation with them that I started with my own teachers. The conversation I started with Chip in graduate school continues to this day and helps sustain my teaching and making.

In my application to Yale, I wrote about an image that I saw that I wanted to make into a photograph. I was sitting waiting for the traffic light to change when I saw a woman in the car next to me sucking her thumb and twisting her hair. I was in awe of getting to watch someone comfort themselves in the assumed privacy of their car, and I wrote that this vulnerability was what I wanted to photograph. In my interview, Chip asked me why I didn't just take the photograph right then instead of remaking it. "The world is more interesting than anything you could ever imagine," he said. This was a point Chip consistently made; it was the first lesson I learned in graduate school.

What Chip was pushing me to articulate was how I worked. A way of constructing photographs that are based on observations that utilize revisitation and performance. He didn't pose this question to produce the answer that he would give. The question was to highlight and care for an instinct that is foundational in my work then and now. As a teacher, I feel one of my jobs is to listen closely to my students and their work and protect the instincts they come into the class with. I need them to question their approach, ways of thinking, and methodologies. By the time they leave my class, I want the instincts they came in with still there, just challenged, developed, and cared for. Looking back, that is what Chip was doing on the first day I met him. He had paid close attention to my application, looked at my photographs, and read my essay. He noticed that this way of working made sense to me. Chip's way of working was different. However, we both agreed that the world is far more interesting than anything we could imagine.

The image of the woman sucking her thumb in her car was a picture about self-soothing and privately finding comfort. I considered making that photograph as a companion to the reflection above. But the need and curiosity to make that photograph are no longer present. As a parent of two young children, I have shifted my focus from figuring out how to take care of myself to taking care of my children. I decided instead to submit this photograph of me breastfeeding my child. Our bodies are mirrored and tangled; the image reflects on the expansive relationship of care and comfort between parent and child. In my mind, the intimacy and immediacy of making this photograph put Chip's belief into practice—to always be an observer of what is happening around us.

Untitled, 2019
Archival pigment print
10 × 7½ in. (25.4 × 19.1 cm)

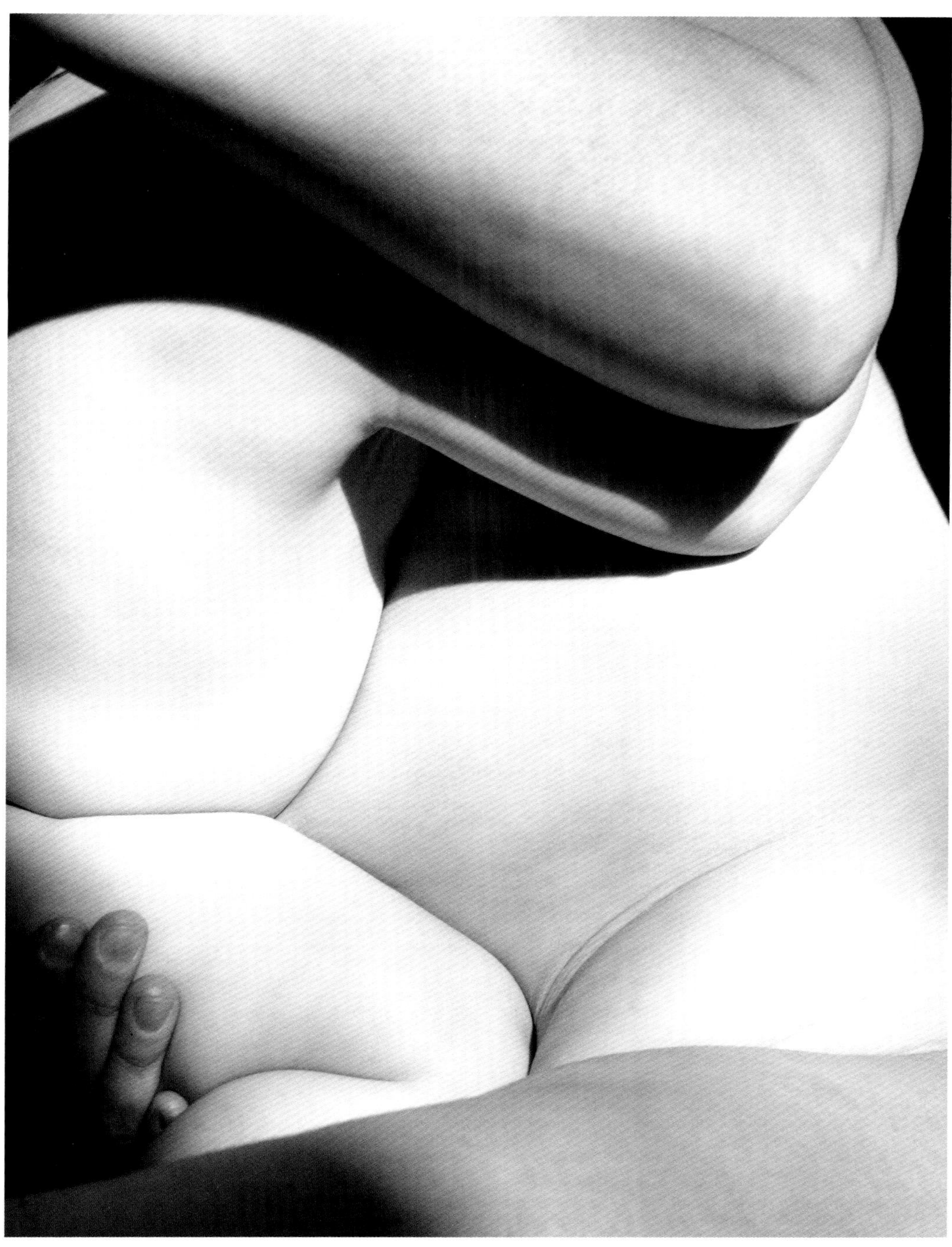

One of the many things that I learned from Chip Benson didn't materialize all at once but rather slowly over time and through a series of artworks that I have made over the years. These pieces have been conceptual in nature, but one thing they all have in common is how they play out the arrangement of scales in black and white. What Benson achieved through his halftone separations expanded my understanding of the tonal values of prints. Whereas I used to think that black-and-white prints require a black tone and a white tone with all the grays in between, Benson's prints showed me that you could hang out in the lower values of those scales, and it would create a depth of feeling that changed how I look at prints and their potential to describe half, whole, and even quarter registers of light on surfaces. The range of values in Benson's prints is expansive; he rendered prints as deep space with color and light activating the infinitesimal. I can't help but think about Benson's clocks along these lines and how they found new ways to communicate the riddles of time. Benson's clocks didn't have ordinary clock faces; they kept time by some other spatial measure that he had conceived of; they were like meta clocks keeping meta time, if you can imagine such a thing.

A PHOTOGRAPHIC TONE (SEASLAWE), 2017
Archival pigment prints
5 parts, 9⅞ × 14 in. (25.2 × 35.6 cm) each

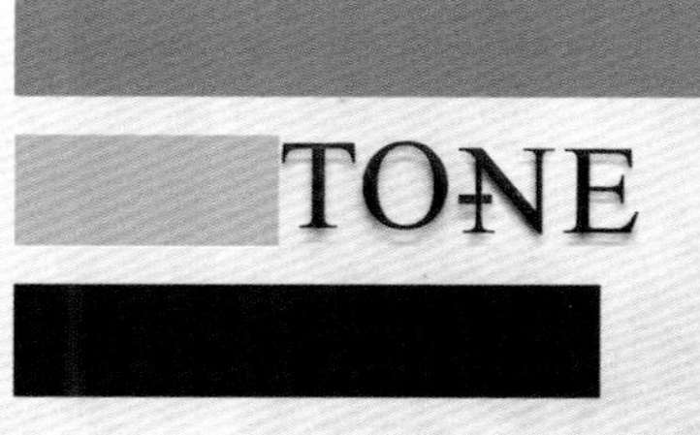

Most of the attention to Chip Benson's work has focused on the craft of printing and bookmaking. When Chip was my professor, he invited us to the opening of *The Printed Picture* at MoMA but spent most of our class time sharing reflections on his life. His insights have stuck with me as much as any technical thing he taught me. Probably the most influential reflection he shared, for my work, was that a good photograph has "life" in it—the sense that something happened before or after the moment pictured. When I traveled to Afton, Wyoming, in the early spring of 2009, I met some ranching families whose children played soccer on the local high school team. I explained to the coaches that I was beginning a project about how people lived in areas of the American West that were famous for being wild. That afternoon, I set up my camera on their heated AstroTurf field, recently installed by a local mining company, and photographed the students practicing. There was one moment when all the boys bunched together, looking up at the ball that was outside of the frame. The colorful field and their sporty outfits contrasted with the snow-covered landscape behind them. Most of the boys seemed expectant. The tallest one was calm. There is life in that photograph. It implies as much as it describes.

Soccer Practice, Star Valley Braves, Afton, Wyoming, 2010
Pigment print
36 × 46 in. (91.4 × 116.8 cm)

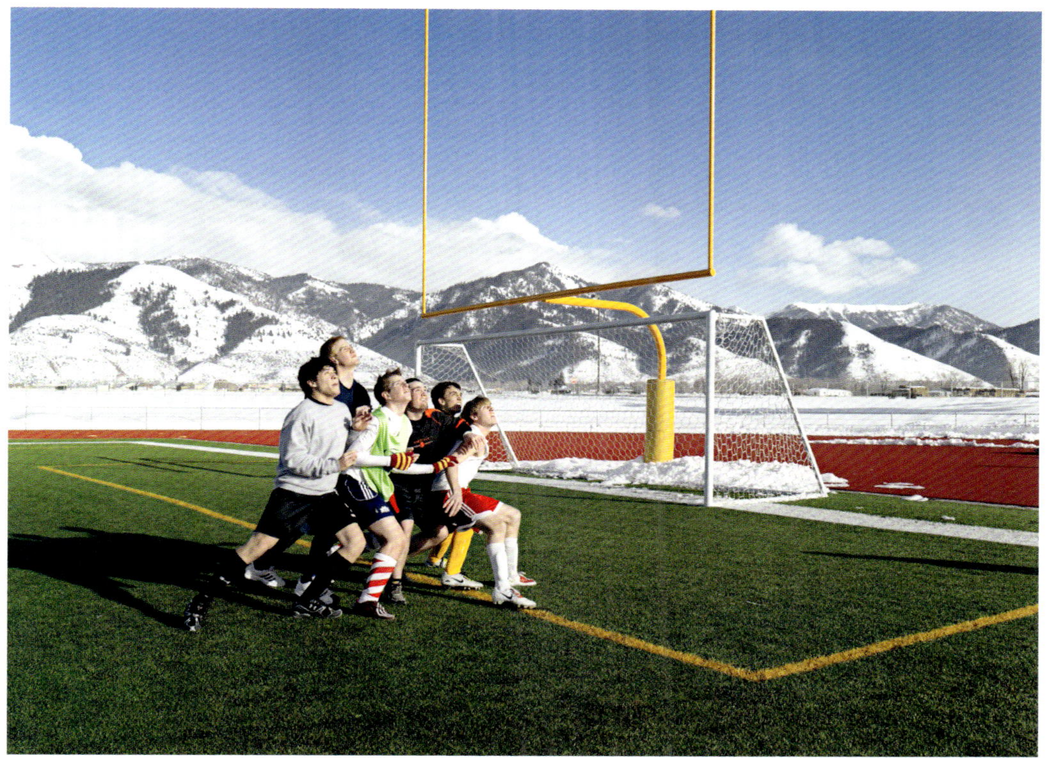

Michael Hoffman introduced me to Richard Benson in the late spring of 1978. I had recently returned to the US from the Atelier de Taille Douce of Saint-Prex in Switzerland, having finished my Thomas J. Watson Fellowship, during which I had been researching the photogravure process with the idea of reviving it. I had contacted Hoffman to see if Aperture had any interest in this research. He immediately invited me to meet with him in New York. During the meeting, he telephoned Chip and arranged for me to go to Newport and show him what I had been doing. Chip had received a Guggenheim Fellowship to research ink and photography, and with funding from Georgia O'Keeffe, he had purchased an etching press to pursue his own research into photogravure.

My meeting with Chip went well, and he agreed that I could come back later in the summer and try to make some photogravures for Aperture of Paul Strand's work from his original negatives. I returned in late August, thinking I would stay for a week or two and make a couple of photogravures. Making photogravures from Paul Strand's negatives that could be "equivalent" to Strand's gelatin-silver prints was no small challenge. I stayed for two years.

While in Newport that fall, I made a photogravure print of *Fisherman, Gaspé*, which Aperture published to accompany a special slipcased copy of *Paul Strand: Sixty Years of Photographs*, and Chip and I made *Iris, Maine* together. (I prepared the plate, he etched it, and I then proofed and printed it.)

Since I had shown extreme perseverance and had modest success with a couple of Strands, with Chip's counsel, we decided to try producing an Edward Steichen portfolio for Aperture. The idea originated with the 1967 reissue of Strand's portfolio *Photographs of Mexico*. On the basis of that, Steichen had originally approached Michael Hoffman and Aperture with the idea of creating a portfolio of his images. It had been an unrealized project until I came along and was willing to attempt it.

I began work in the winter of 1979, still borrowing Chip's studio, which he called the "Dark House." There were untold difficulties as we attempted to reestablish working methods for the complex process of hand-pulled, dust-grain photogravures that were all but forgotten. At some point, Chip and I went to the Metropolitan Museum of Art to make full-scale copy negatives of a selection of Steichen's prints that were in the Alfred Stieglitz Collection. At the time, the Meriden Gravure Company had a large horizontal process camera installed in one of the museum's subbasements with a darkroom, so we were able to make large-format copy negatives of Steichen's *The Flatiron*, *The Pond—Moonrise*, and *Richard Strauss* without having to remove them from the premises. (Years later, Steichen's original *Moonrise* print was sold from the collection for a record amount at auction.) By 1980, I had all twelve plates made and proofs selected as "go by," or *bon à tirer*, prints. So, it was then time for the next phase. For this, I left Newport and returned to the Atelier de Taille Douce and worked with the intaglio printers there. It took another year to produce the five hundred prints of the initial printing of twelve plates.

What I usually tell people is that in Switzerland, I learned about the refinements of printing, printing ink, and printmaking as they pertain to photogravure. And from Chip, I learned about photographic materials, their response to light, the chemistry, and how to use that to arrive at a consciously desired, rather than random, result. I also learned, by example from Chip, a freedom to pursue the ideas and interests that speak to me the strongest.

Paul Strand, *Old Fisherman, Gaspé*, 1936
Dust grain photogravure
6⅛ × 4⅞ in. (15.6 × 12.4 cm)

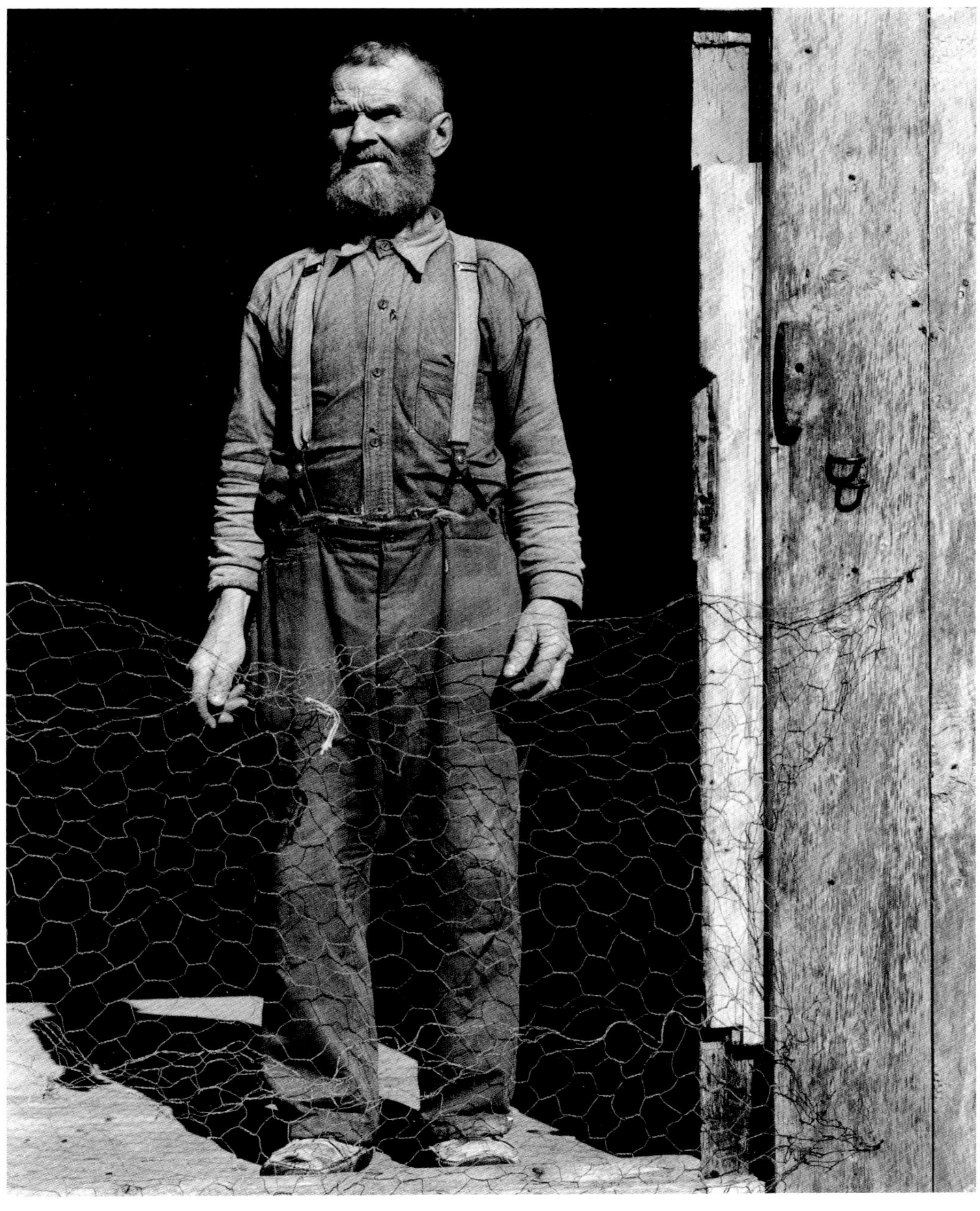

When our graduate class had Chip for the required bookmaking class, we took a field trip to GHP Media to tour the West Haven facility before printing our thesis book. He showed us around the printing presses and took us over to the digital offset Indigo Press. He described that we could make a different kind of book with this machine, one where each book's page sequence would be randomly generated, so each book would be essentially unique. I also remember Chip telling us how he had printed an entire edition of a book, by himself, using a Heidelberg press that was installed in his basement. This dedication to the printed image by any means necessary really struck a chord with me. At the time, during my last semester at Yale, I had just started to use chance, modular systems, and random activity as conceptual frameworks to generate images—which Chip found amusing and kindly ribbed me about frequently.

Fast forward five years, and I got the opportunity to publish my first book, *Wildlife Analysis* (2013), with some inspiration from Chip's ideas and techniques. My publisher and frequent collaborator, Conveyor Arts, generated an algorithm so that each book in the edition of five hundred was unique and utilized the capabilities of the Indigo printing press. This was paired with my decision to design and reprint the entire book in a color darkroom with an enlarging easel as my only design tool for the layout and 8-by-10-inch color darkroom paper as my template. In total, there were 105 unique analog C-prints that made the book edit, out of more boxes of paper than I care to remember. It took about two years to complete, and all the while, I was figuring out how and why this should even be a book. I honestly believe that without having had Chip as a teacher, this book wouldn't exist. He taught me to listen to, and trust, my instincts. Even when things might seem like they're going off the rails, if you have curiosity and conviction in what you're doing, things might go all right.

Untitled, 2011–13, from *Wildlife Analysis*
(Jersey City, NJ: Conveyor Arts, 2013)
Set of sixteen unique analog C-prints
10 × 8 in. (25.4 × 20.3 cm) each

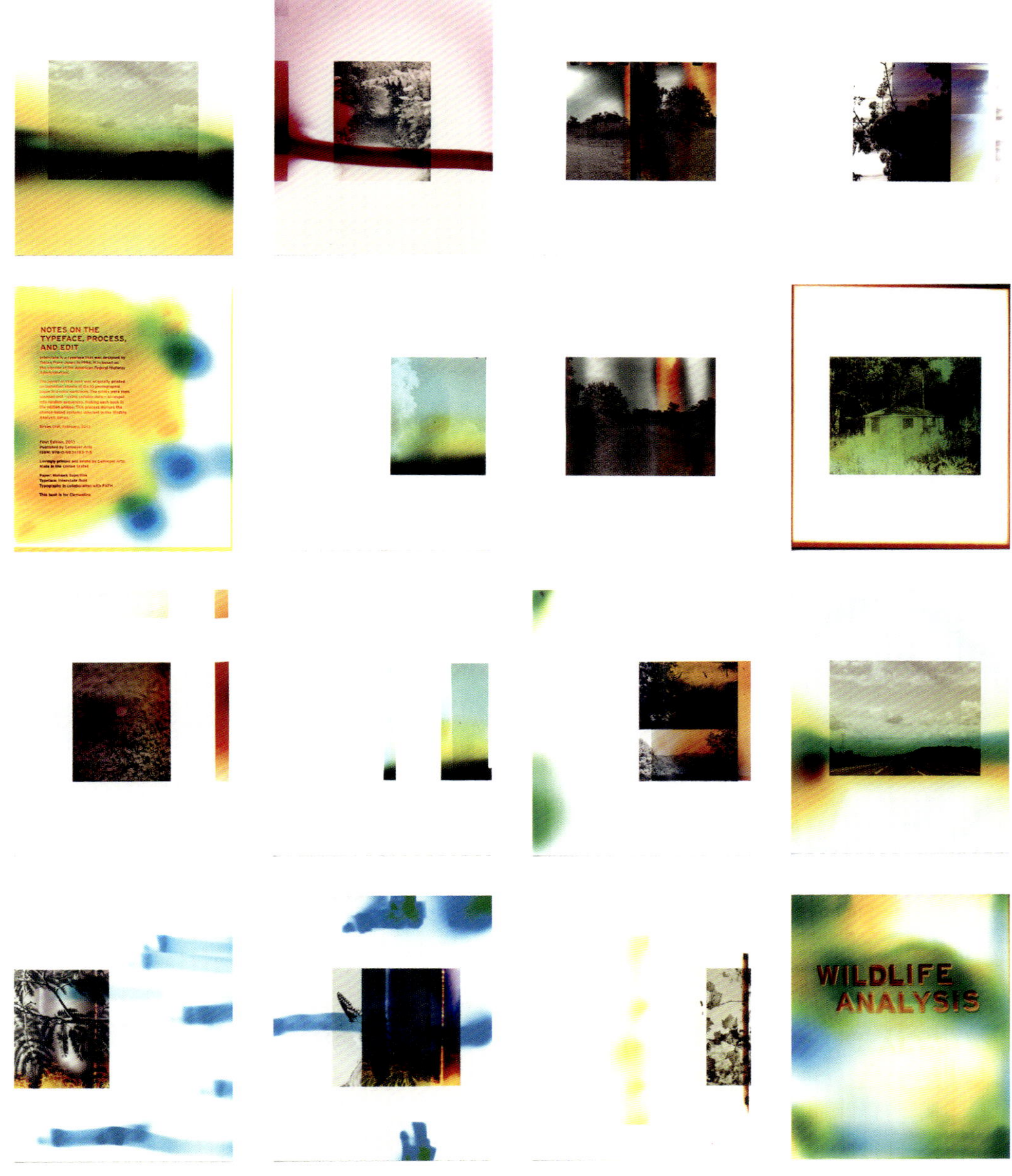

When I started Chip's class at Yale, I thought I was going to learn technical photography skills. His very first assignment left me totally confused. Although I had done everything that he asked, I hated the pictures. I remember looking at the contact sheet in the darkroom with him, trying to find the image that was "good." He told me, however, that there's no such thing as an empirically "good" photograph. He helped me understand that photography is not just about passively capturing something in the world, but rather caring passionately and deeply about something enough to photograph it. I spent the remaining years of graduate school learning to use photography to engage with the world, not just the medium itself.

One of the things that Chip and I both cared about deeply was New England architecture. I was specifically interested in how it set the stage for domestic dramas. In 2016, he and Elizabeth Kahane, photographer and philanthropist, invited me to Newport to photograph for my series *Out My Window*. Although he had just learned that he was sick, he still generously spent days with me, introducing me to his friends and neighbors. This picture is of Elizabeth and Bill Kahane's house, which happened to be previously owned by Dodo Hamilton, the grandmother-in-law of Chip's son. These kinds of coincidences happened with all my shoots in Newport. Chip knew everyone in town, and everyone was willing to help with my project because he had given it his blessing. If I saw a house that I wanted to photograph, I simply had to ask Chip for an introduction and I was invited to photograph there (and often offered a glass of wine on the porch afterwards). Chip and the Kahanes showed me that Newport wasn't a snobby town of mansions on the Cliff Walk, but a warm community of neighbors who were willing to trust a curious photographer. While Chip taught me to be a technical perfectionist, he, more importantly, showed me how to fall madly in love with the people and places I photograph.

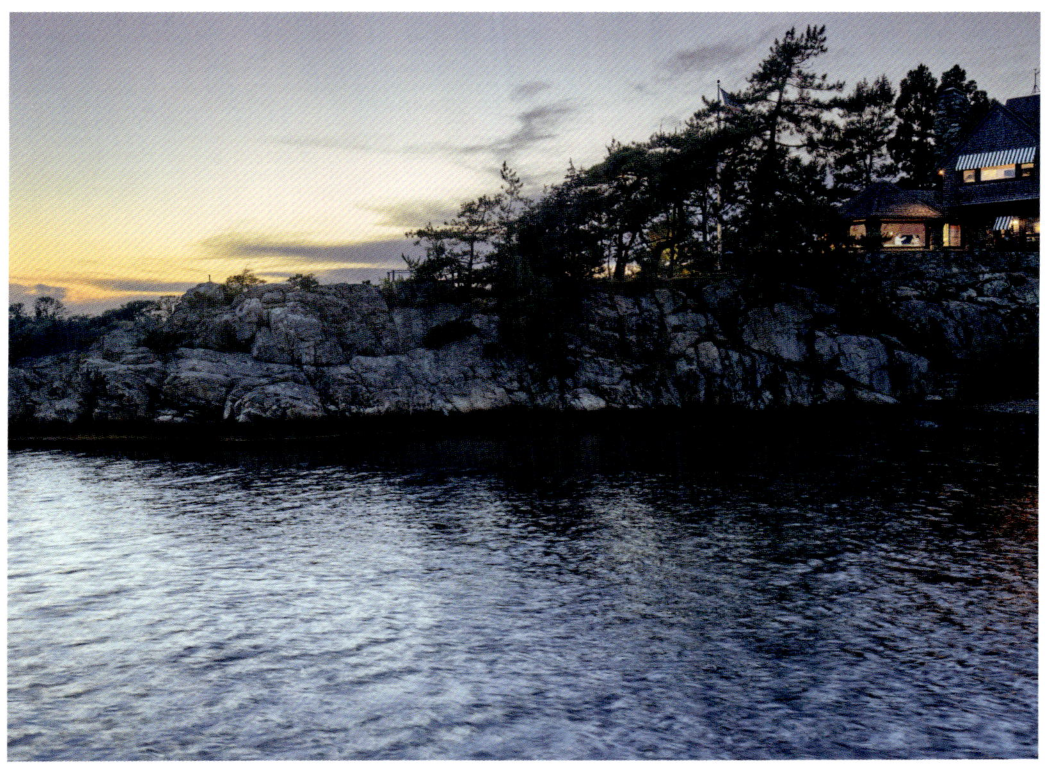

Out My Window, Newport, Wildacre, 2016
Pigment print
34 × 45⅜ in. (86.4 × 115.3 cm)

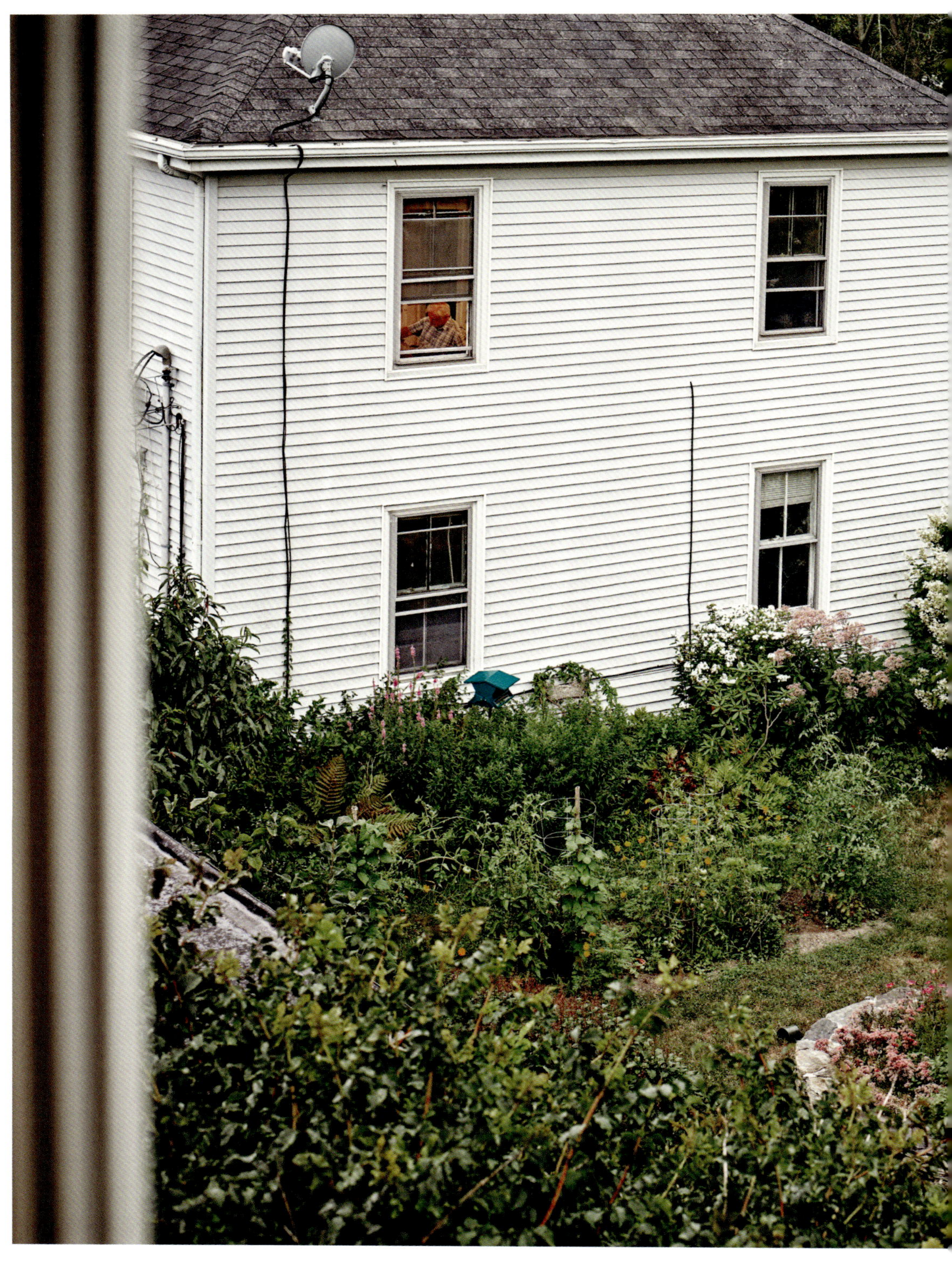

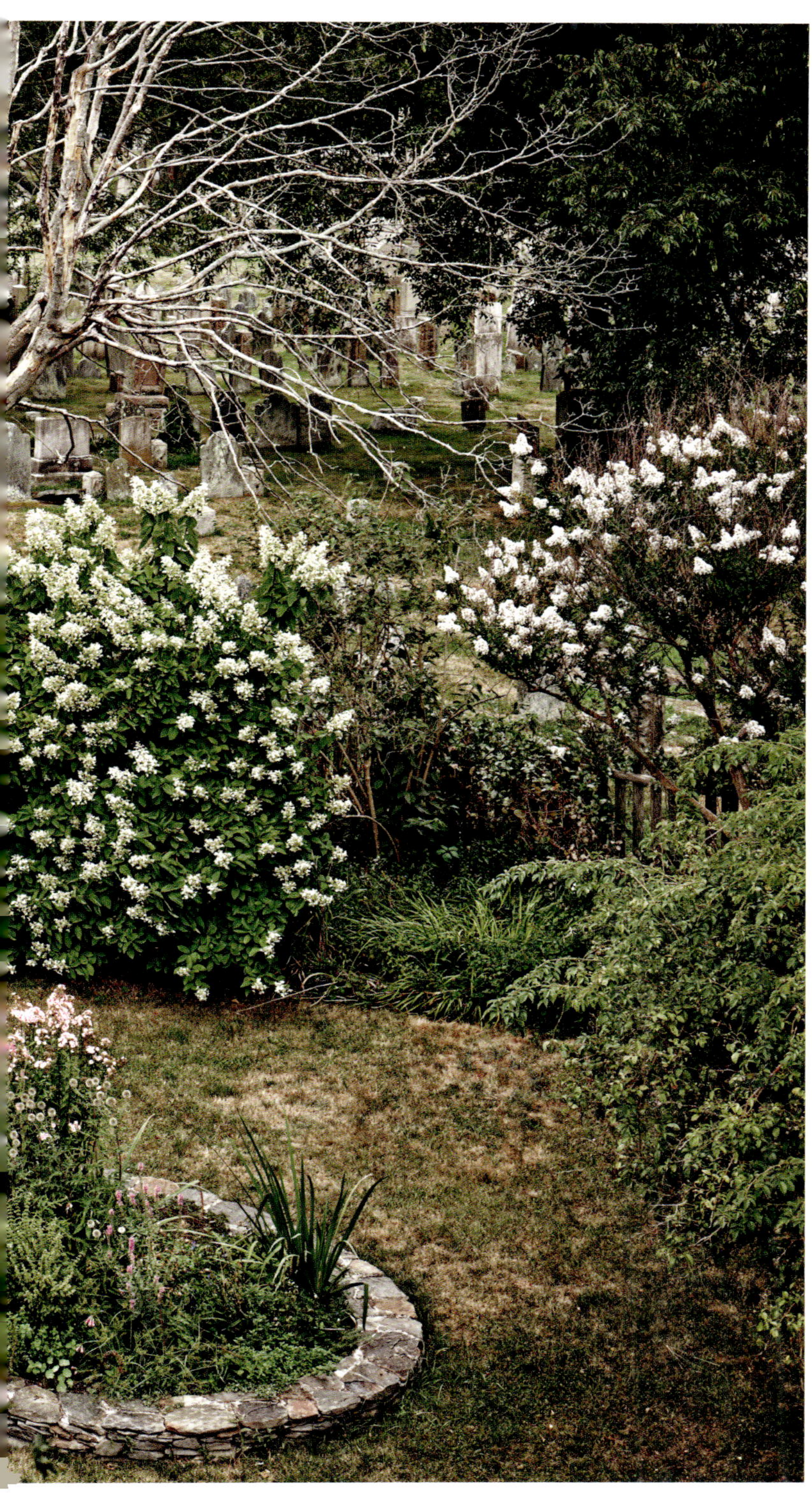

Out My Window, Newport, Thomas's Garden, 2016
Pigment print
34 × 45⅜ in. (86.4 × 115.3 cm)

As a testament to Chip's ingenuity, admiring former students sometimes cite his experimental process of separating a photograph into
numerous halftones and printing them in acrylic paint on aluminum.
It's exactly the kind of thing that captivates the imagination of a young
photographer in love with the processes and materials of photography.
The most widely known picture that was printed with this technique
is likely his untitled photograph reproduced in Stephen Shore's *The
Nature of Photographs* (1998). When looking at it now though, I am struck
not by its technical virtuosity but by the great lengths he went to make a
uniquely beautiful print (the picture's subject, a hydraulic excavator
bucket, seems a suitable metaphor for his effort).

Chip's print—particularly in contrast with its reproduction in
Shore's book—illustrates with comic exaggeration how the way a
photograph is printed affects its meaning. It also exemplifies an ethos
that imbued his final words of advice after graduating from Yale:
"Somehow you should try to figure out how to beat this new technology
into making things that physically are very beautiful—are *physically*
beautiful." His commitment to the physical print amid the changes
wrought by digital technology has deeply influenced my own work.

My picture of bananas was printed on a desktop inkjet printer with
a half-dozen hand-mixed inks. The tone of the final print was controlled by adjusting the concentration of pigments in each ink mixture
rather than by digital means, like applying a curve in Photoshop. The
process is manual, iterative, and admittedly goofy, but it allows incredibly fine control. It also requires more direct contact with the materials—
ink and paper—than digital printing usually permits. I don't mean to
advocate that we cling to ossifying processes, but I do believe that if
photographic prints are to endure for another 190 years, we must bend
the arc of technology away from "you press the button, we do the rest"
and toward "making things that are physically very beautiful."

Ausgerechnet Bananen, 2020
Pigment print with hand-mixed inks
14 × 9⅞ in. (35.6 × 25.1 cm)

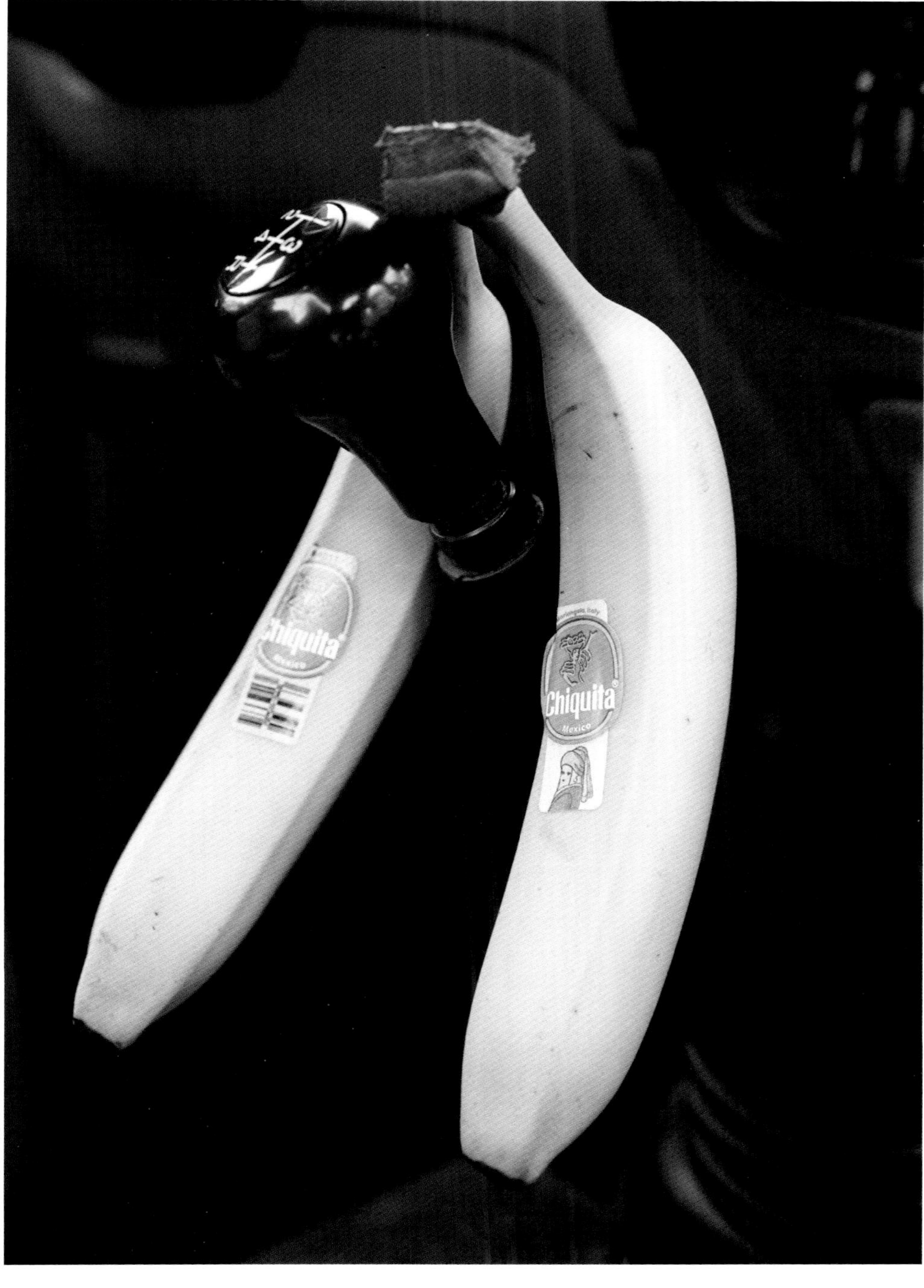

Richard Benson did the halftone photography in two books that had a significant influence on me in my early days as a printer: *English Drawings and Watercolors, 1550–1830 in the Collection of Mr. and Mrs. Paul Mellon* (1972) and *The American Monument* (1976) by Lee Friedlander.

The Mellon book was a typical museum publication printed at the Meriden Gravure Company, where Benson worked at the time. Printed on uncoated paper, the book is luminous and clear with a beautiful, soft color and tonality. The Friedlander photography book is also printed on uncoated paper. It was a radical idea at the time to use uncoated paper to print contemporary photography. The printed results look like actual photographs, not reproductions. The pictures have a strong presence and clarity, and they retain the sensibility of the originals, though in a new way.

Before the advent of our present digital system, all high-quality printed reproductions of original artwork had to be photographed directly into halftone—the tiny dots that created the illusion of tonality and resulted in the film matrix from which a printing plate was made. A large vacuum-back camera held high-contrast film in contact with a transparent halftone screen, and the screen's apertures exposed light onto the film in proportion to the light reflected from the original artwork. The exposed film was then developed by hand in a chemical tray, a process that required a high level of skill and judgment. It also depended on the technician having an insightful interpretation of the original artwork into ink on paper. Those processes and decisions determined the quality of the printing plate used on the press.

Both the Friedlander and Mellon books employ a monochrome technique called "double impression," which uses one halftone negative to make one plate for the printing press to print the two successive colors in register—black and either a light gray or a warm buff gray. This halftone photography technique to make the printing plates is the same for both books, as dissimilar as they are in content. That this old technique was used in a new way was inspiring to me and is the foundation of my effort in making illustrated books.

Chip's guidance, teaching, and encouragement in my early days at the Meriden Gravure gave me insight into a printing aesthetic that he imagined. It has endured as a model for all of us who make illustrated books.

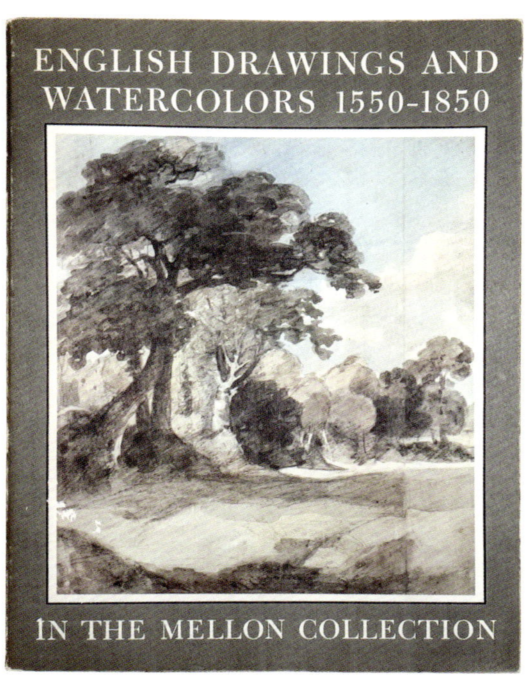

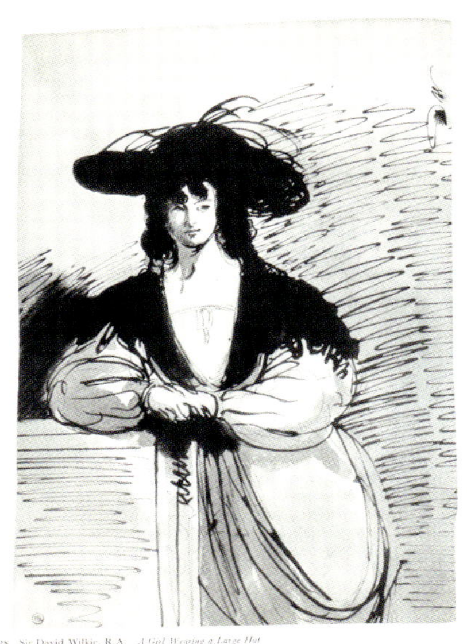
128 Sir David Wilkie, R.A.: *A Girl Wearing a Large Hat*

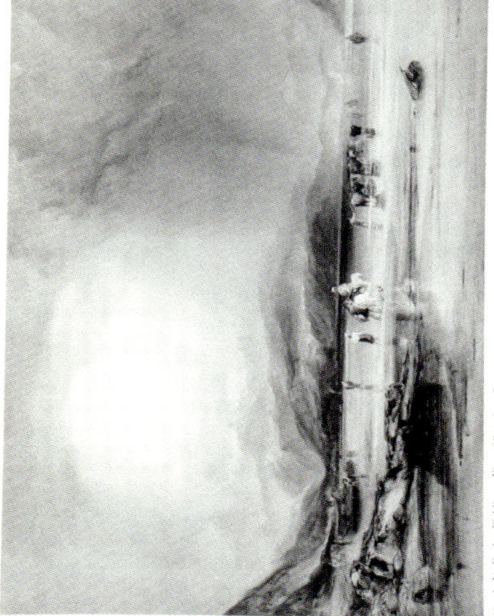
129 A. V. Copley Fielding: *View of Snowdon, 1834*

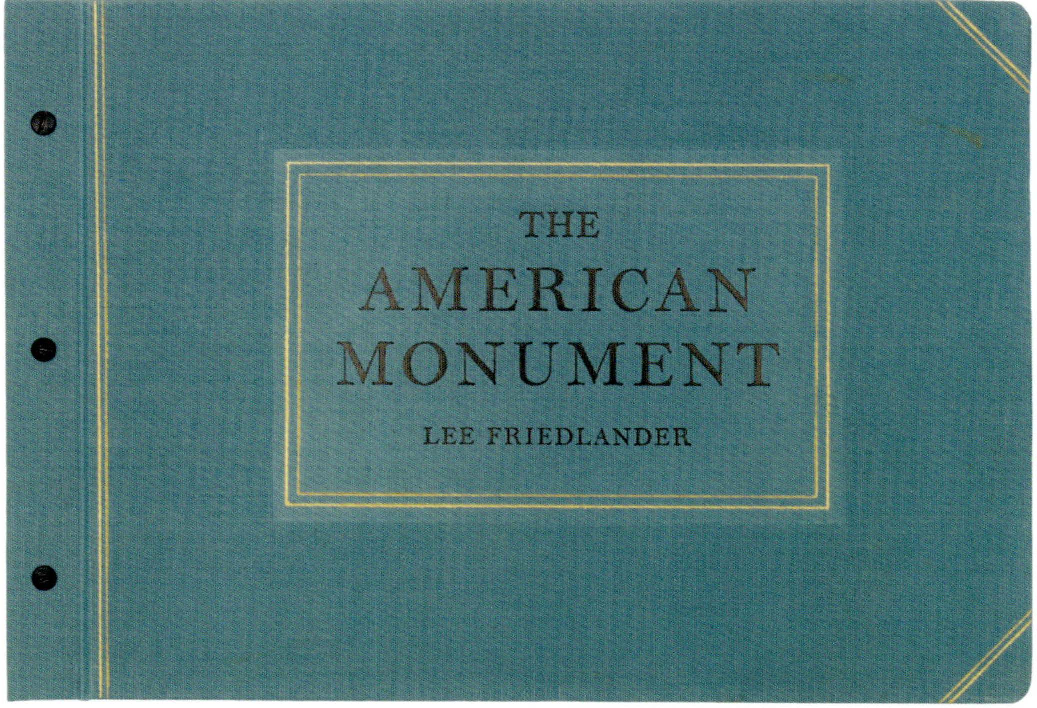
THE
AMERICAN
MONUMENT
LEE FRIEDLANDER

Lee Friedlander, *The American Monument*
(New York: Eakins Press Foundation, 1976)

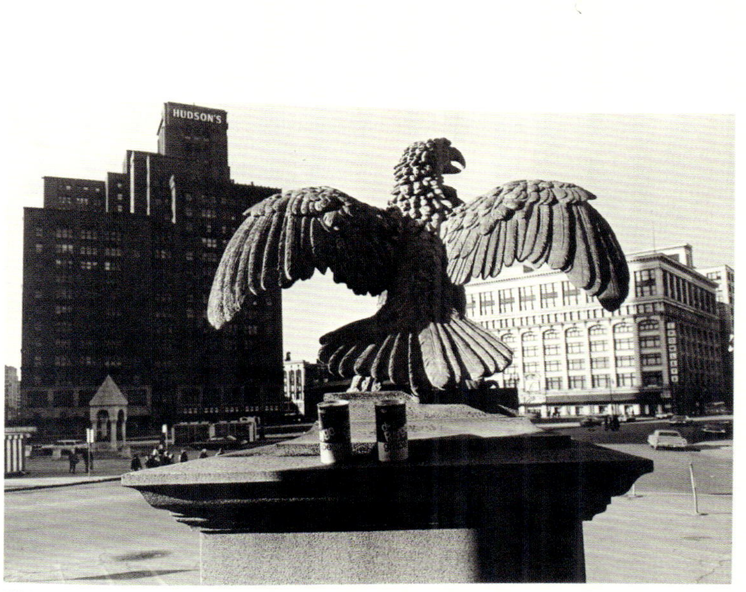

57. To Michigan Soldiers and Sailors. Campus Martius, Detroit, Michigan

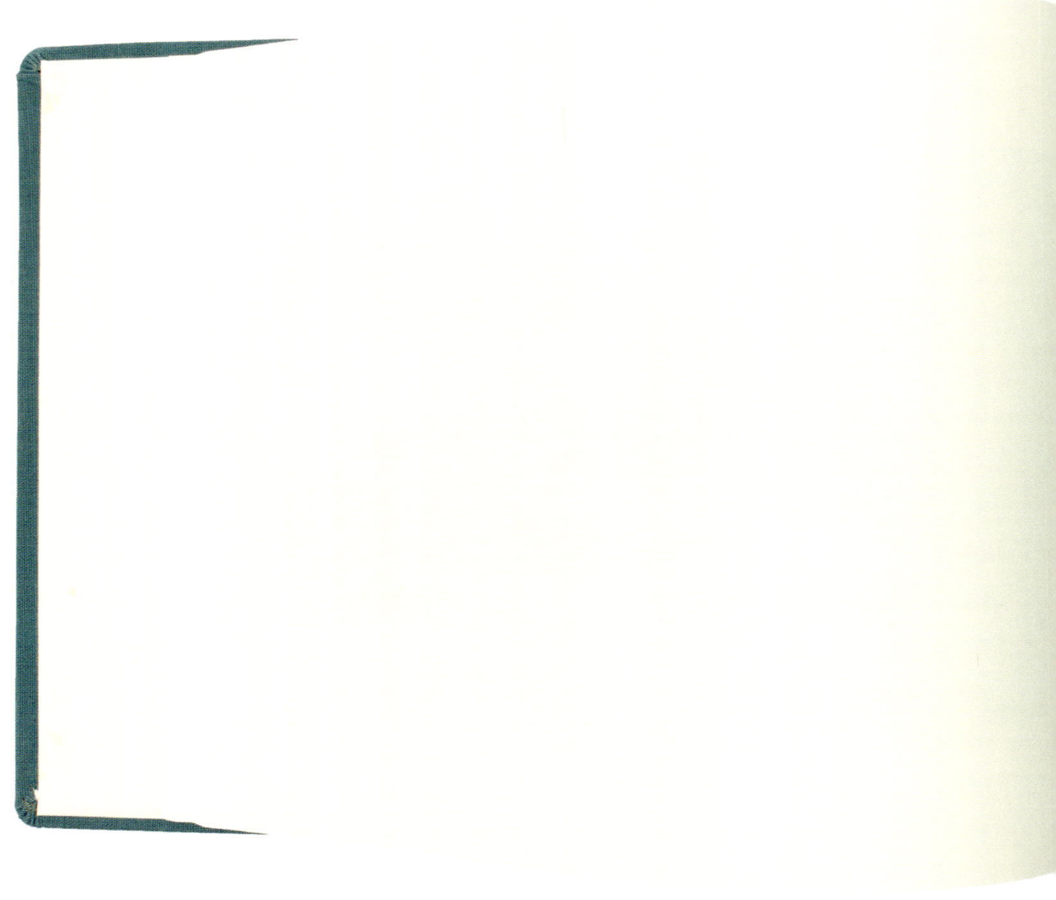

Lee Friedlander, *The American Monument*
(New York: Eakins Press Foundation, 1976)

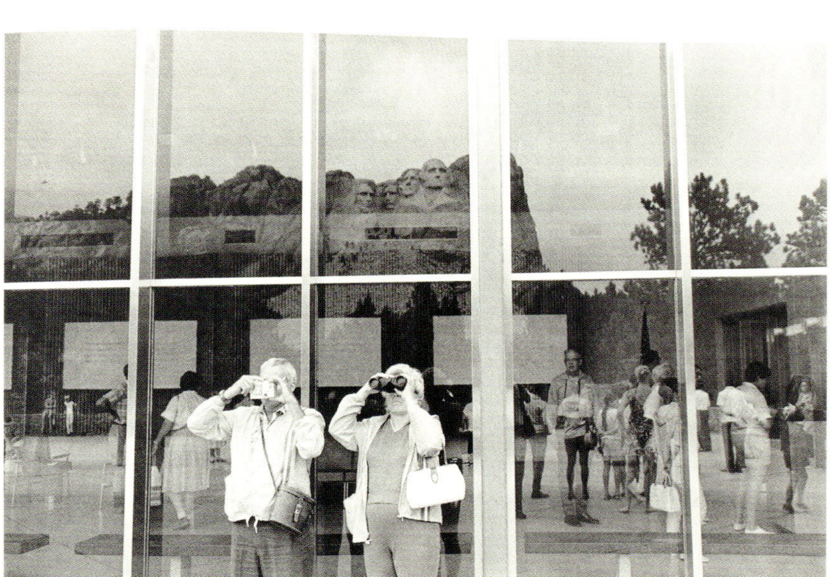

99. Mount Rushmore, South Dakota

Richard Benson's celebrated journey with the "printed dot," and its transformative implications for photography, was sustained through his decades-long relationship with Leslie George Katz and the Eakins Press Foundation. Three milestone publications in particular—*Lay This Laurel* (1973), with photographs by Benson and a deeply insightful essay by the polymath Lincoln Kirstein; Lee Friedlander's ground-breaking monograph *The American Monument* (1976); and *'O, Write My Name': American Portraits, Harlem Heroes* (1983), with photographs by Carl Van Vechten—paved new pathways for photography and its representation in printed ink. The Benson/Katz affinity that found its zeitgeist in the medium of the photography book defined Benson's lifelong contribution to American art, not to mention outfitted his workshop with a printing press and all the related equipment he needed to set new technical standards and invent new ways of using familiar processes. The relationship was mutually beneficial—Benson under-stood the importance of patrons in his quest to reinvent printing, if not contemporary photography altogether, and Katz needed a craftsman who could fulfill the press's mission to produce books that "in content and form defend human excellence."[1] Of Benson, Katz wrote that he "confirms authenticity by fanatical devotion to techniques of simula-tion that gratify the manifold hunger for illusion. But it is always with the precision of an observer who knows how things should look, not a magician, that he extends the horizons of the eye."[2]

An inventor at heart, Benson dismantled existing, and sometimes outmoded, printing techniques and reassembled them to serve his savant-like understanding of how ink and paper can be combined to transmute the esoteric nature of the unique print into a democratically accessible medium of multiples—a process fundamental to the nature of photography. But this was clearly a fraught ambition for Benson, who sought to elevate what he saw as photography's inherent mediocrity—"Something's wrong with photography, and I've got this idea that it's because the physical thing we end up making just isn't good enough"[3]—to something akin to painting, wherein the artist's hand employed the tools of the medium to make something that conveyed the hard work that was always so important to him. With one project (as in the case of his printing of *The American Monument*), he might employ a "slip-dot halftone" on press to make thousands of copies of individual images—"slip-dot" entailing his own invented offset technique in which the same halftone plate is used for two impressions to create a broader tonal range. (An initial pass of black ink is laid down and allowed to dry; then, the second pass of gray ink—intentionally out of register—is laid down on top.) At the same time, he might be painstakingly translating his own negatives into "paintings" on sheets of aluminum that require a dozen or more layers of acrylic paint to build one-of-a-kind prints. In both cases, it's safe to say that no one else could replicate what he was doing. Benson pushed the relationship between "original" images and printed multiples to a place that is still being sorted and understood. He once wrote: "I think it is possible that once we can see the growth of photography clearly, it may not appear as the revolution that we think it to be today, but as simply another very fine and very advanced means of making images on paper."[4]

As a printer, Benson sustained a productive tension between hard-wrought unique prints of photographs and conventionally accessible manufactured trade editions, and one can sense a similar tension in his own work as a photographer. We see in his efforts an obsessive dedication to the thing at hand—"a picture is probably the most complicated thing you can make"—as well as to the hand itself. "The 300 line screen negatives would be developed and etched by hand and the inks carefully mixed to match the colors of the original prints. . . . It is important to understand that the sort of book I am proposing has never been made before."[5]

His trade as a printer was inseparable from his work as an artist photographer, and vice versa; but it is his work as a printer for which he is most widely known. Benson's first solo exhibition took place at Washburn Gallery in New York in October 1976. The photographs presented included palladium prints of the pictures he made for *Lay*

This Laurel of the Augustus Saint-Gaudens memorial to Colonel Robert Gould Shaw (as well as a selection of photographs he made of Daniel Chester French's *The Four Continents*, which had been commissioned by the Metropolitan Museum of Art). In an accompanying essay, Lincoln Kirstein wrote of Benson: "His graphic records are quite selfless, just as the lettering on an arch or a gravestone tells nothing of the hand that cut it, but gives all honor and attention to the names and deeds remembered. . . . [I]n the record of Saint-Gaudens' marvelous memorial, we find the camera used to its peak accomplishment in one of its most honorable, unique and valuable services, that of imaginative documentation."[6]

While the analogy to cutting stone in "honor and attention" must have resonated deeply with Benson, given his family history and love of making things by hand, it must have been difficult for him to digest the suggestion that his art was in the service of anything other than his own artistic vision. Therein lies the essence of Benson's creative life. As he once said: "Photographs have such a clear connection to the world, through the description of the lens, that we often assume they can exist apart from any physical container; my experience has been quite the opposite—that the specific manner in which any photograph is printed can have a tremendous effect upon its meaning."[7]

In his 1977 Guggenheim Fellowship application, Benson wrote: "My plan for this Fellowship is to further my research on the development of hand ink printing and hand photo-offset printing. I would be printing photographs taken by myself. . . . I feel that a Fellowship would allow me to raise photographic ink printing to a practical and versatile level and that this would be a significant contribution to the field." In his supporting letter of Benson's successful application, Katz wrote: "In my opinion it is possible that Richard Benson may turn out to be the most gifted and accomplished photographer-printer of his generation."

The most ambitious of the Eakins Press collaborations with Benson is Carl Van Vechten's *'O, Write My Name': American Portraits, Harlem Heroes*, which features inimitable, intimate portraits of the people who

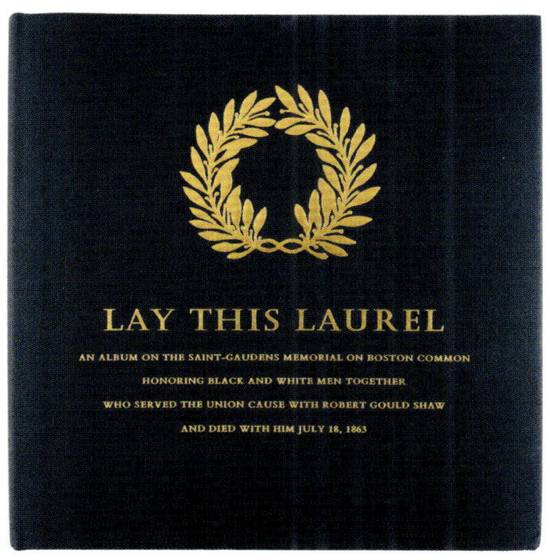

LAY THIS LAUREL
AN ALBUM ON THE SAINT-GAUDENS MEMORIAL ON BOSTON COMMON
HONORING BLACK AND WHITE MEN TOGETHER
WHO SERVED THE UNION CAUSE WITH ROBERT GOULD SHAW
AND DIED WITH HIM JULY 18, 1863

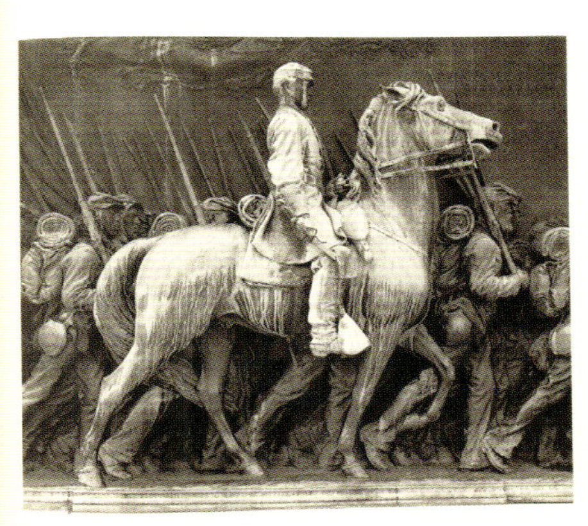

THE SAINT-GAUDENS ON BOSTON COMMON
Moving, marching, faces of souls!
Part-freers of a destiny
Swaying us on with you—(slowly, restlessly—)
(Relentlessly), towards other freedom.
The one, in front, carved from what
Your country was made for—
You—images of God carved in (ebony),
Above and beyond that moving mass
The shadow of a saddened heart—never light abandoned.
—Moving marching faces of Souls!
CHARLES IVES

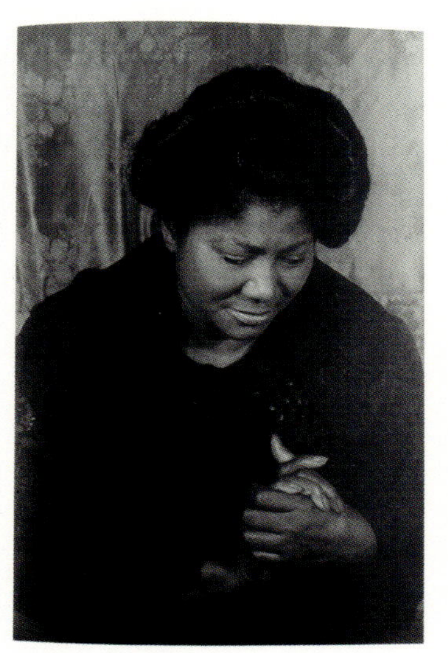

'O, WRITE MY NAME'

Photographs by Carl Van Vechten

AMERICAN PORTRAITS

HARLEM HEROES

MAHALIA JACKSON
1911–1972

There are certain women singers who possess, beyond all the boundaries of our admiration for their art, an uncanny power to evoke our love.... And when we encounter the simple dignity of their immediate presence, we suddenly ponder the mystery of human greatness....

RALPH ELLISON
(from the essay "As the Spirit Moves Mahalia")

Once a maid and factory worker, she became the world's foremost Gospel singer through the application of her musical passion, self-discipline and management skills. An inspiration to the civil rights movement, her singing reflected the religious and secular roots of black music.

1962

Carl Van Vechten, *'O, Write My Name': American Portraits, Harlem Heroes* (New York: Eakins Press Foundation, 2015 edition)

shaped the Harlem Renaissance. A dizzying array of public and private donors, consolidated through the agency of the press, allowed for the purchase of a printing press and all the necessary accompanying hardware. Benson's experiments in printing Van Vechten's notoriously technically inconsistent negatives resulted in a portfolio of resplendent hand-pulled gravure prints with tones as rich as "the black on a butterfly's wing," as Katz put it. The process also refined Benson's prescient understanding of choosing techniques that resonated not just with the historical images at hand, but also with the spirit and intent of the artists who made them. He once delivered a clear forecast of the ubiquity of inkjet printing today, stating: "There is no question in my mind that the future of photography will involve printing with ink on paper, eliminating the current dependency upon chemical processing and thus making photography a more traditional and lasting graphic art. The sort of endeavor we are contemplating could show the way."[8]

'O, Write My Name' received a $47,000 grant from Georgia O'Keeffe (another patron of Benson's who was deeply interested in how ink could be used to render photographs) and subsequent support from the Ford Foundation, J. M. Kaplan Fund, National Endowment for the Arts, Gilman Paper Company, and many others. The project evolved between 1975 and 1983, when it was ultimately published, in the midst of Benson's most inventive period. This was when he was working toward his printing tour de force, the book *Photographs from the Collection of the Gilman Paper Company* (1985), which would lead to him receiving the MacArthur grant in 1986.

Richard Benson spawned a generation of technicians who elevated the art of the printed photograph without losing touch with its essentially utilitarian essence—after all, books have a purpose. "A book, like a shoe, a coat, or a baseball mitt, is made for use or wear if it is serious," Katz once wrote. "Repeated use only deepens its character."[9] Benson also influenced a generation of photographers with his teaching by example. In the process, he transformed how people will experience photography for posterity. Even as the medium redefines and reinvents

Carl Van Vechten, *Mahalia Jackson*, 1962
Gravure (above) and gravure plate (below)

itself in ever-tightening cycles, Richard Benson has left behind a world that bears the indelible marks of his mind and his hand. As he once wrote:

> If you ask any biologist what is more miraculous—the mind or the hand—you will undoubtedly be told the mind takes the prize. This remarkable wet thing that we carry around inside our heads is the most complicated known object that we are aware of; it is the force behind all the great stuff we have made. The hand does its work in response to the directives of the mind and the senses, and in the realm of art, the result is some physical object that can be accessed by all of us and that—when cared for—can outlive its maker. Then, even though a mind once stood behind it, the physical thing is all that remains.[10]

1. Excerpted from Eakins Press Foundation mission statement, 1966.
2. Leslie George Katz, "Appreciations" in *Message from the Interior* (New York: Eakins Press Foundation, 1993), p. 8.
3. Quoted in Calvin Tomkins, "A Single Person Making a Single Thing," *New Yorker*, December 17, 1990, pp. 44–52.
4. Excerpt from Benson's 1977 Guggenheim Fellowship application.
5. Excerpt from Benson's proposal for "Gilman Paper Company Limited Edition Book" (ca. 1981).
6. Lincoln Kirstein, introduction to *Richard Benson: An Exhibition of Palladium Prints* (New York: Washburn Gallery, 1976), pp. 3–4.
7. Richard Benson, *The Physical Print: A Brief Survey of the Photographic Process* (New Haven, CT: Jonathan Edwards College, 2005), Preface and Introduction, np.
8. From Benson's proposal for "Gilman Paper Company Limited Edition Book" (ca. 1981).
9. Katz, "Appreciations" in *Message from the Interior* (New York: Eakins Press Foundation, 1993), p. 8.
10. Richard Benson, "Lee Friedlander and the Western Landscape" in *Lee Friedlander: Western Landscapes* (New Haven, CT: Yale University Art Gallery, 2016), np.

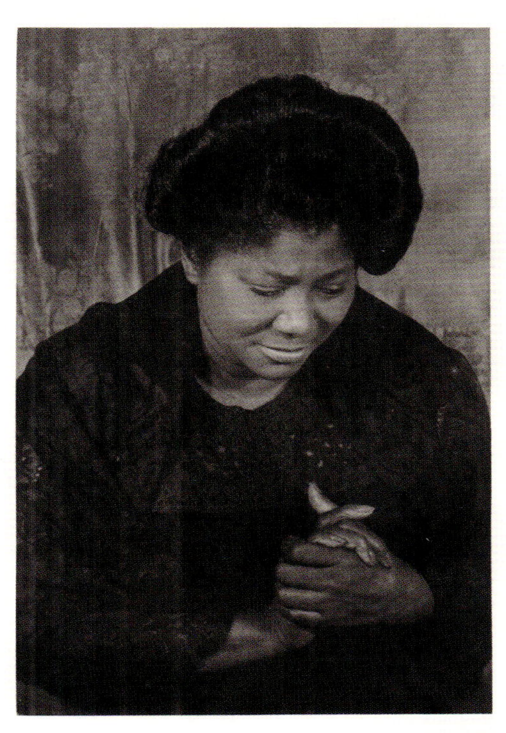

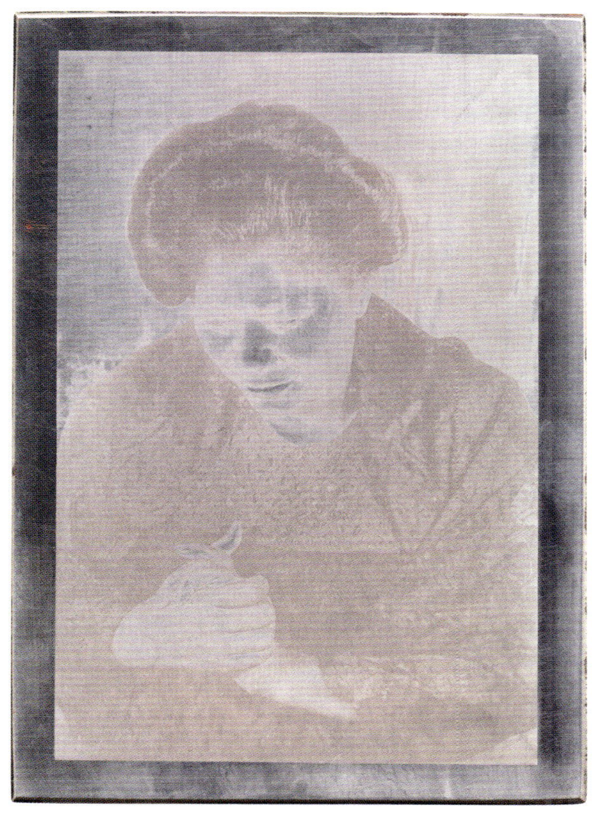

Ironically, it was Richard Benson, a maker of things and obsessive doer of much, who introduced me to one of the most influential texts in the history of photography. I was sitting with him in the somewhat tattered lounge-cum-darkroom area in the basement of the Yale Art and Architecture Building, poring over my contact sheets made just prior to arriving at graduate school. It was early in my very first semester, and I presented to him a few black-and-white contacts of 4-by-5-inch view camera negatives, made at my family's junkyard back home. The pictures were of stacks of old tires, which must be recycled in a very specific and costly way, a difficult process that was, to say the least, a bane in the life of my grandparents, who once had mountains of them in the back. I was pretty proud of my detailed description and my use of swing and tilt to cut the focus across the frame of the photograph, just so.

But Chip informed my eager self that the pictures just didn't work. This was hard for me to grasp. He asserted: "This is just a *study*. There is no *period* in this sentence." He went on to explain that I should read *Camera Lucida* by Roland Barthes, a slim book that incidentally the critic Jerry Saltz handed me at critiques a few months later, having arrived at the exact same conclusion himself. There was something to this. Chip went on to explain that this was just a study of the tires, a well described document. "Now if there was a big squashed bug right there, *that* would be a picture," he explained in simpler terms. The bug would be the punctum, the single thing that the meaning of the picture rests against and is derived from. A period on my visual phrase was what was needed to turn it into a statement with some power and risk. Otherwise, all I would have would still be just a pile of old tires. And that is not enough. The mere study of a thing is not enough; there has to be some tension, something at stake. In this case, that imagined bug's short life would have given the photograph that meaning—made it a memento mori, even.

Speaking of remembering death, a few weeks before the material world lost Chip, my grandmother also passed away. It still gives me some measure of comfort when I look at my daughter and know that some of her genetic material lives on inside this little person, and that my grandmother is there, in a way, when I stroke my daughter's hair at bedtime, just as my grandmother would do for us when she put my sister and me to bed. In the same way, I see Chip when I look at my colleagues and his former students. He lives on in us today, but only in the best parts of ourselves, when we are curious and obsessive as artists, and kind and generous as teachers, partners, parents, and people.

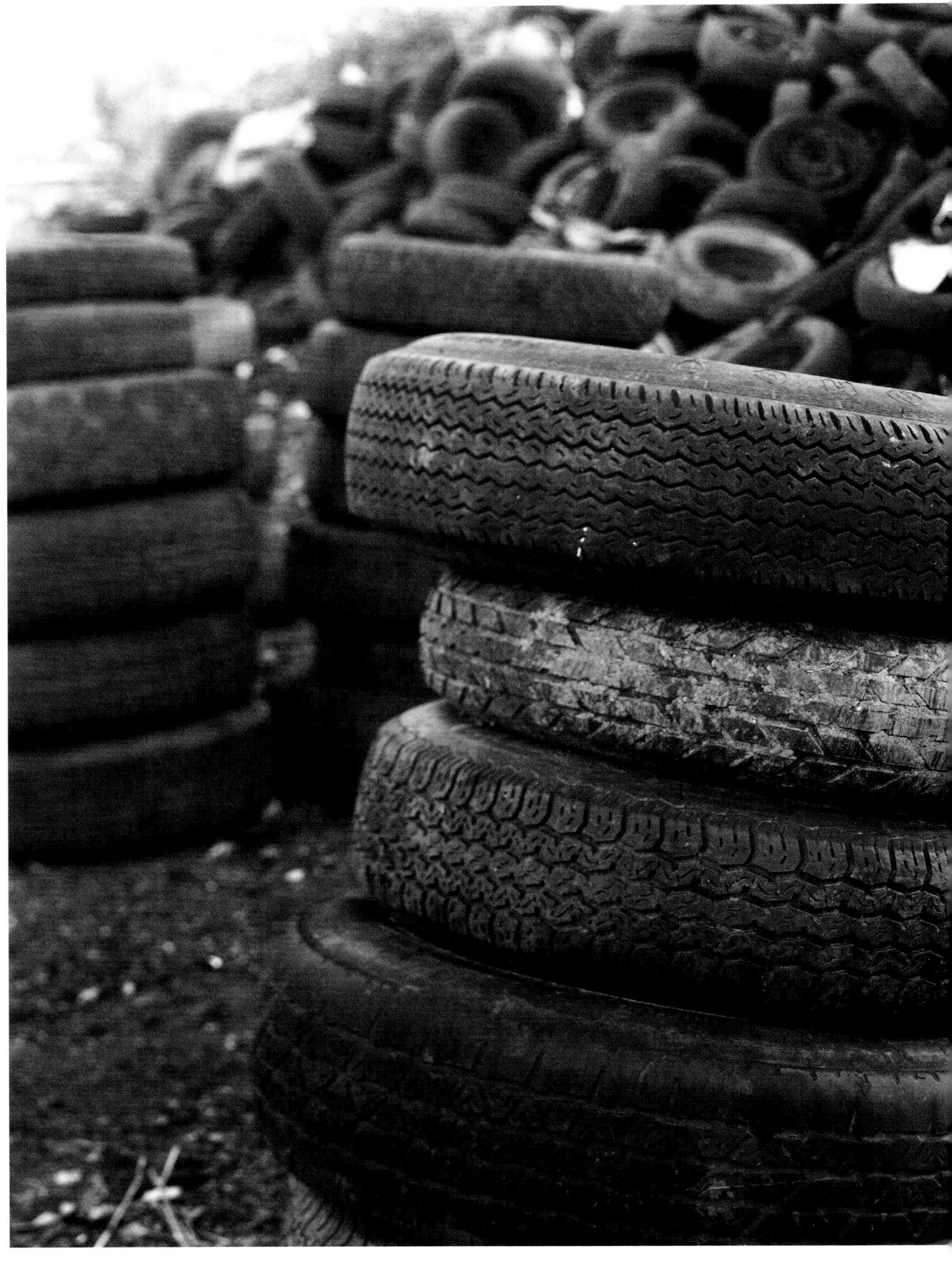

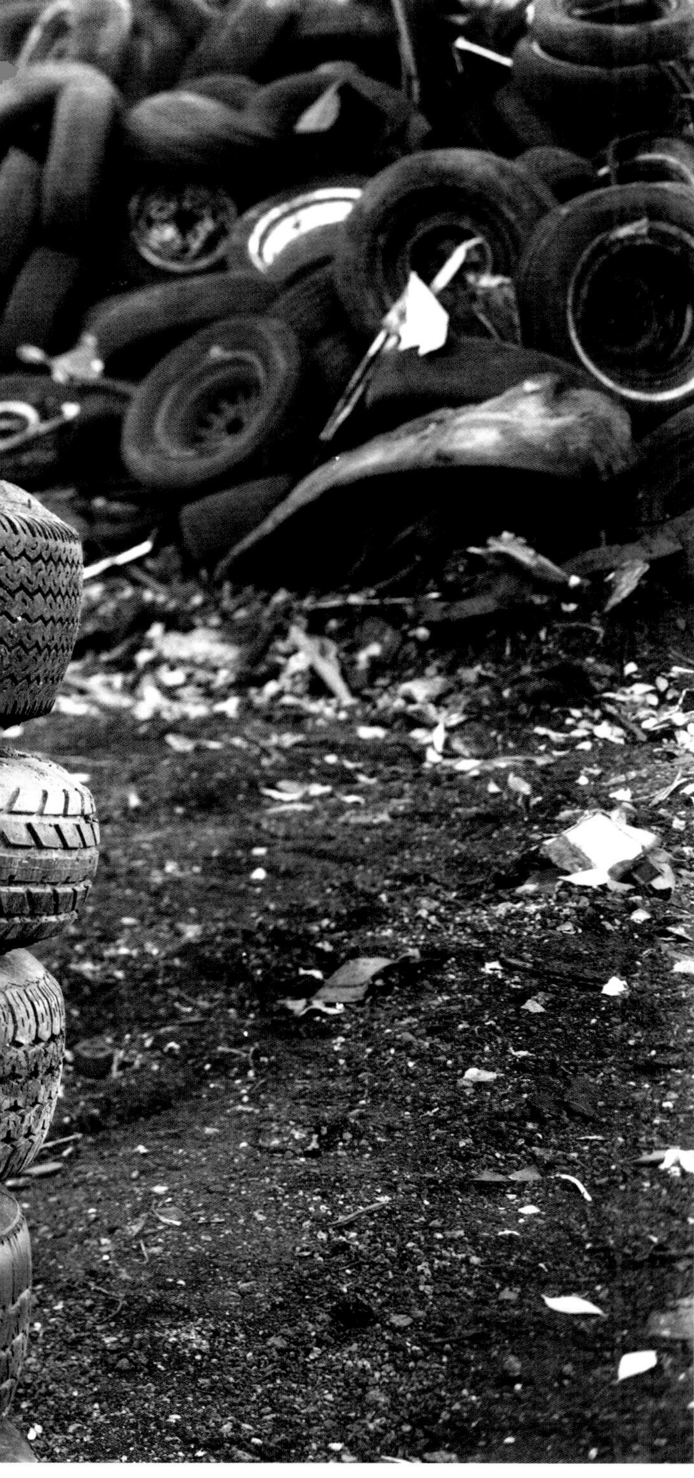

Stacked Tires, Joe's Junk Yard, Penna, 1998
Gelatin-silver print
16 × 20 in. (40.6 × 50.8 cm)

I was making the photograph shown here, of a building with its skin removed, its guts revealing a map of its life. I smiled, realizing how this scene contained so much of the stuff that Richard loved. Later, I even imagined what would have gone through his head when he saw it: a visual taxonomy of that split second when his brain deconstructed and rebuilt the picture. This diagram is my clumsy attempt to illustrate that moment. He hadn't been my teacher for more than twenty-five years, yet there he was.

Richard met everything and everybody on even ground. He valued those who "lived by their wits," as he often said, and he had no time for, or interest in, power or social hierarchy. He would speak with the same amount of excitement and reverence about the guy who figured out how to winch his first Heidelberg press into his basement as he did of Walker Evans, Lincoln Kirstein, and Paul Strand, or his pals Lee Friedlander and John Szarkowski. To him, they were all luminaries. Each object, person, or landscape was unique. He recognized their stories, history, strengths, and weaknesses, and he found beauty in it all. Simultaneously, he was able to identify what was not working. He could look at you and hear the chipped gear or bad lifter and just add a drop of oil or tighten a screw; few things were beyond repair.

When I think of him now, I don't see him; I hear him. He was like his voice: warm and full of humor, with a healthy dose of gravel. It was magic to see him at work, dancing around a press or a steam engine, pulling levers like Dr. Frankenstein. He was honest and direct: "Kimball, why the fuck would you ever do that?" was a regular refrain. It is impossible for me to point to a single lesson or moment where I recognize Richard's influence on me or my work. By his example, I learned to trust myself and my process, and I found a way not just to see the world but to be in it.

In a *New Yorker* profile of Richard, Calvin Tomkins began by asking him if he had reinvented photography, and Richard immediately rejected the notion. He then went on to talk of his family, always his family, and then to explain the new printing process he had devised. The article ends with Richard saying, "Okay, so maybe I did reinvent photography, but nobody noticed." We did, Richard. We did.

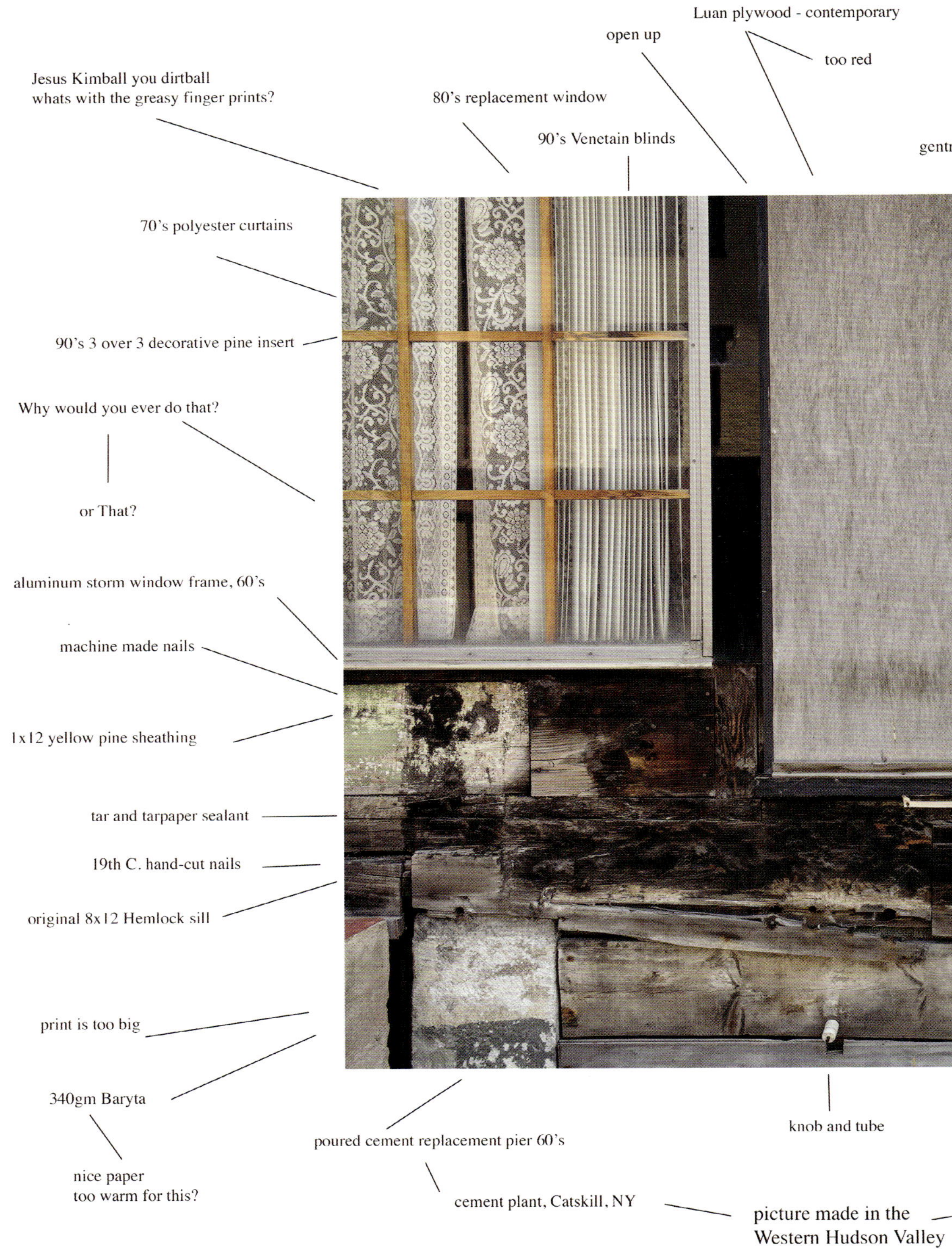
Luan plywood - contemporary
open up
too red
Jesus Kimball you dirtball
whats with the greasy finger prints?
80's replacement window
90's Venetain blinds
gentr
70's polyester curtains
90's 3 over 3 decorative pine insert
Why would you ever do that?
or That?
aluminum storm window frame, 60's
machine made nails
1 x 12 yellow pine sheathing
tar and tarpaper sealant
19th C. hand-cut nails
original 8 x 12 Hemlock sill
print is too big
340gm Baryta
nice paper
too warm for this?
poured cement replacement pier 60's
knob and tube
cement plant, Catskill, NY
picture made in the
Western Hudson Valley

Way Street (with imagined annotations by Richard Benson), 2016
Archival inkjet print
30 × 45 in. (76.2 × 114.3 cm)

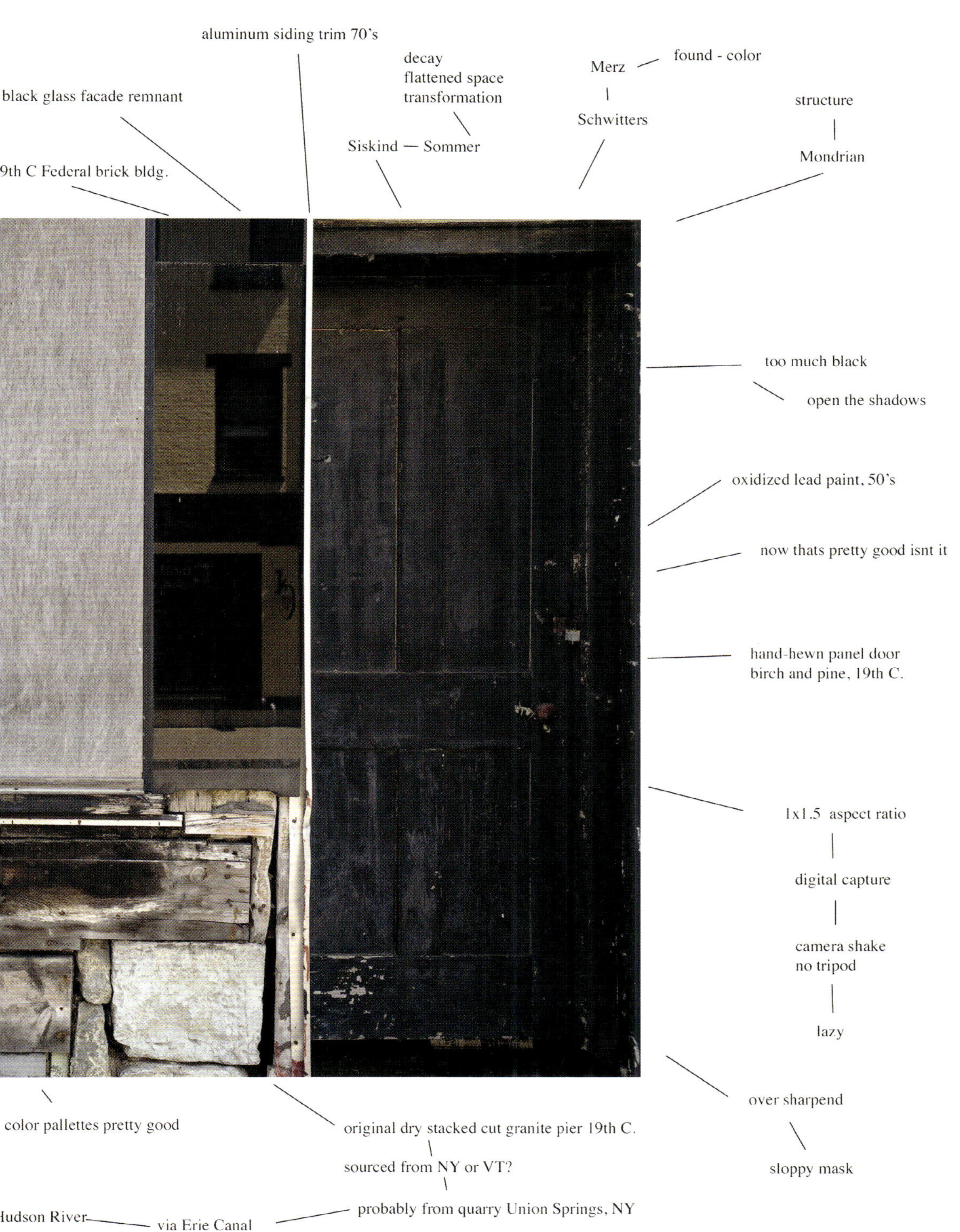

I first met Richard Benson in 2003, as a college dropout, deep in the basement of my first real job at Esto Photographics, Inc., in Mamaroneck, New York. I didn't literally meet him, but I worked near a copy of *Photographs from the Collection of the Gilman Paper Company* (1985). I had taken on a tedious task for myself and two of my high-school buddies. We were in the thick of cataloguing a hundred thousand or so negatives and slides by Ezra Stoller. The task, though rewarding, was monotonous and required many visual and mental breaks. Aside from losing 687 ping-pong games in the warehouse, I spent many hours carefully flipping through each of the 480 pages of the Gilman book. Chip, with the help of Thomas Palmer, had made this incredible tome that mesmerized me, with images for which I previously had only a dim appreciation. Otherwise reproduced in history books as bland monotone halftones, the glorious masterpieces from the Gilman Collection had dimensionality, the eerie glimmer of a silver shadow, and even the subtle foxing of age. I regularly flipped through the pages until I came to Steichen's *Moonrise, Mamaroneck, New York* (1904), later made famous for its record-setting sale at Sotheby's. I usually thought of it as mundane and gushy, and at the Met, seeing it in the halls with preservation levels of luminance reinforced my blasé attitude toward it. But in Chip's reproduction, viewed under the strong copy-stand lights, the hand-colored hues really sang. I had recently moved out to Orienta Point on the North Shore of Long Island Sound, where D. W. Griffith had his film studios and Steichen and other artists spent their weekends or summers in Mamaroneck. One night there was a strong moonrise over Mamaroneck, and I admit that I took a photo of my landlord's bird feeder refracting the moon. I later learned that Steichen had made his famous moonrise at the golf course at the end of my block. That book was there because Chip seemed to know everyone on the Boston Post Road between Beantown and Broadway. Ezra, like many other photographers, had befriended Chip after seeking out advice on some photographic pursuit and bought the Gilman book. The reproductions in that book were so remarkable to me that I had to figure out who Chip was and how I could meet him.

It turned out that he happened to teach photography, just a short train ride away, in New Haven. I slowly learned that any photographer I seemed to care about had also been at Yale: from Walker Evans to Mark Steinmetz and An-My Lê. I spent the next three years doing everything I could do to get there, including finishing up college at RIT. At the invitation of a friend, I attended a critique on Chapel Street. Upon entering, I walked through a hallway decorated with press sheets and a banquet table celebrating the retirement of Richard "Chip" Benson as the dean of the art school. I was initially afraid I had lost my window to study with him, but it turned out that he now had more time to teach his printing class for the second-year students. I was going through a phase of wanting to return to the basics and photograph in black and white, using an 8-by-10-inch camera with the hopes of documenting a contemporary scene in Mamaroneck with the richness of a Benson quadtone. In the first week of class, he immediately cursed at me and said I wasn't allowed to photograph that way. He said that I was a photographer of the present and that I had to use the tools of today to achieve the best image possible. I leased a digital camera and never looked back. I now mostly photograph with an iPhone, in black and white, then print the images as tritones, using a digital press at Meridian on the fanciest paper I can afford. Once I was printing a title there for ROMAN NVMERALS (a small publishing enterprise I started), when I saw a few of Chip's oversized postage stamps sitting on pallets at the plant. I called him and left a message. He immediately called back—especially interested in having us come by his house to see his latest innovation: a 4K TV. After he made sure that I was gainfully employed and feeding my family, he plopped each of us down in front of a giant TV. He had figured out how to send uncompressed files to the screen for an exquisite viewing experience, beyond what the printed page could hold.

Recently, I was cleaning out the offices of Esto for its move to Brooklyn after being in Mamaroneck for forty-plus years. One of the last things left to pack were five or six press sheets, with a blank sheet on top. A message was scrawled in pencil: *Ezra, Here is a group of pictures for you—I don't remember which ones I sent before, so I hope these are ones you like. All best.—Chip*

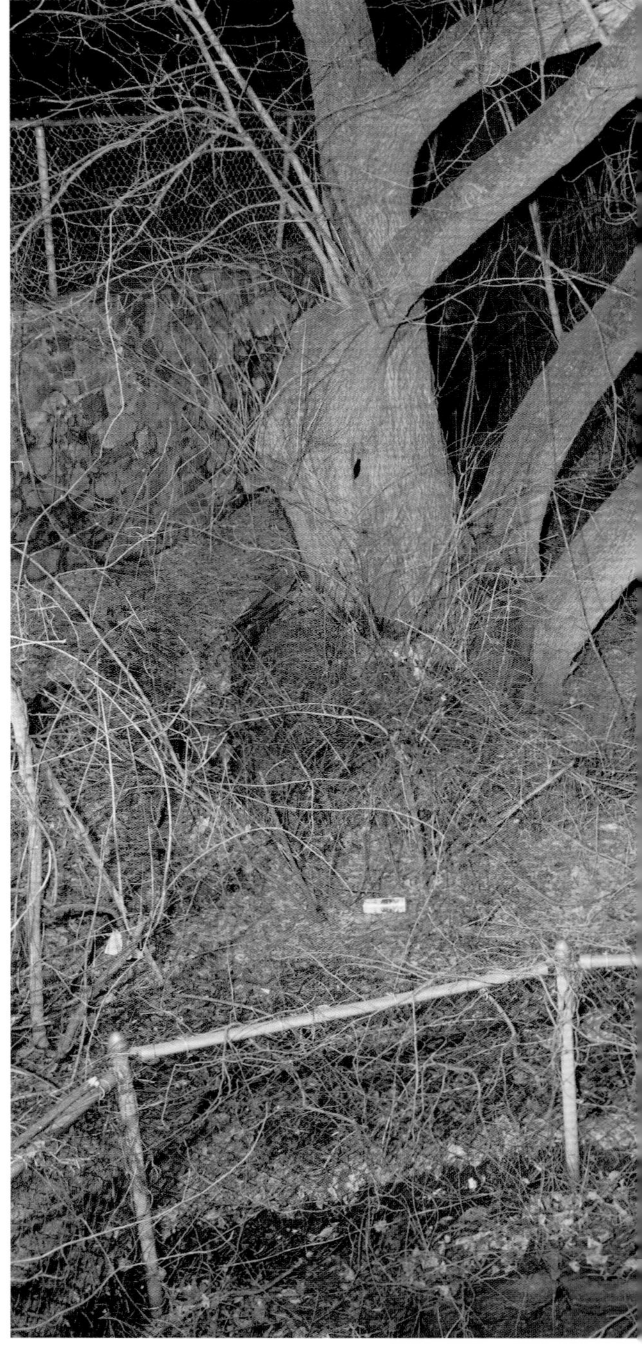

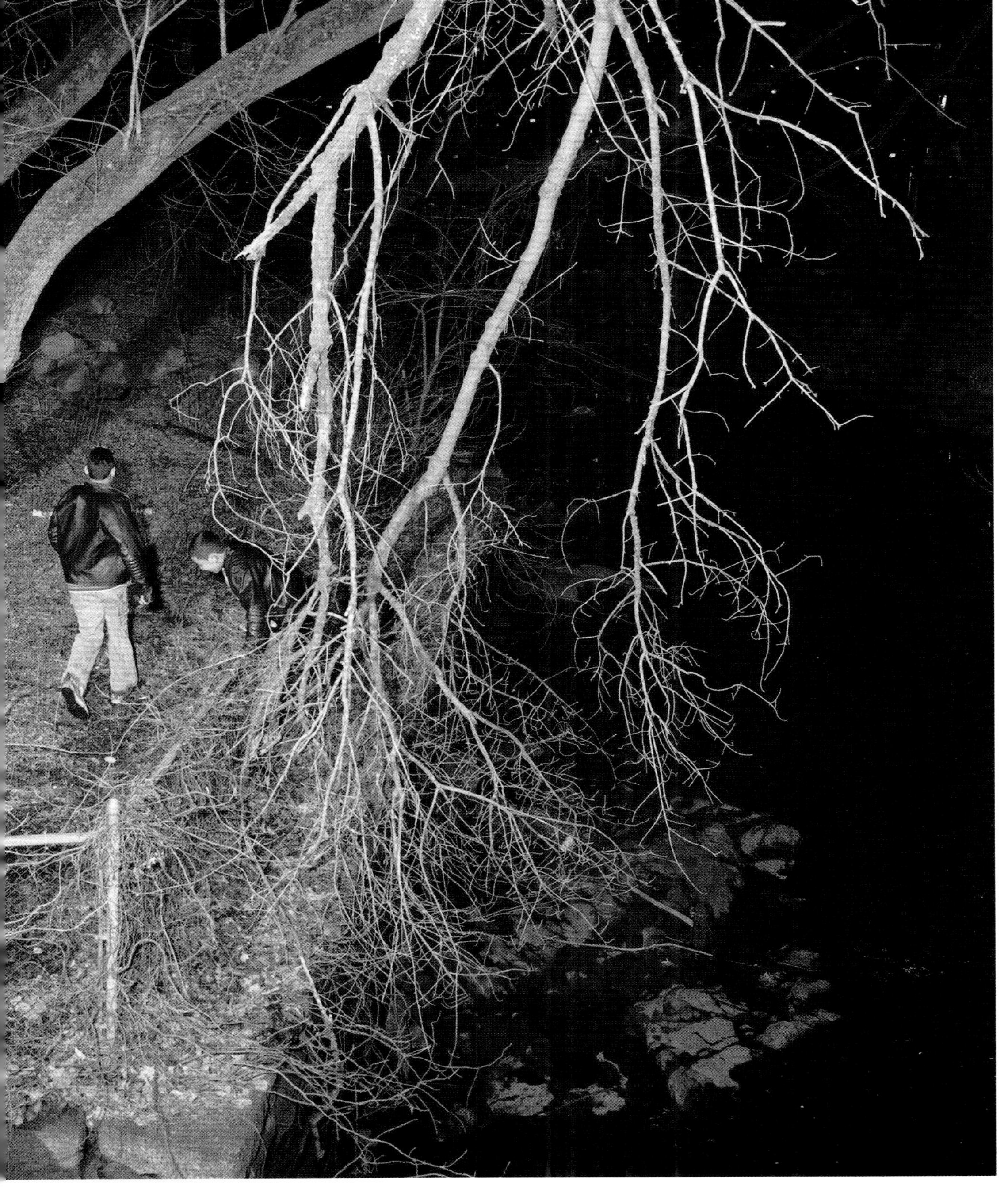

Kids Running in Woods, Mamaroneck, 2008
Gelatin-fiber print
24 × 32 in. (61 × 81.3 cm)

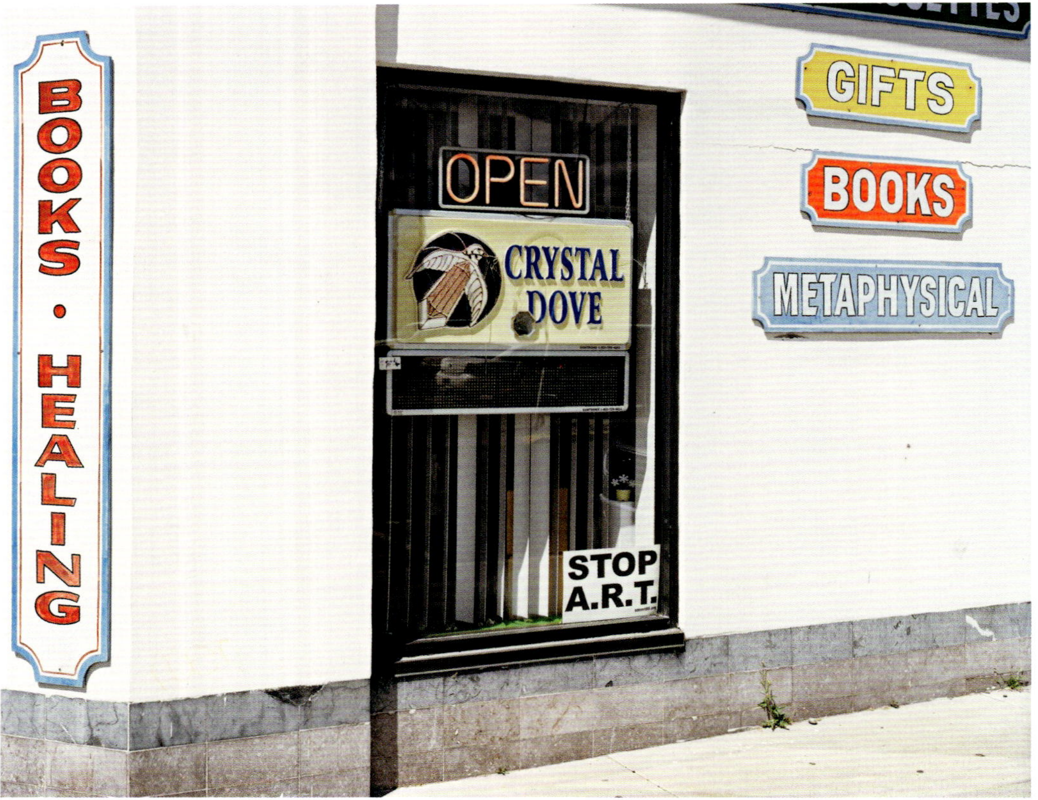
BOOKS · HEALING
OPEN
CRYSTAL
DOVE
STOP
A.R.T.
GIFTS
BOOKS
METAPHYSICAL

525 (For R.M.A.B.), 2017
Archival pigment print
21 × 26 in. (53.3 × 66 cm)

In my first semester of graduate school, I was stumbling through the process of learning how to scan a negative, how to "tune it" (as Chip would say) in Photoshop, and how to make an inkjet print. The results were less than desirable, and on seeing them, Richard told me so using language that was filthy, hilarious, and oddly inspiring. At the same time, he promised to help me out if I brought some files to his office. I have no memory of what we actually did on the computer, because our conversations inevitably turned to what was in my pictures and how that could look in a print. He made it sound easy, but that was only because he had worked his head off for his whole life trying to figure it out. He told me how a former client had challenged him to render a shadow in a reproduction that was like the black of a butterfly's wing, and we once marveled at a white in a painting he said would be next to impossible to achieve in any photographic process. In his mind, the act of printing was to be at the service of the subject itself and not our ideas about that subject. To him, this was the difference between Photography and Art. As I understood them, his lessons were concerned with how attention and presence could be held up, made visible, and celebrated in the continuous present of a photographic print. Most of my work is concerned with the things human beings make and how our desires and ideas are made manifest in those physical objects. Like a photographic print, things in the world are often perceived as either concealing or revealing how they were made. I think the art is in the between—and I think that's another thing I learned from Richard.

In my first year of graduate school in 1981, we met with Richard Benson on Tuesday mornings. There, Richard would give impromptu lectures on topics of interest. He was working on the spectacular Gilman Paper Company book and would bring samples of its complicated printing process. He also shared stories from the Atget series of books he was doing with MoMA, subsidized by Springs Industries. Eventually, discussions led to the issue of financing for most contemporary illustrated books. Richard revealed the tiny sliver of the budget that publishers could allocate toward production and how crucial some decisions were.

In 1993, when I learned that I was about to have a book, *Grapevine*, published in England, I asked him for printing advice. Richard promptly answered that I should get Jackson-Wilson, the printers based in Leeds, to send him the proofs in Newport when done. His willingness to oversee the project triggered the company's excitement enough for it to attempt a tritone version similar to the one they had just done for Jonathan Cape of Lee Friedlander's *Nudes* book. After seeing both sets of proofs, Richard preferred the tritone version and recommended a warmer third color. Jackson-Wilson, thrilled by Richard's participation, had its own interest in the photographs and, along with the publisher's consent, decided to showcase *Grapevine*'s printing and aimed for the highest possible quality.

In the seven or eight years between my sitting in Richard's classroom and photographing *Grapevine*, I had gone out in search of ordinary America, in no small part due to his teachings. My prior work had been semistaged portraits of fellow graduate students—a group that Richard was not interested in. Eventually, I found how contagious Richard's championing of the world around him, and especially of this country, was. While we might share some subject matter, I could never attain his level of optimism, which was a reflection of the noble person he was.

Untitled; from the series *Grapevine*, 1988–92
Gelatin-silver print

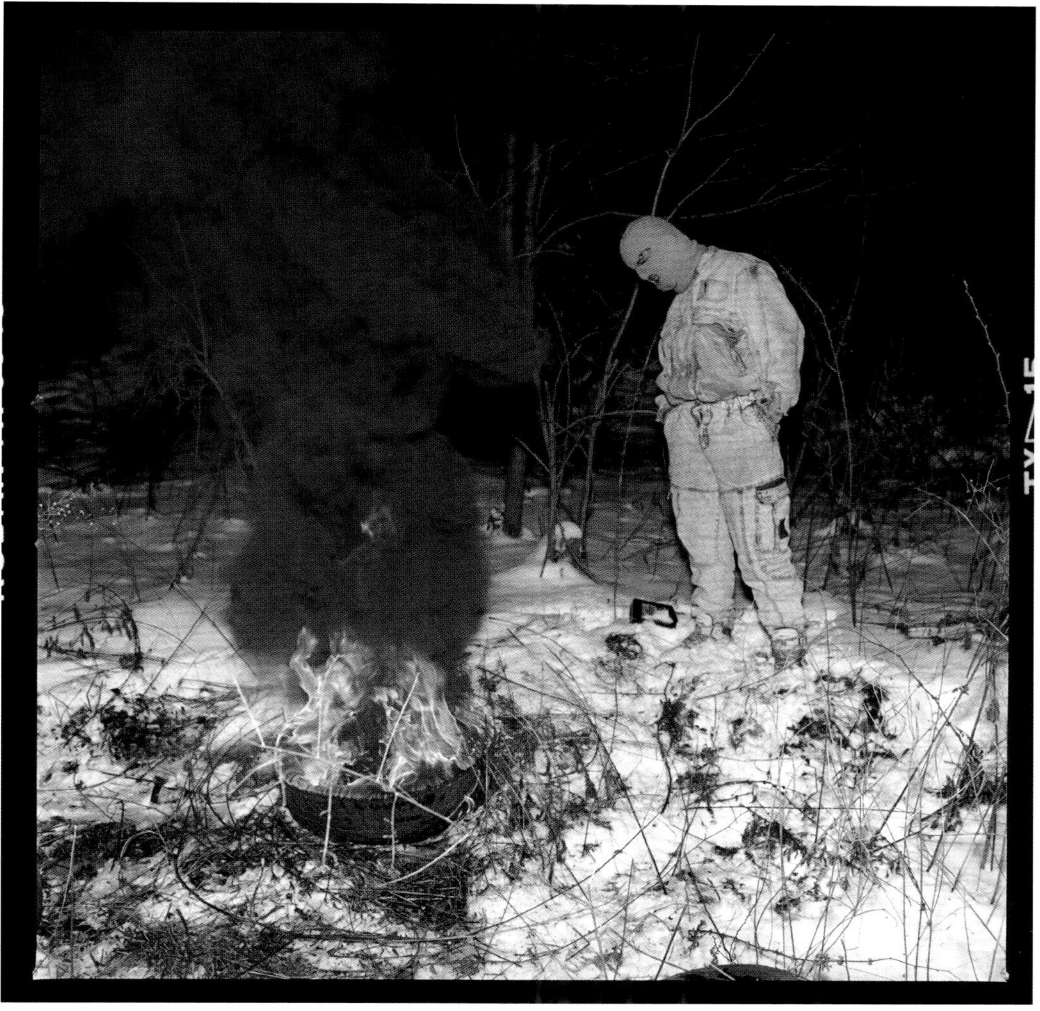

GRAPEVINE

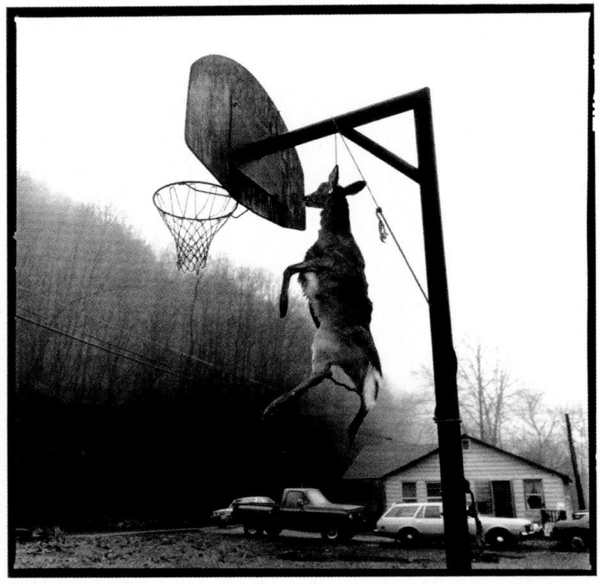

photographs by **SUSAN LIPPER**

Grapevine (Manchester, UK:
Cornerhouse, 1994)

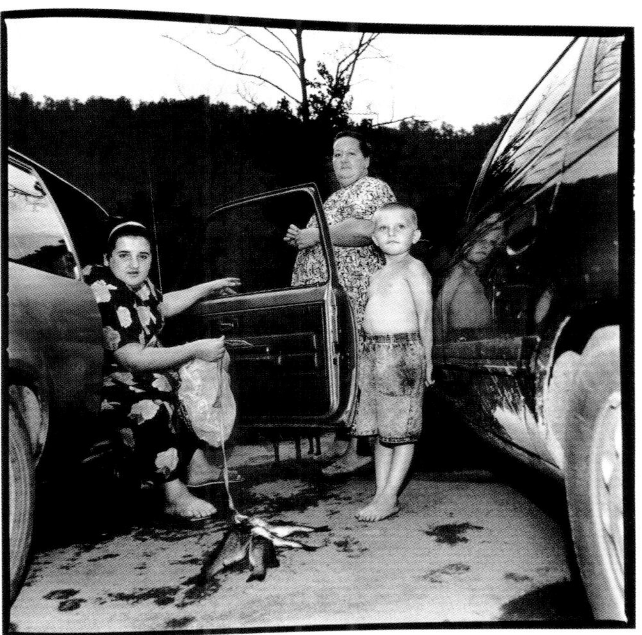

When I met Richard in Hartford, Connecticut, around 1974, he was working making halftone film for Meriden Gravure, among other jobs. I rented darkroom space in the same building he worked in, where other photographers suggested I introduce myself to Richard. I finally did, and as it turned out, this was one of the better decisions of my life. I was teaching at the time, with an occasional afternoon off. I would work in the darkroom and visit Richard often. One day while having coffee he said, "Lopes, if you keep coming here, I'm going to put you to work." And so he did, as I began to learn many of the alternative processes and do small jobs.

One day, he informed me that he was seriously considering relocating to Newport, where he would open a shop for photo- and print-related projects. Surprisingly, he asked me to join him. It was an easy decision to relocate. In January of 1976, I began working with him. Among the first projects were the Paul Strand portfolios published by Aperture. Working with Ann Kennedy and Michael Hoffman, Richard would prepare guide prints for later edition printing. Soon, Strand's health began to deteriorate, and things had to move more quickly. Richard then began making trips to France. Fast-forward to when the edition printing began: Although we had separate darkrooms, we worked in tandem to speed up the printing. Richard worked the enlarger and would hand off a batch of prints, which I would process and wash. I continued to work on spotting prints and eventually cutting the mattes as well.

The only other project we worked on together was a book authored by James Mellon, *The Face of Lincoln*. This project involved numerous trips to copy the best prints of Lincoln's face, which encompassed all the processes of the time, from albumen to platinum. This was preceded by several teaching sessions with Richard on copying with an 8-by-10 camera. I traveled with Mellon to create the copy negatives, which were developed in Newport. Richard then took the film and made 16-by-20-inch enlarged negatives and positives for minor spotting. These were then used to make film for the book printing. This was an important

James Mellon, *The Face of Lincoln*
(New York: Viking Press, 1979)

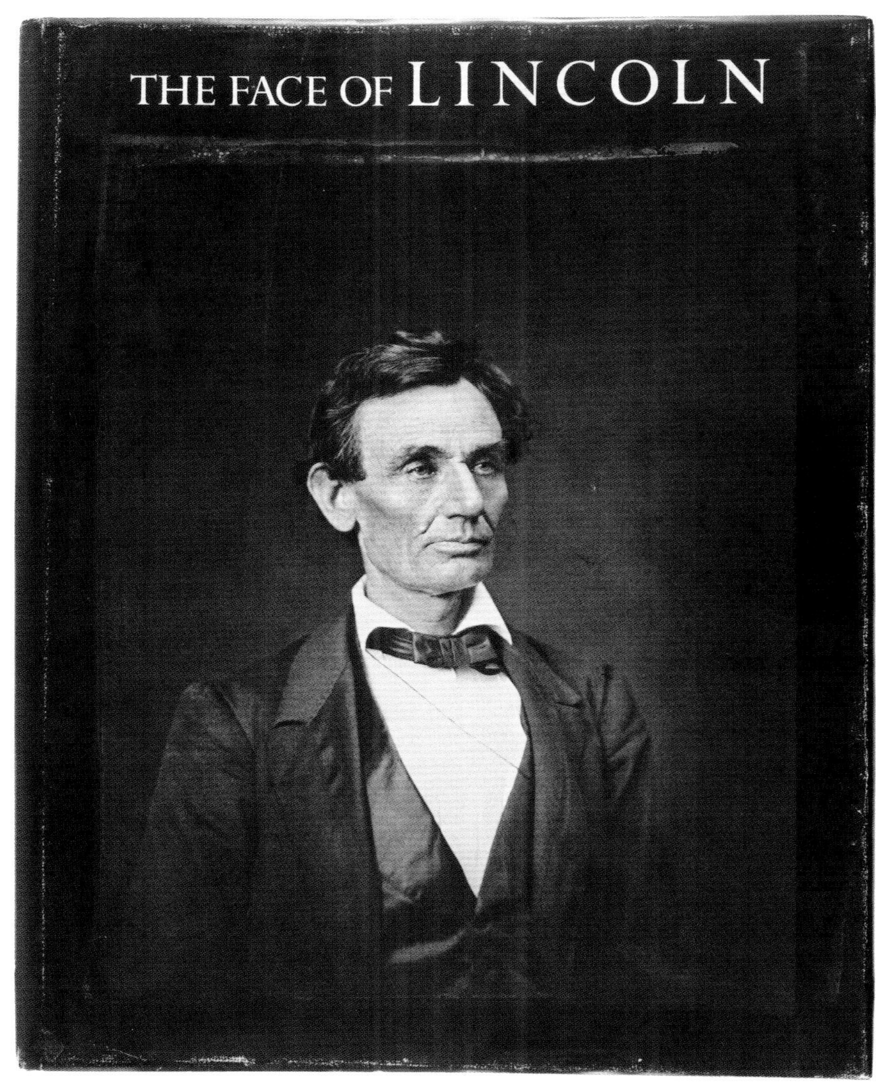

step as Richard taught me the process of making enlarged negatives, which would become a foundation for later work in the shop and my own business.

Most of the time we worked separately, with Richard on the print or book sides, and I exclusively on the photo side. My first solo job was one of Edward Weston's iconic photographs, *Breast*. Richard always made the film and watched over the proofing process. This was a collaboration, as Cole Weston was present to look at prints as well. By this time, I was able to print the edition without supervision and this is generally how the shop worked. When there was spare time, we would talk pictures and Richard would give me occasional photo assignments. One favorite was a challenge to make a strong "family" image, as one of my favorite Strands was the portrait of the Italian Luzzara family. He was pleased with the result.

As I became more independent, Richard was able to continue his book work, making his own pictures, and conducting his experiments. This helped the shop survive, as we were able to take on more work. After several years, Richard was offered the job at Yale. He very generously handed the business to me and guided the process for a bit. This was Chip: generous by nature, willing to share his knowledge, able to see better than anyone I know. Essentially, I was able to make a career from his sharing of knowledge and friendship.

James Mellon, *The Face of Lincoln*
(New York: Viking Press, 1979)

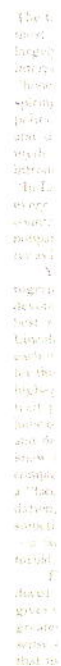

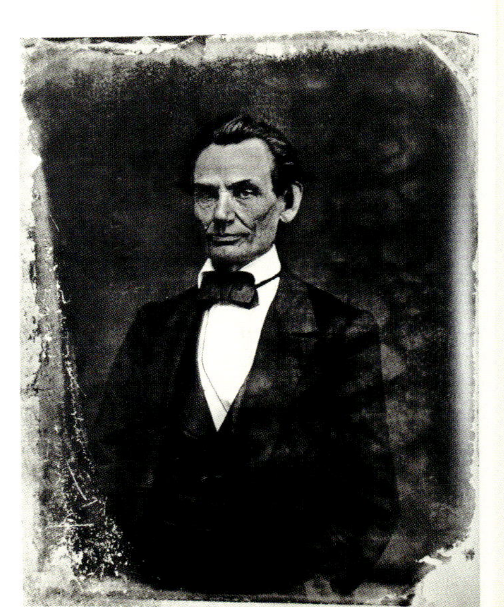

THE FACE OF
LINCOLN

Compiled and Edited by
JAMES MELLON

A STUDIO BOOK · THE VIKING PRESS · NEW YORK

Each print was an adventure, a case study of the possibilities and parameters of the medium, both a dance and a wrestling match between image and object. Richard Benson took apart the image and saw the underlying structure in sections and in layers of depth and tone. I'd show him a work print, and he'd tell me that the poetry of the photograph hinged on the relationship between the white sheet and the window. He'd be unhappy with the gray tone of the window. The window needs to be black, he'd say, really black, and the sheet needs to be luminous, almost weightless, to make us believe in the small magic of the girl standing on her head. I began to understand that a photograph is an unfinished approximation—words of a poem in a jumble—until the picture is resolved as an object.

The rigor, slowness, and specificity of printing with Richard, the deep dive into the layered nuances of tonality, changed my work. His teaching invited a heightened, yet quieter, precision in my seeing. I began responding to quotidian drama and small gestures. A slower, more ambiguous narrative emerged.

My methods and subject have changed dramatically since 1989 (though the deep themes remain). When I began my project *Woven*, I spent a year learning by trial and error. I shifted from making singular analog view-camera frames, used in my previous project *Fallen*, to stitching together multiple digital files to create 5-by-10-foot photographs. I'm indebted to Richard for this sense of experiment and invention that forms the core of the resolution between form and content, image and object.

Untitled, Woodbridge, Connecticut, 1989
Gelatin-silver print
16 × 20 in. (40.6 × 50.8 cm)

Notes from printing with Richard, 1989

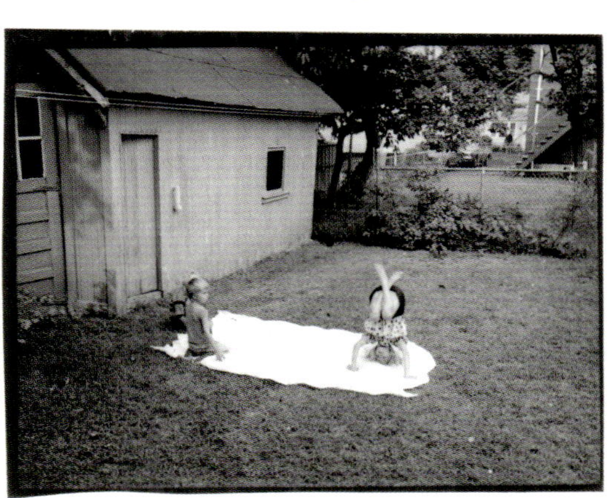

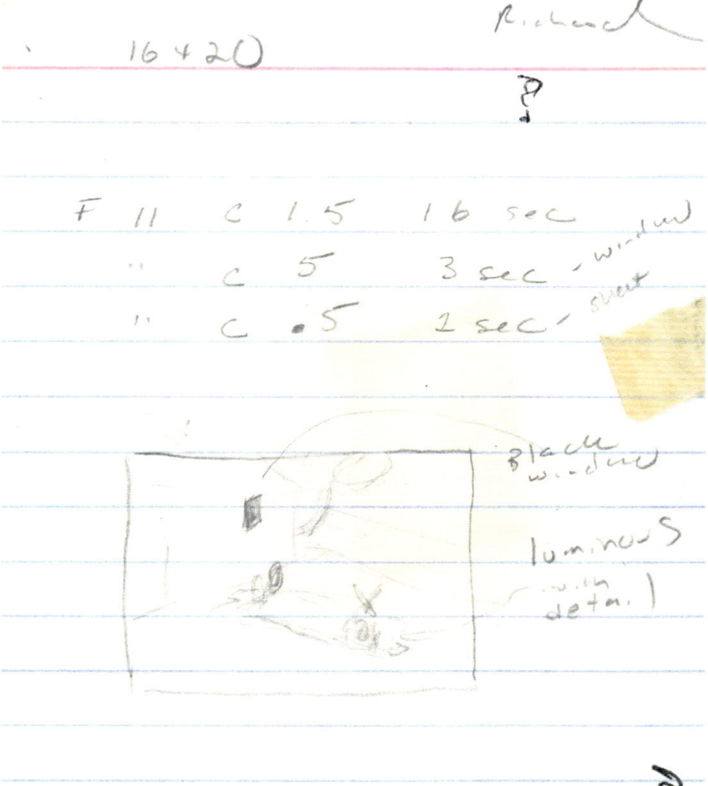

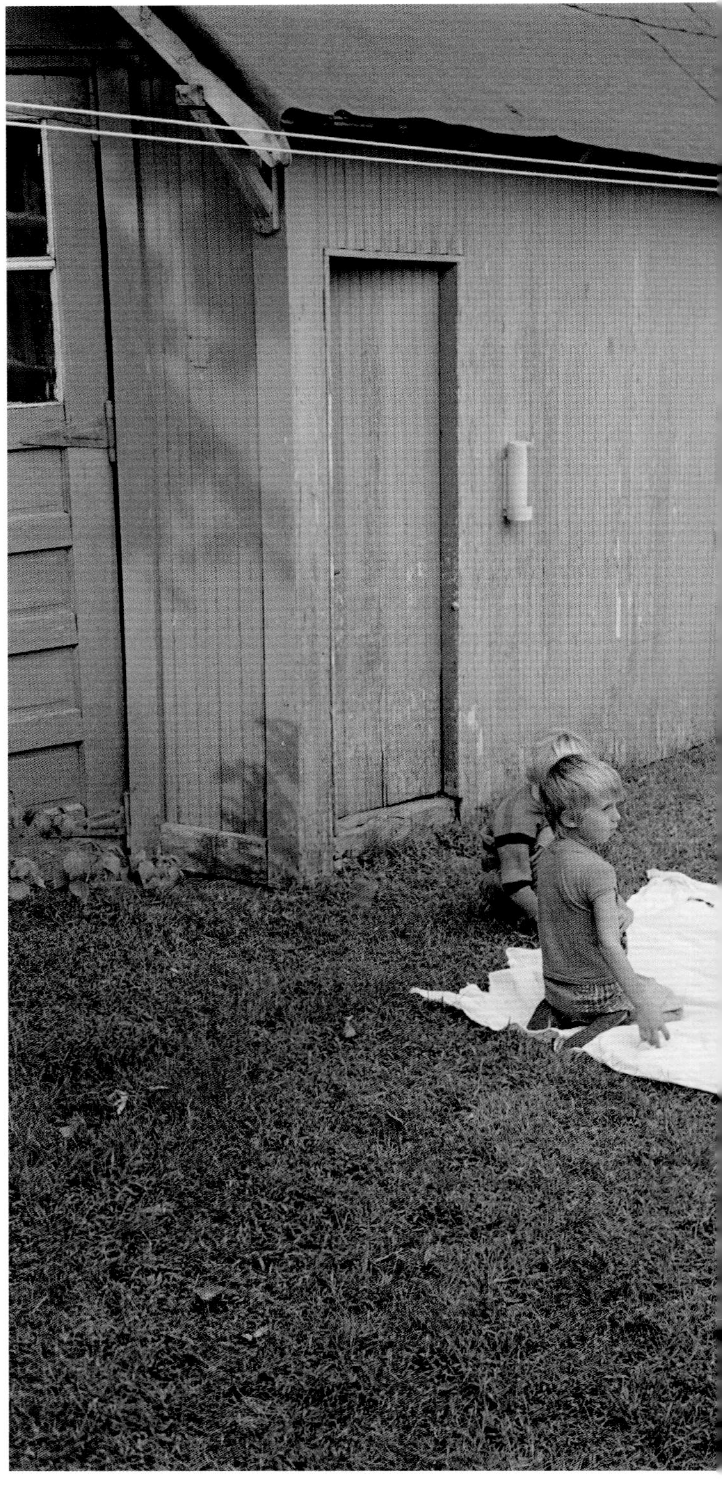

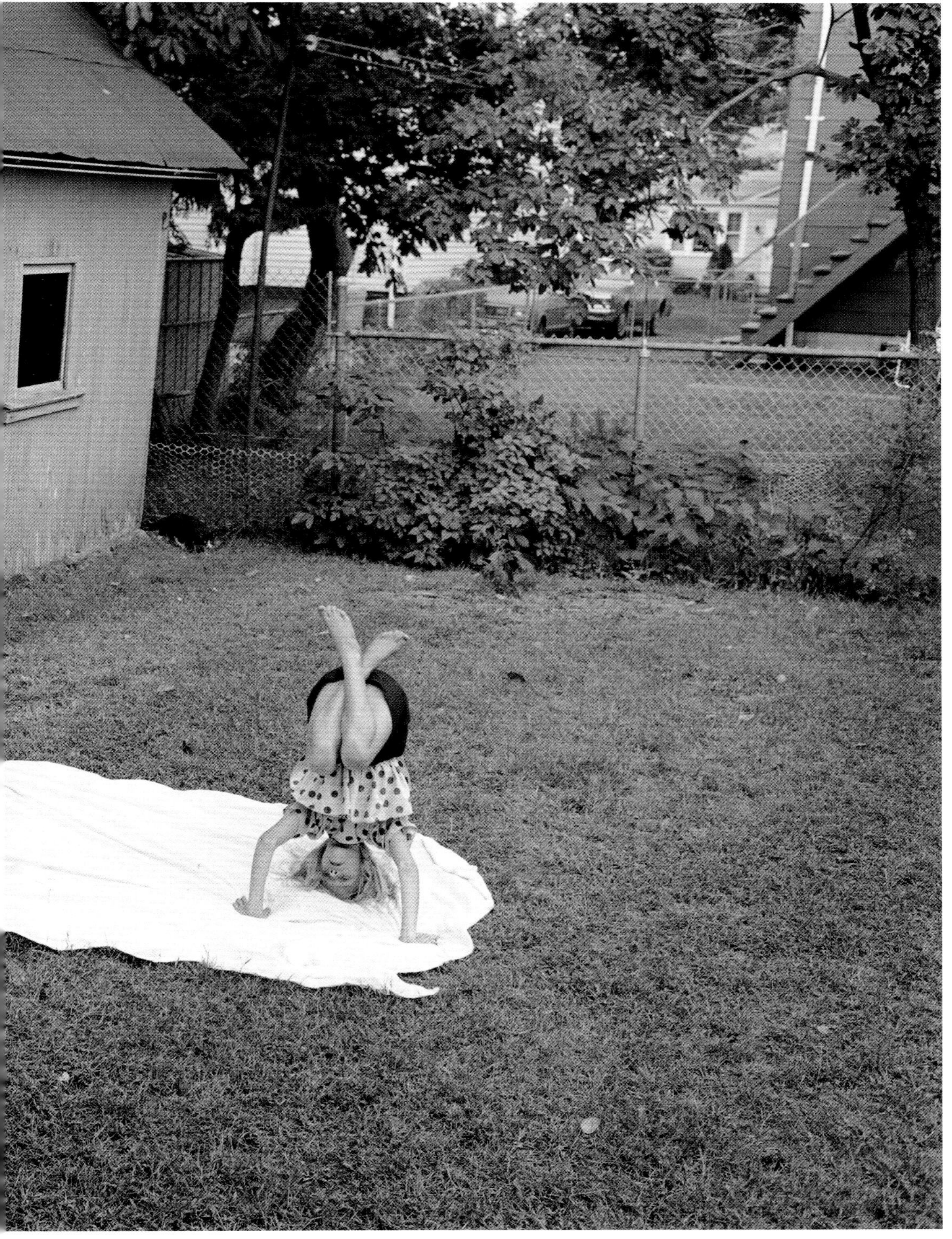

Untitled, Woodbridge, Connecticut, 1989
Gelatin-silver print
16 × 20 in. (40.6 × 50.8 cm)

I first met Chip Benson at the Meriden Gravure Company (later called Meriden-Stinehour Press) in the '80s. This was an incredible printing company that developed many innovative printing techniques. Chip and others worked with a group of craftsmen in prepress and with the press room to push the art of photographic reproduction ahead of any other competitors. Chip was gone by the time I joined the company, but his legacy was always felt. Bob Hennessey followed in his footsteps, and we all benefitted from the culture of excellence and creativity that the company engendered. I've maintained a lifelong connection with Bob Hennessey because of our connection to the Meriden Gravure Company.

Remember that this was all pre-digital and the efforts were analog: operating the cameras, stripping negatives to flats to generate plates developed by hand, silhouetting images with a paintbrush. Printing was done on offset machines with only one ink unit, and with complex jobs running through the presses multiple times. It was a labor-intensive craft and required everyone to know the process from beginning to end.

Meriden was a place that cultivated cooperation and allowed for input on all levels. Chip went on to spread his knowledge to many other printers and people. His enthusiasm for making things was infectious and inspiring.

After I set up Allethaire Press with Emily Oppegard, my business partner and press operator, Chip recommended that Jeffrey Fraenkel give us a try for one of his collection books, *Seeing Things*. Inspired by the Gilman Collection process, we worked with Bob Hennessey to create a book of special tritones shot from the original prints and printed using eighty-eight combinations of PMS colors. These were all done pre-digitally, with negatives that we contact-exposed to plates—which could thus be manipulated during exposure under the UV light. All were printed one color at a time on a small-format Heidelberg press. We press proofed every image, matched them against the originals, then sent them to San Francisco for review. It was a great challenge and luckily successful in the end. I always think of making that book as my graduate school education.

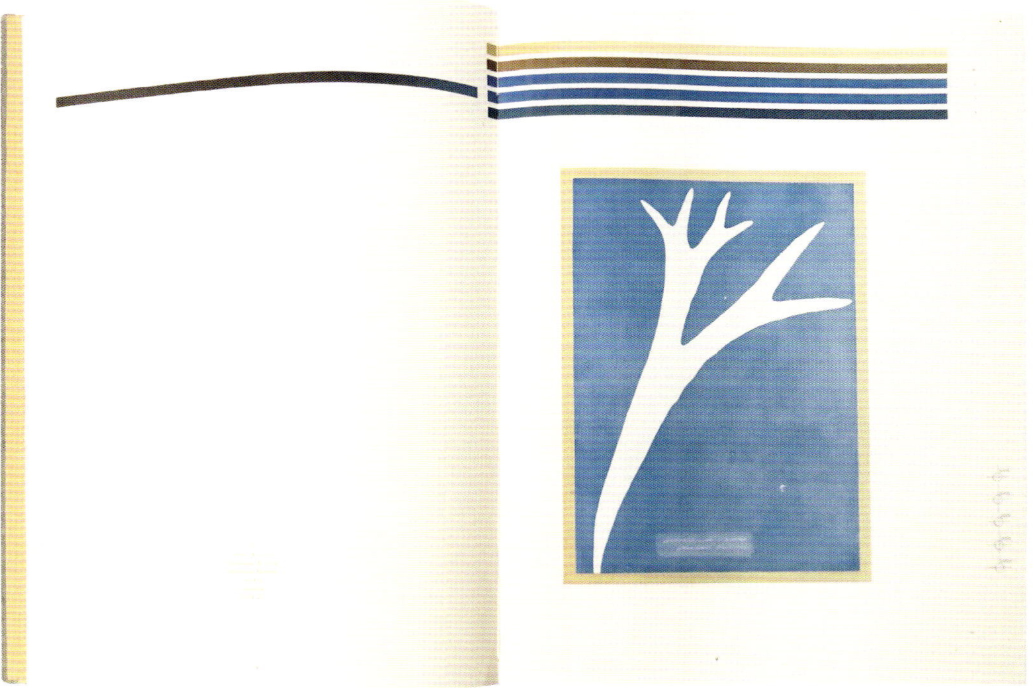

"In October 2008, MoMA published *The Printed Picture* by Richard Benson, which traces the changing technology of making and distributing pictures from the Renaissance to the present." Although these words introduce the accompanying exhibition, now archived online, they are not entirely true. Both the book and the exhibition begin not with the Renaissance but with a moment perhaps thirty thousand years earlier, when human beings registered their existence through handprints and hand stencils on the walls of caves.

The first chapter of *The Printed Picture*, "Relief Printing," reproduces an image of the cave at Chauvet in southeastern France. Yet to have displayed a version of this image in the exhibition smacked of an inauthenticity inimical to Benson. Since we couldn't have the cave, he suggested we represent this most ancient method of relief printing with a process familiar to most parents and nursery school teachers: dipping one's hands in paint and pressing them against a smooth surface (ideally, from most adult perspectives, not a wall).

I was surprised and touched when Richard encouraged me to do this with my daughter and son, then ages five and three. I'm embarrassed by how much I overthought the exercise: primary colors were too obvious, right? Was it sufficiently messy to acknowledge children were involved while still meriting a place on the wall? I suspect Richard would have chided me for doing anything other than simply *doing* it, and yet our handprints were the first images seen on entering the exhibition. It was the first time I had brought myself, or my family, into my work, but seeing our marks on that wall alongside a letter from his great-grandmother and his brother's flawless calligraphic alphabet, I began to grasp how much work is enhanced if family—and, by extension, life—is allowed in.

Sarah Meister with Madeline and Lee Meister, Handprints, 2008
Acrylic paint
14 × 16⅝ in. (35.6 × 42.2 cm)

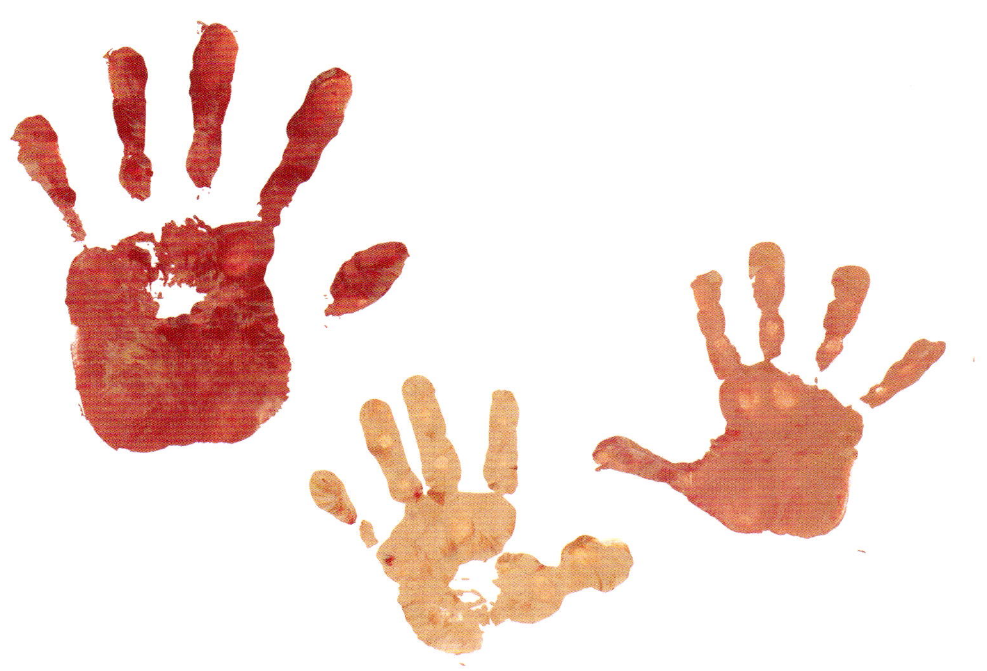

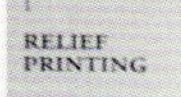
1
RELIEF
PRINTING

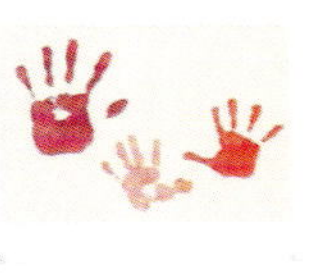

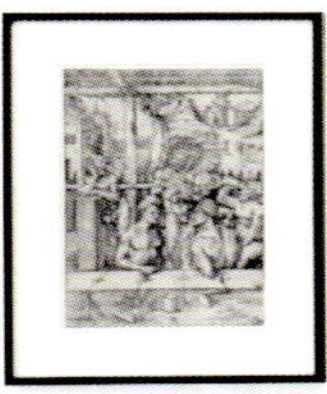

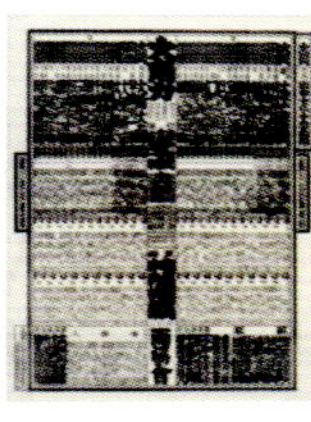

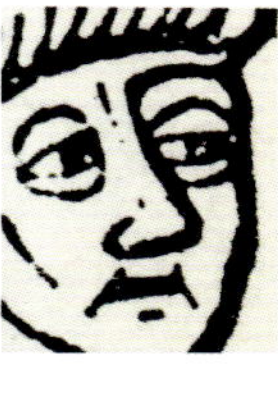

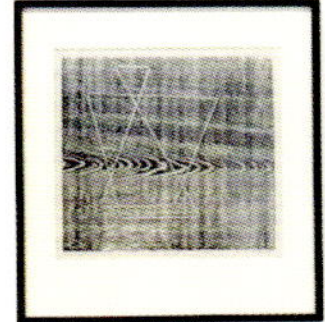

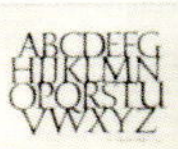

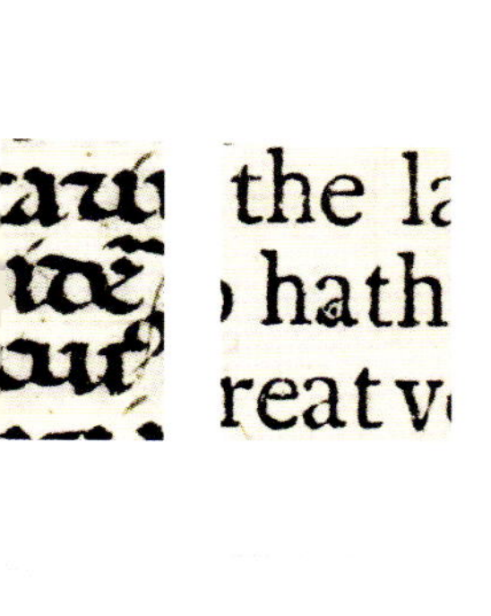

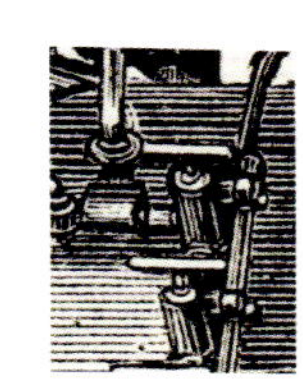
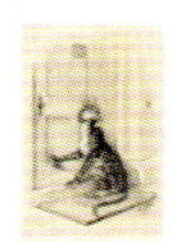

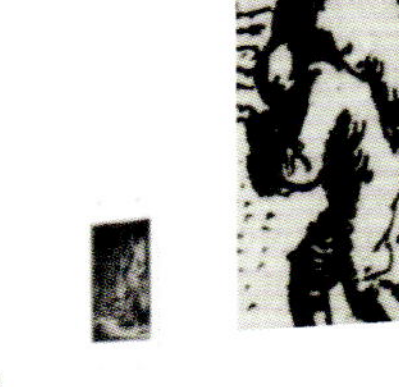
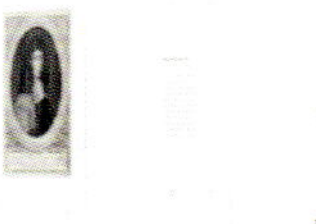
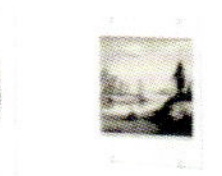
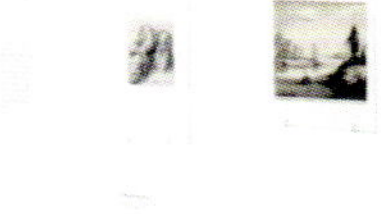

Installation view of *The Printed Picture* at the Museum of Modern Art, New York, October 17, 2008–July 13, 2009

Richard Benson's work, especially in the field of photomechanical reproduction, demonstrated that materials and technique carry meaning and that ink on paper can convey the creative intent and purpose of a physical print. His approach provides a model for seeking more from the printed page, a license to capture some of the experience of holding a photograph in your hands.

In the digital age, making *Bill Brandt | Henry Moore*, a book about analog photography, became, for us, about holding onto the material presence of the print. How could we recreate the experience of looking at a photographic print in a moment of time? Moved to catch the light, turned over, and brought close and far, a print in our hands creates a physical engagement that is dimensional and embodied.

Benson's material legacy informs the book, which was published with the Yale Center for British Art in 2020. Our team was assembled to realize a book that conveyed an immediacy of encounter. Photographers Richard Caspole and Robert Hixon worked against the grain of their usual photographic practice at the museum to help us achieve our ideas for how Brandt's prints could be reproduced as material objects, rather than disembodied images. We sought out the expertise of Miko McGinty, Thomas Palmer, and Daniel Frank, who had all worked with Benson to ensure process and materials reflected our ambition to set a new standard for how photographs appear in print. By highlighting elements of sheen, texture, gloss, emulsion cracks, and paper creases, the resulting illustrations project an unmediated experience of a photographic print through time.

Encompassing the production of two very different artists, the resulting volume is more than a surrogate experience subordinate to the direct encounter of a print by Brandt or a sculpture by Moore. Instead, it is an assertion that the experience of art through photography and the printed page is fundamental, central, and unique. This idea is pure Benson: audacious but backed up by the work.

Bill Brandt, *Henry Moore*, 1948
Gelatin-silver print
9 × 7¾ in. (22.9 × 19.7 cm)

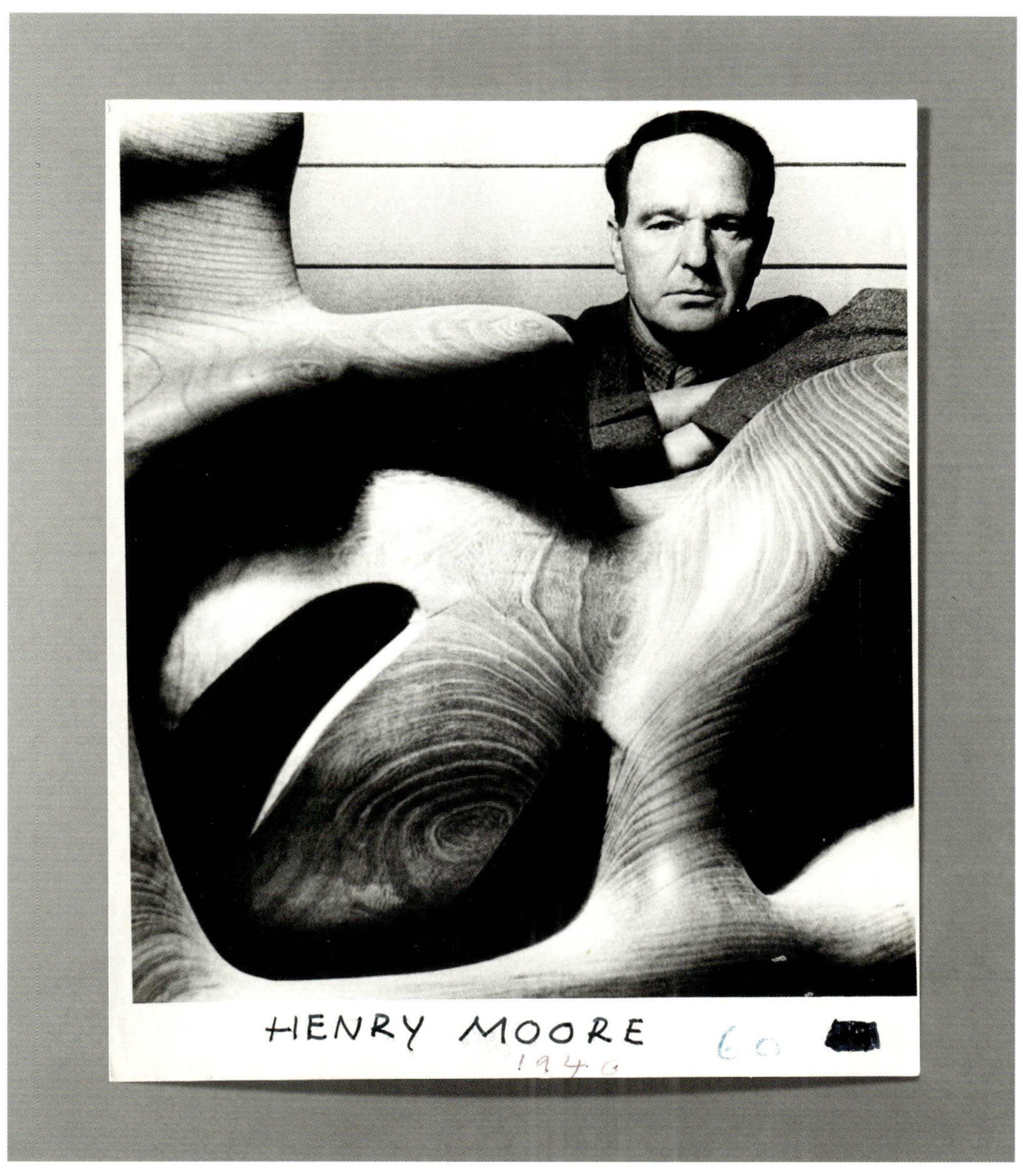

I've long been obsessed with the camera's sneaky ability to convincingly transform meaning in a manner that is surprising, seductive, and even poetic. I've chased this elusive prize for most of my life, employing an 8-by-10-inch view camera and the nineteenth-century hand-coated platinum-palladium printing process. As a young person entrenched in the medium, I was advised to find Richard Benson, which led me to Yale.

I showed up every week at Richard's Tuesday class with an array of platinum-printing problems. Supportive of my efforts, no matter how failed, he answered every question, once leaving class to walk me down the block to Hull's Art Supply to be sure that I bought the correct print-coating brush. In regard to the far more difficult job of producing a good photograph, Richard made a major and permanent impact on me when he said that a state of confusion was "exactly right" for a creative endeavor. I am cautious by nature. This proclamation freed me to embrace mistakes and surprises, relinquish control and meet the world at least halfway, putting aside, for example, my view-camera assumptions about sharpness, composition, and depth of field.

I have lived the decades since my time at Yale dancing back and forth between the many well-grounded technical lessons of Richard's weekly classes and the uncertainty inherent in the creative process. Sometimes things land well and I'm simply ecstatic. More often, photography provides the job that I go to every day, as if I were a baker or a banker. Most days, I'm happy to go to work. The best days are those eye-openers that can happen only with a leap of faith, a foray into the unknown—that exactly right option, as articulated by Richard Benson decades ago.

Remanzacco, Italy, 2019
Platinum print
10 × 8 in. (25.4 × 20.3 cm)

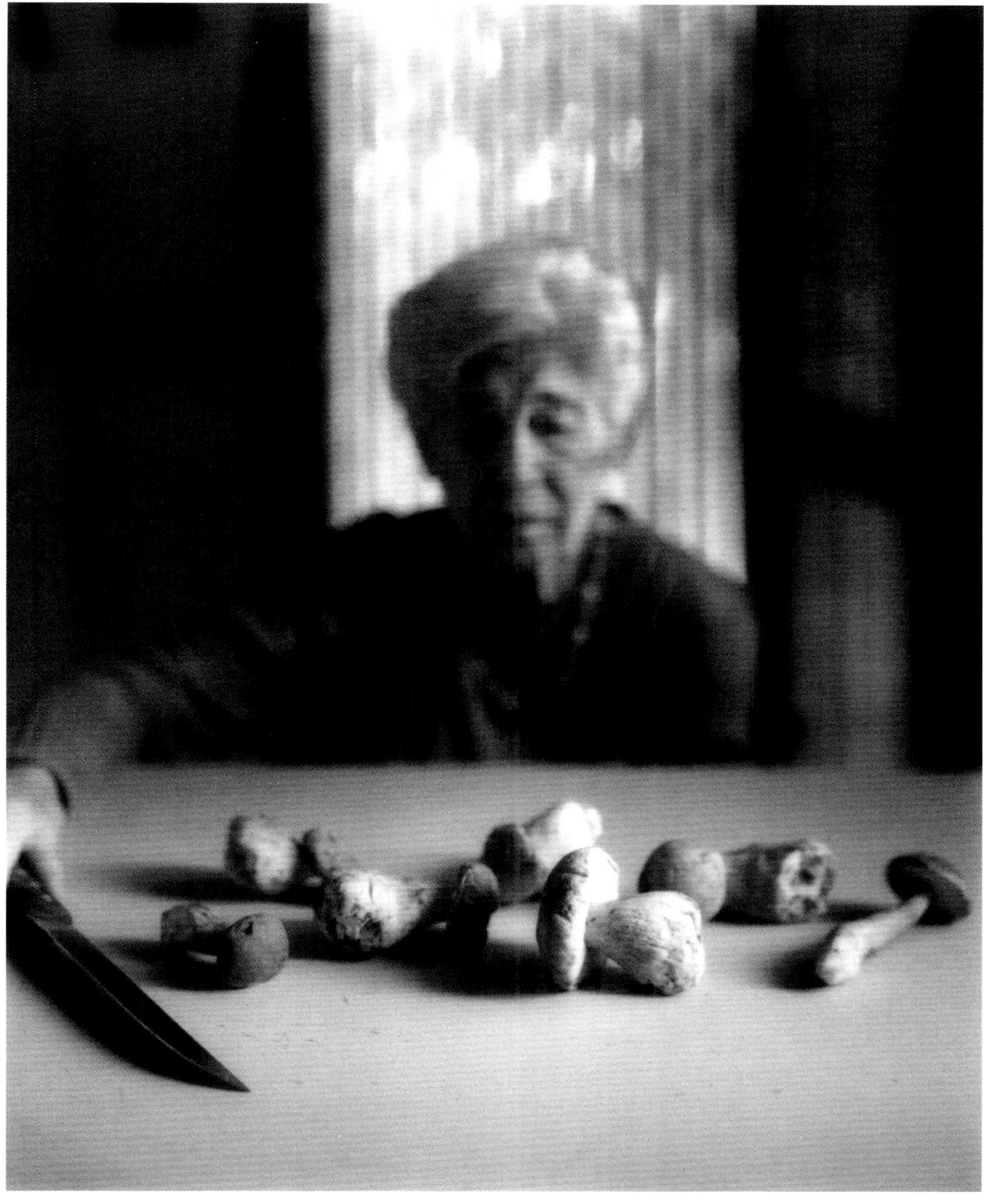

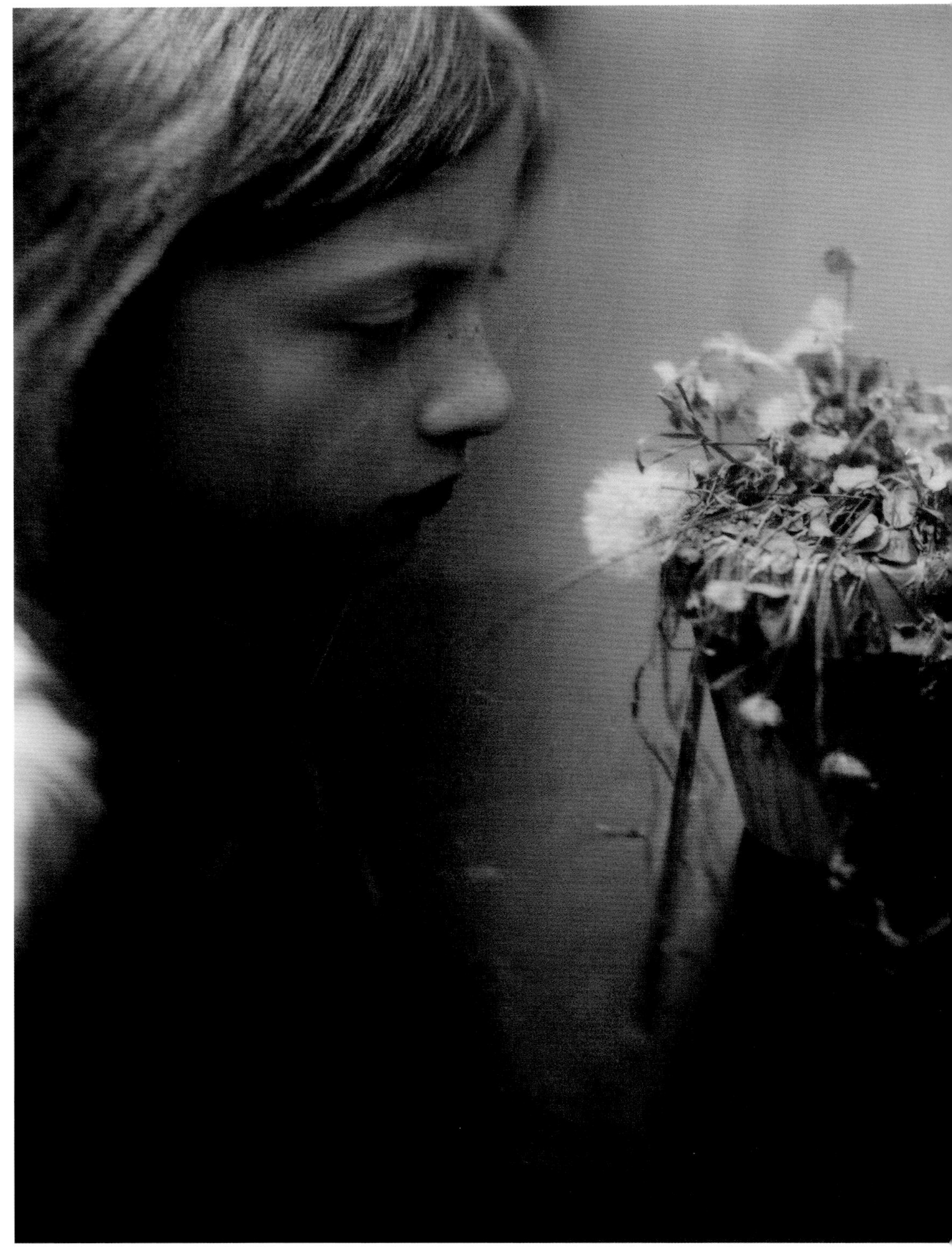

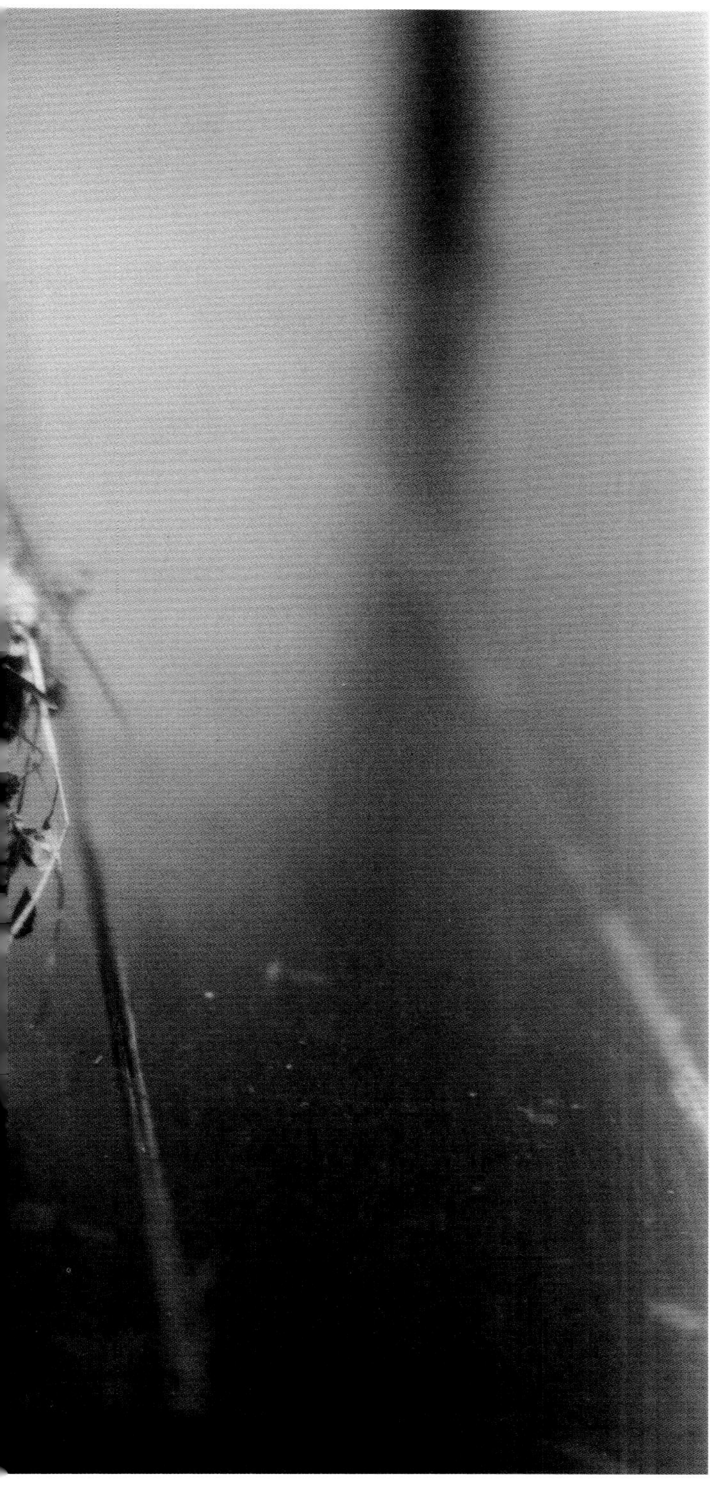

Ithaca, New York, 2018
Platinum print
8 × 10 in. (20.3 × 25.4 cm)

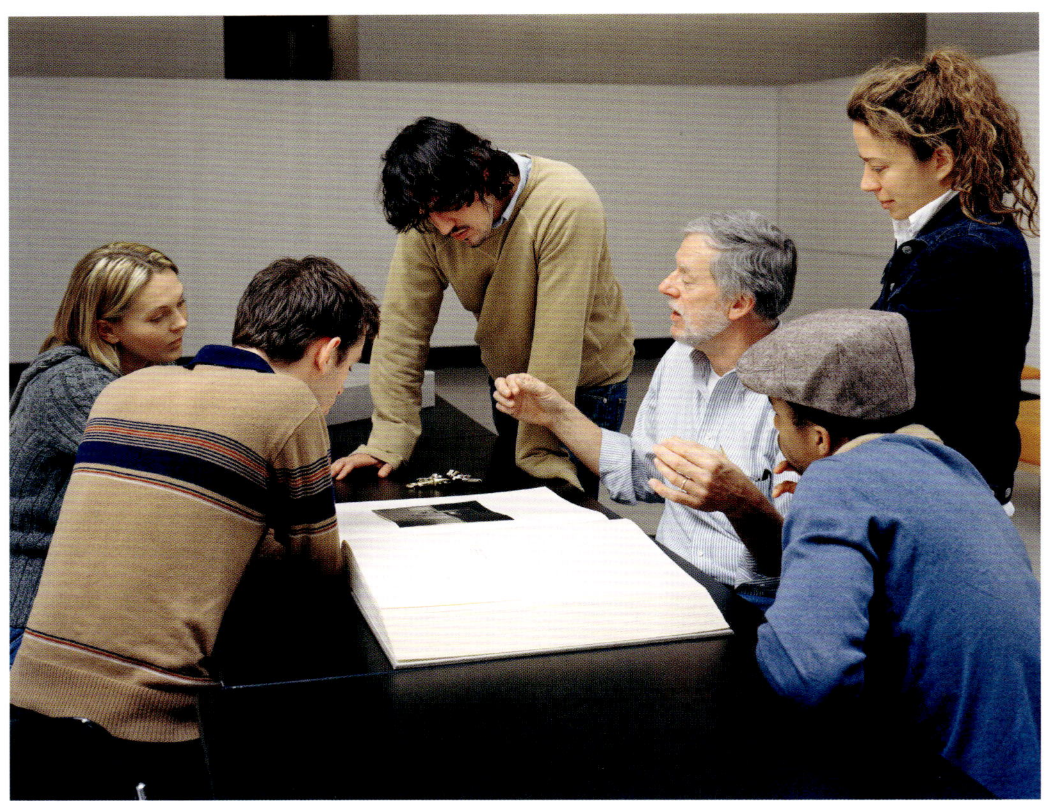

Chip describes the making of the Gilman book to the Yale School of Art 2004 MFA photography class (clockwise from front left: Matthew Connors, Jonnie Andersen, Ted Partin, Richard Benson, Samantha Bass, and Wardell Milan), 2002
Archival pigment print
30 × 38½ in. (76.2 × 97.8 cm)

As someone who attended twelve schools before graduating from an alternative high school, to say that my relationship with education before I got to Yale was fraught would be an understatement. I was left with little faith in the idea of academic institutions, but when I heard about Richard Benson—how he dropped out of Brown University to work with his hands and yet had received a MacArthur Grant and was the dean of the Yale School of Art—I applied to the MFA program, thinking I would not be accepted but figuring I would not regret trying.

My time at Yale and my work as an artist and professor have all been heavily influenced by the example that Chip set for us there, an experience that altered my perception of what is possible. Chip was wonderful at animating the process of creation, of making complex ideas comprehensible. He was a deeply moral person in the sense that he expected people to be their own authentic selves, and he had no tolerance for bullshit, but he was also an incredibly patient and generous teacher who gladly offered insights or advice or answers to questions. He both taught and modeled the need to look deeply at things and to consider the physical configuration of an object to determine meaning, concepts that influenced my thesis project, *Art School*, as well as my art-making and teaching.

This picture, of Chip showing our class the Gilman collection book, is meant to be a portrait of this process of close looking in action, of being not only an artist but a thinker. The plates that he made to reproduce the photographs are extremely precise, and at the same time their success relies on multiple passes of the paper through the press. Each of these passes is a chance to correct and adjust as well as to build on the successes and failures of the previous pass, a lesson in and of itself.

Chip often spoke about the physical properties and manifestations of photography. His emphasis on the elements of the medium forced us to consider the deep roots of photography, its ongoing evolution, and its meaning. The biggest gift Chip gave me was an appreciation of the technological magic involved in chemical processes; of materials like silver, ink, paper; and of the way pixels translate a film image into a gorgeous print. Chip's ideas continue to influence how I think about photography. One could say that he was involved in the art of alchemy.

To make my picture *Book: Boy with Fruit by Caravaggio* (1993), I photographed the lush ink in a reproduction of the painting *Young Sick Bacchus* (1539), placing an old volume on art history underneath a window with incoming light falling on it. This light had reversed the ink's reflections on the page, transforming them—all naturally—into the equivalent of a photographic negative. This effect became all the more startling when I developed the 4-by-5 film negative and saw Bacchus, in the darkroom tray, as a photographically positive image. At the time, that discovery made me think about old-fashioned spirit photography. Now, though, I think what I saw happen between the tabletop, the window, and the darkroom has more to do with the spirit of Richard Benson.

The events leading to my photograph began when Caravaggio made his painting centuries ago, using color oils to create an image measuring 26 by 21 inches. A second stage occurred when it was copied photographically. Eventually, the painting was reproduced at a small size in the pages of an art book, which I came across and photographed at a funny angle with black-and-white film. I digitally scanned this negative recently to prepare for its inclusion in this book.

The journey of an image, from its historical creation by Caravaggio to now and into tomorrow, is the kind of story that Chip loved to meditate on, read about, and relate to the rest of us. No one did it better.

Book, *Boy with Fruit by Caravaggio 4 × 5 Film Negative*, 2021
17 ⅞ × 22½ in. (45.4 × 57.2 cm)

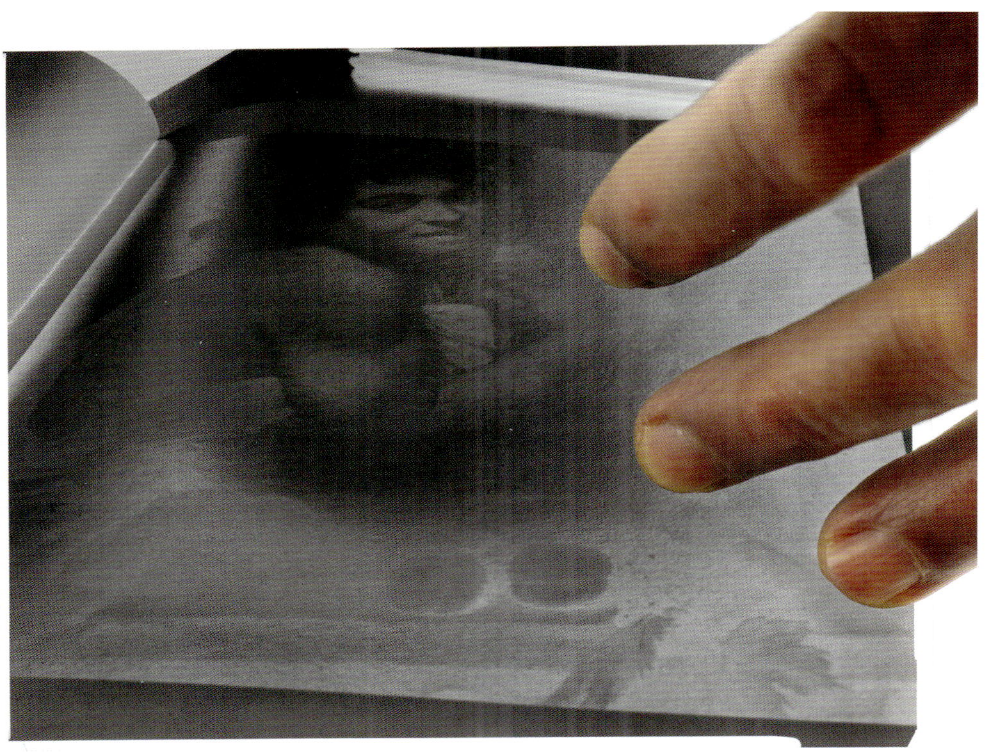

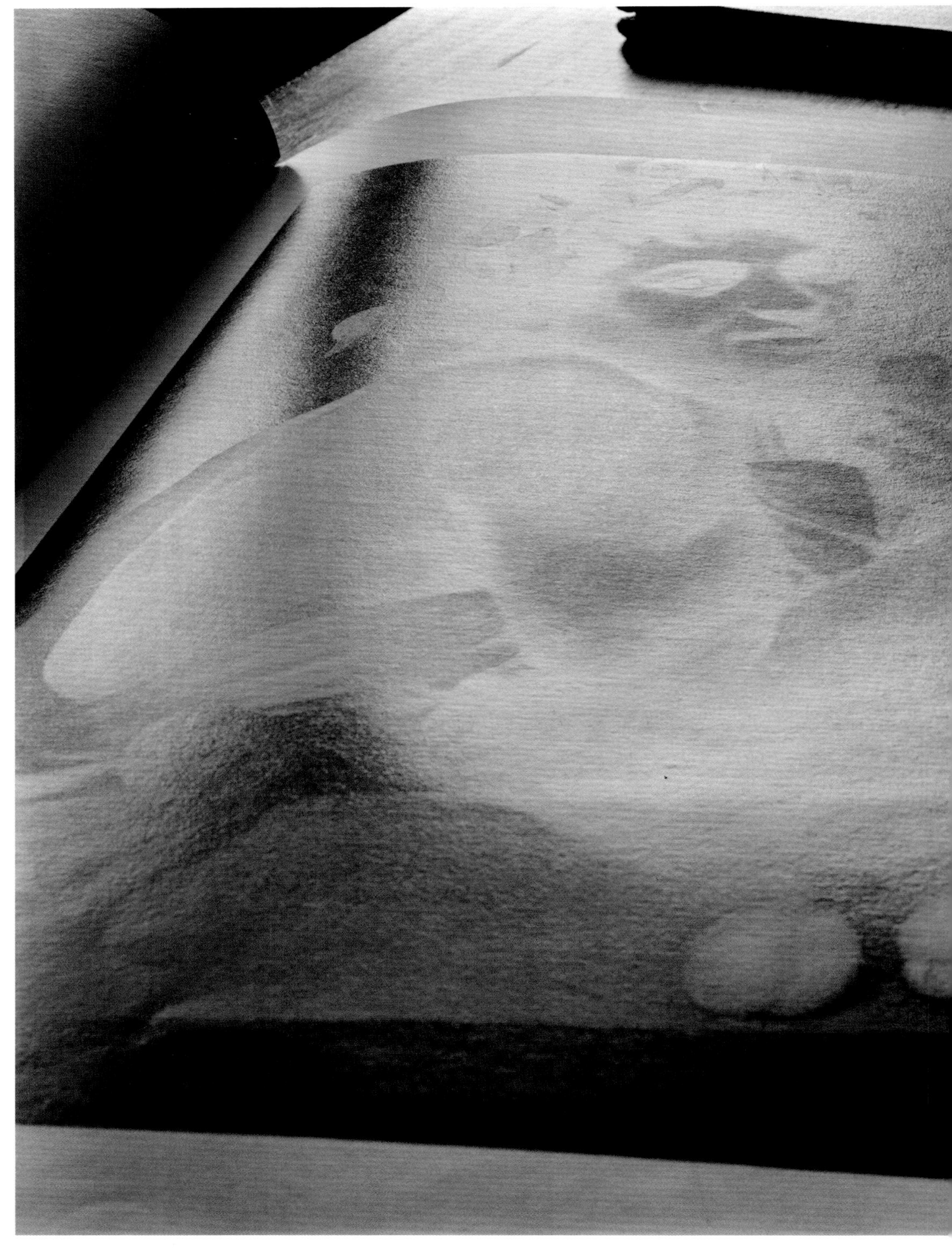

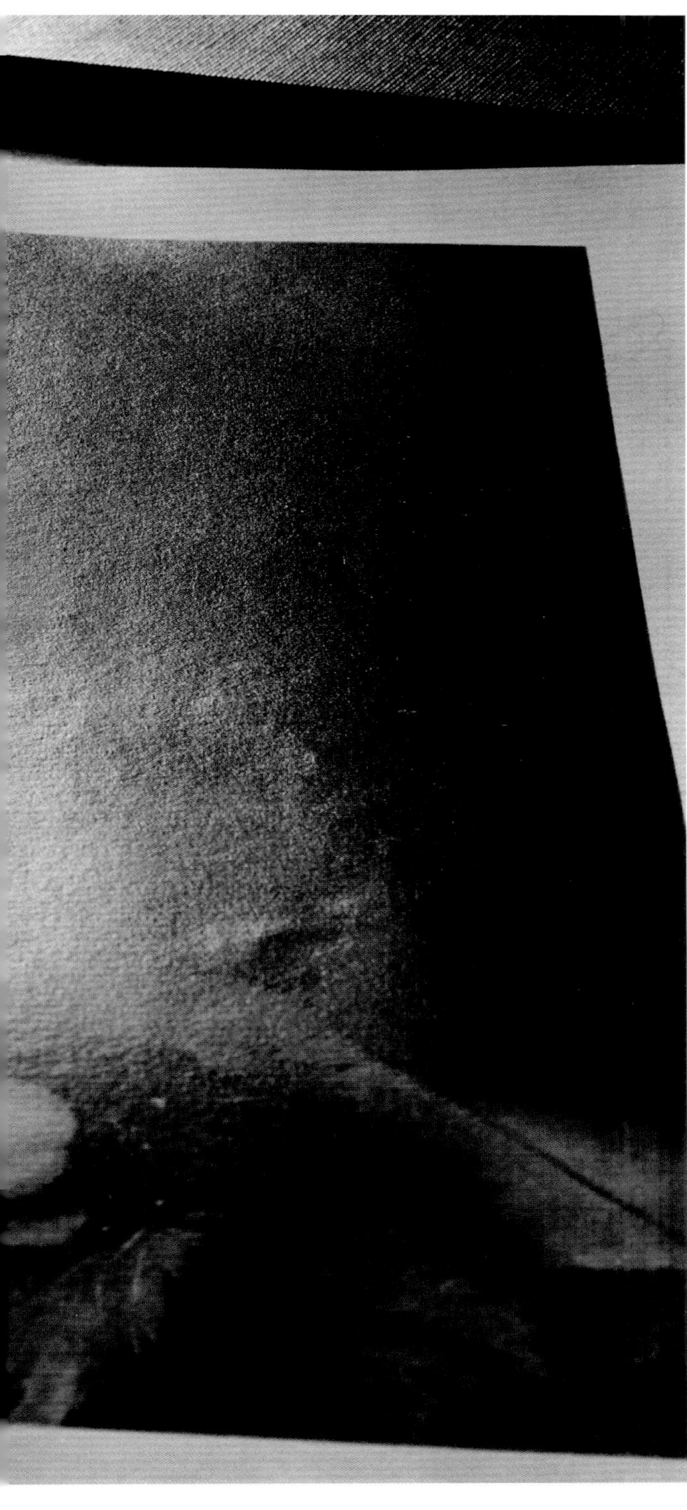

Book, Boy with Fruit by Caravaggio, 1993
Archival pigment print
30 × 40 in. (76.2 × 101.6 cm)

For my first critique at Yale, in the fall of 1998, I was feeling a little lost, unsure if I wanted to continue with straight photography or experiment with the medium. Chip had then recently been gifted two wide-format inkjet printers from HP (the first-ever at the School of Art), and while most of the students in the photo program at the time were making traditional darkroom prints in both color and black and white, I was interested in producing a monochromatic series of close-up facial portraits in pink, of Yale football players. I discussed this idea with Chip, who was intrigued not so much by the concept but by the color conversion, of rendering black-and-white analog images in a mono-chromatic pink through the inkjet process. The experience of working late to make a set of 30-by-40-inch prints on the HP opened up for me a different way of thinking about image-making. Chip described, with his typical verve when talking about any mechanical printing processes, the process of inkjet, explaining how the system that shoots pigment through nozzles is more akin to printmaking and lithography. He pushed against the notion of adhering to just one traditional method of making photographs, noting that it's often more interesting to think of ways to work fluidly in between methods, to see what different results you can find in combining them. At that stage of my learning, it was a radical realization: that there is no hierarchy in terms of traditional methods versus emerging ones, and that there is still a great deal of potential in trying to think about them as all part of the same array of possibilities. This was the first lesson.

The second lesson from Chip was less technical but has also left a lasting mark decades after. As part of his legendary class about book-making, Chip invited us to visit his home in Newport, Rhode Island, and we spent a memorable afternoon in his workshop, looking at the famous books he had helped to make of works by Eugène Atget, Lee Friedlander, and Paul Strand. He talked in great detail about the process to make the separations from the original negatives and about the mechanics of offset halftone printing. What was most astonishing was the mechanical clock that he had been laboring on, which he

Untitled, 1998
Archival pigment print
30 × 40 in. (76.2 × 101.6 cm)

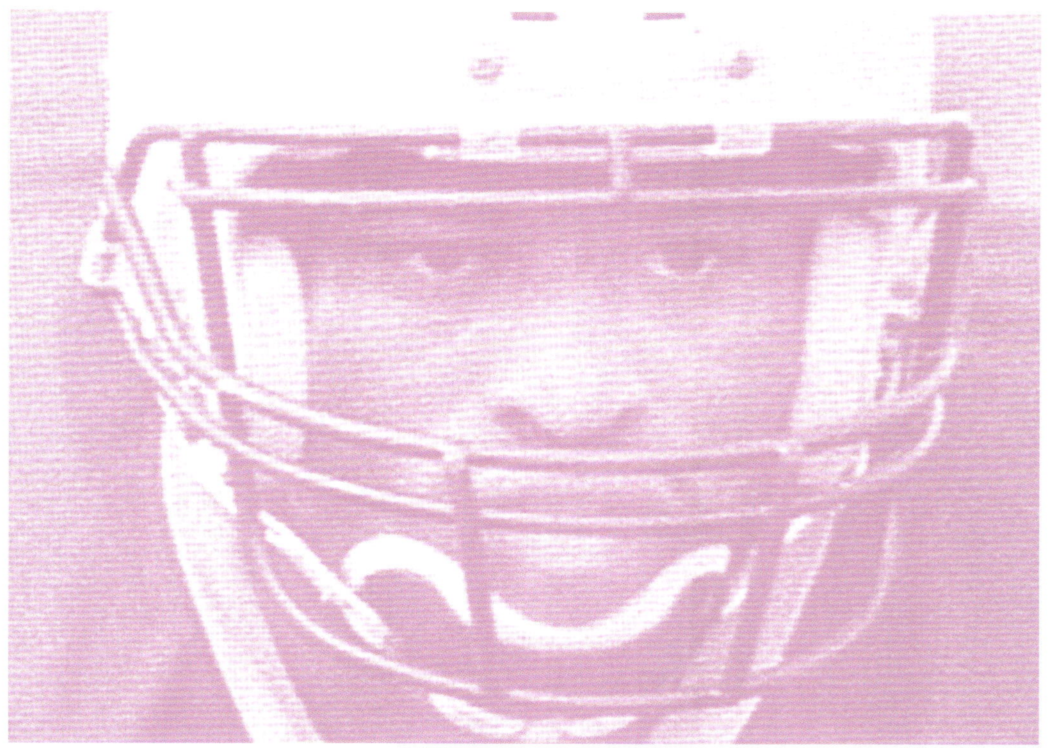

described as tracking time with a precision close to that of an atomic clock. Though there was an audible ticking, there were no obviously visible markers, such as hands or dials, of an apparatus that displayed time. I realize now, reflecting on this encounter, that there was something extraordinary about the poetic metaphor contained in this machine: that it was enough for it to be able to accurately trace the passage of time, effectively indexing the mundane yet mysterious phenomenon. It was less important for the instrument to express what time it actually was.

I found myself returning to this notion in 2017, long after that encounter, when I started a series of seascapes. These particular images were taken with a traditional 8-by-10-inch view camera on a day trip in Point Reyes in California during the morning and afternoon, and I was trying to find a vantage point high enough to depict the changing surface of the ocean. The choice of using large-format negatives is to achieve a high level of description even with a large-scale print, so that the depiction of the wave patterns can confuse the planar aspect of the film or print itself. The prints are analog prints on gelatin-silver paper, produced in a traditional darkroom. This is important because the indexical connection to light is still present. The intention was to use the sea surface as a ground for gradations of color applied through a hand-tinting technique, itself a historical process used since the beginnings of the medium. This process produces a layer of color that is integrated with the emulsion, seemingly part of the image. The sequential structure of the series, taken at slightly different moments during the early morning and later periods of the day, reflects a deliberate use of the camera's unique ability to render change over time.

I connect this work to both of the formative lessons I learned from Chip. The first is the discursive spirit he carried through his making process, not preferencing traditional modes over newer ones, allowing for discovery between processes. The second is that the act of making is itself a form of marking time. These are lessons that I still carry with me in my own teaching and approach to photographic pedagogy.

Pt. Reyes, October 21, 2017, 7:47 AM, 2017
Hand-tinted gelatin-silver print
60 × 50 in. (152.4 × 127 cm)

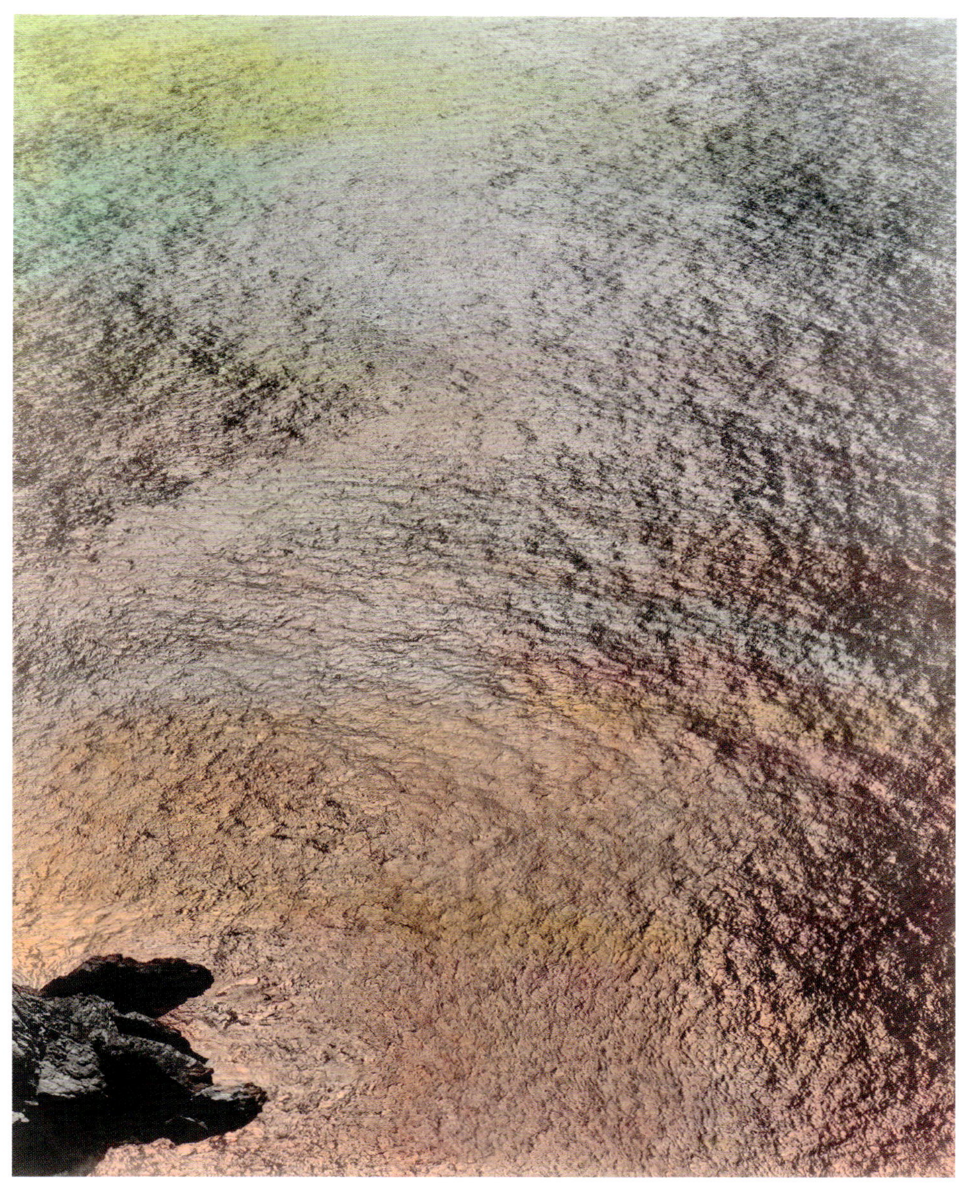

I first met Richard Benson in the spring of 1977, when we—along with Irving Penn (!)—were invited to New Haven to participate as guest critics at the final review of the Yale graduate photography program. As it turned out, we got along well and, two years later, after I'd been installed as director of graduate studies of that same program, and following a national search, Richard was hired to teach with me.

I was determined to shape a strong department at Yale and had decided that having Richard on the faculty was the first, and possibly most important, step I could make toward that end. His mastery of photographic technique and printing methods was incomparable, of course, and central to his hiring. But I also felt that his geniality of spirit, which, during those days on the critique panel, had seemed limitless, and—from his end—impossible to check, could only help in establishing what was effectively a new, independent department of photography in the School of Art. Not to mention that, when we spoke together, it seemed we each understood not only what the other was saying, but, also, everything he meant. I wasn't completing a pedagogical superstructure, by asking Richard to teach at Yale, but joining with an unexpectedly kindred spirit who, like me, had spent his adult life energetically puzzling out aspects of the mystery of photography, and only seemed to gain more appetite for the chase as he went on.

I think it's worth pointing out that Richard originally came to Yale with a full-time appointment and, along with the job, had accepted the requirement of establishing residence in New Haven. As that first year ended, however, he told me he couldn't continue to be away from his family in Newport for so much of the week, and therefore would have to leave Yale and his classes. Something neither of us wanted to happen.

As a result, we figured out a "part-time" role for him that had him teaching more than most of the tenured faculty in the School of Art (and, I'd hazard, at Yale in general), but allowed him the time he wanted in Rhode Island. And on we went, with Richard, as usual, acting as honorably as a person could, given his and the school's needs.

Until he became Dean in 1996, Richard participated as a core figure on the critique panel during the weekly review of student work that everyone in the program attended and recognized as central to the teaching that went on there. During that same time period, he also had a prime role in the admissions process. In other words, students

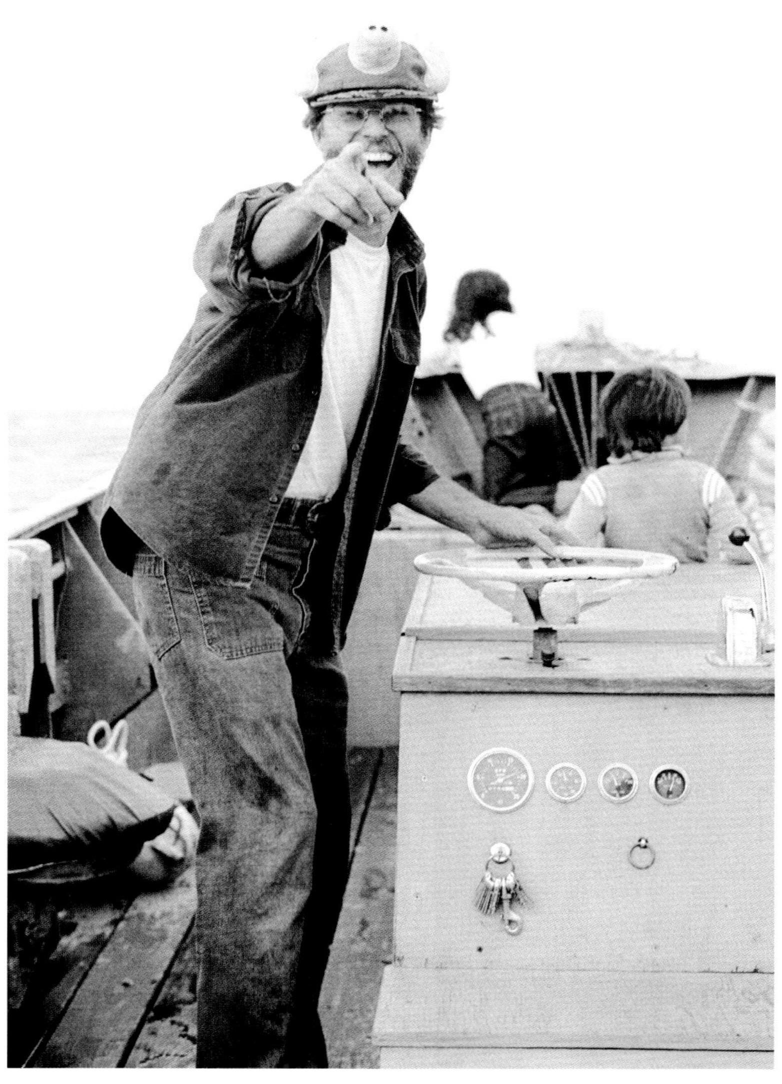

Richard Benson Piloting Miss Piggy on Newport Bay, ca. 1985
Gelatin-silver print

interacting with him before he entered the dean's office, were doing so in distinctly different ways than those he taught after, just as he was necessarily operating with a different kind of agency in relation to the photography program itself.

And how should we count those ways during that seventeen-year period? Since I rarely sat in on either his Book or Photoshop class, I have to base my impressions on the weekly critique, as well as the countless meetings and meals we had over the years discussing photography, teaching, students, schedules, families and the human race in general. The last of which, despite our obvious differences of temperament and outlook, we both measured through jaundiced eyes (though I realize that's an odd image to use in relation to photographers). I think our mutual admiration of ancient Greece played a role in this, but, whatever the reason, the fact is that, for all of his sweet nature, Richard was decidedly dispassionate in the way he viewed human history and fate—something I hadn't anticipated but, perhaps perversely, found endearing.

For all of that, to the students Richard was clearly the Good Cop to my Bad Cop, which the two of us joked about. As stern and sharp as I was as a critic, so was he warm and cajoling. No one got a pass from him, though. How could they, when who knew better than Richard Benson precisely what the physical, hand-directed requirements were to produce, for example, a strong print or to set up a stand camera in search of a clear, coherent picture (back when such a thing was an uncontested good). And, armed with that knowledge, who could argue as urgently as Richard, how, before everything else, photography was born in those physical acts and nowhere else (including, least of all, the photographer's mind)?

His understanding, however, wasn't limited to tripods or platinum printing, or the Photoshop Curve (which he had a hand in developing). Perhaps because he was so broadly curious about how *things* worked, so was he a student of the great human drama of how and why people act the way they do, an ongoing musing that had the side effect of inoculating and rendering him immune to the vague language of hope that many artists, students and otherwise, use to describe and defend their work. Although that never prevented him from dismissing ill-conceived ideas, not to mention photographs, in as charitable a way as anyone I've ever known. In other words, he was, equally, a generous critic, and a valuable, central one, during his time both on and off the critique panel.

As he proved again and again through those later years with the major books and self-printed pamphlets he wrote and curated— on ships and the sea; a taxonomy of everything; his Samoyed, Mookie; a compendious history of printing; and even an anthology of historical photographs made at Yale—as well as his unrelenting work as a photographer, photographic inventor, and, yes, builder of 10,000-year clocks.

Those who knew him will remember and treasure their own particular Richard, or Chip, Benson through the so many things he made and wrote and said, or simply gave us (for me, most preciously, a small, ancient Greek vase). Which is how we'll all live on, it seems. In his particular case, more vividly, brilliantly, purely. For that's how he was.

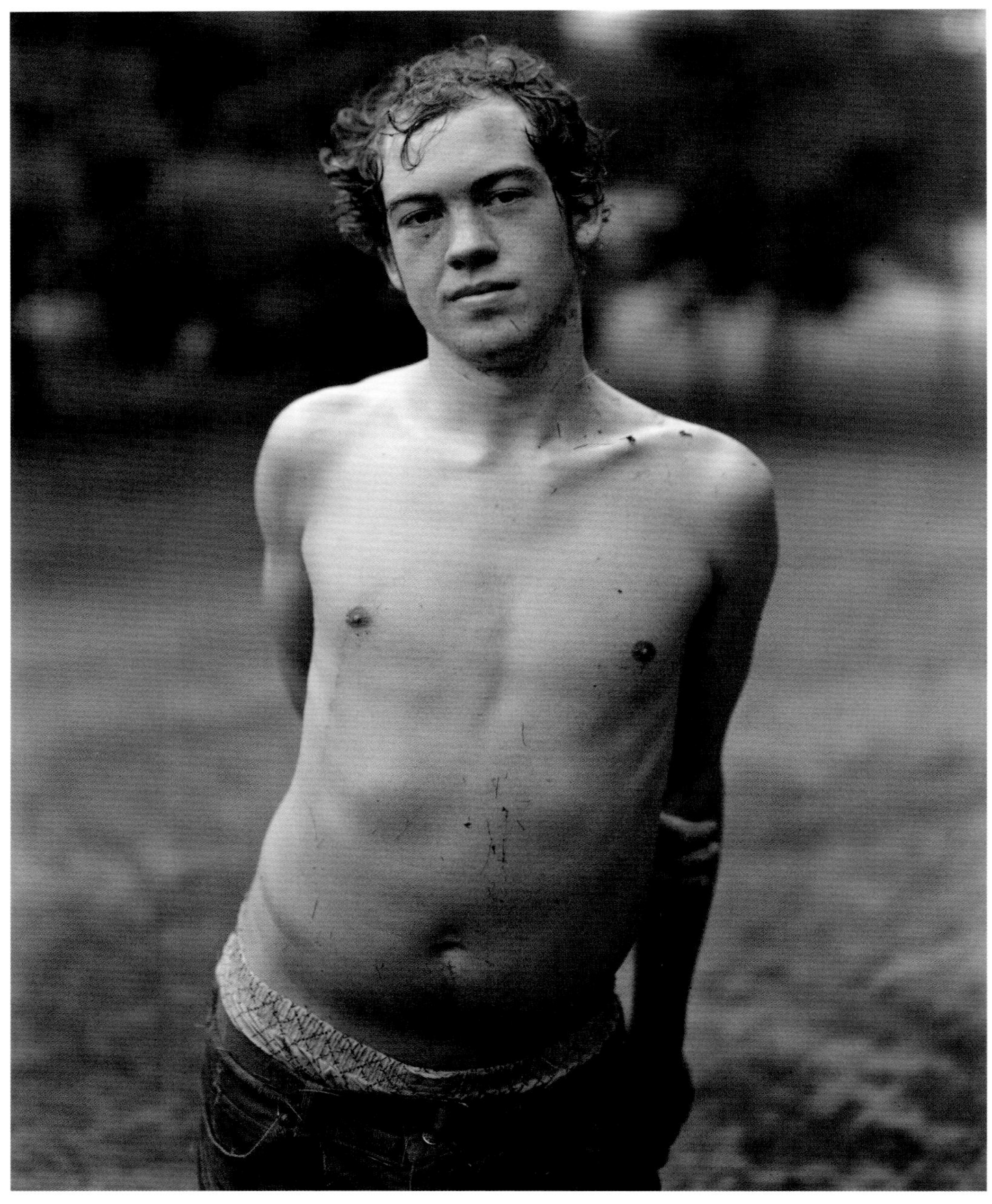

Norfolk, 2003
Gelatin-silver print
10 × 8 in. (25.4 × 20.3 cm)

When I started studying at the Yale School of Art, I had no idea what I was doing, and thought I had really gotten myself way in over my head. After our class's first meeting with Richard, the only thing I was certain about was that I had to spend as much time as possible with this person and hopefully glean some of the incredible wisdom he possessed and wanted to share with us.

I know without a doubt that nothing has shaped me more as an artist than Richard lending me his 8-by-10-inch view camera and 10 ¾-inch Gold Dot Dagor lens (the perfect portrait lens, according to Chip). I saw the world in a way I never had before with this camera. For all the talk about how cumbersome and clunky view cameras are, it was easy to use. It was easy to use because of how Richard taught me to use it. "Just treat it like any old camera," he said. That's what I did, and what I continue to do now, nearly twenty years later.

As if we weren't fortunate enough to be at Yale and working with Richard, he arranged to have John Szarkowski teach a class. Once after class, we left our pictures hanging on the wall and went for lunch. When we came back to the building to get back to work, I bumped into Richard. He said, "I shouldn't tell you this, but when we came back from lunch, John pointed at your picture [made with Chip's 8-by-10] and said, 'Perfect picture!'"

I was immediately embarrassed and blurted out, "Oh wow, thank you." Richard barked back, "What are you thanking me for? *I* don't think it's a perfect picture! What's a perfect picture, anyway?" Another lesson learned.

After the final critique of my first year of graduate school in 2006, I was invited to join Chip and John Pilson for lunch at a restaurant in the basement of the Duncan Hotel. According to Chip, Walker Evans had frequented this space when it was a different establishment. During lunch, Chip started discussing the difficulties I was having in school. My training was in black-and-white street photography, shot with small cameras, but I was feeling a lot of pressure to have a stronger conceptual foundation to my photographic process. My current approach wasn't yielding impressive results, and it was apparent to everyone that I was drowning. Chip then told me something that John Szarkowski once said:

> Some photographers think the idea is enough. I told a good story in my Getty talk, a beautiful story, to the point: Ducasse says to his friend Mallarmé—I think this is a true story—he says, "You know, I've got a lot of good ideas for poems, but the poems are never very good." Mallarmé says, "Of course, you don't make poems out of ideas, you make poems out of words." Really good, huh? Really true. So, photographers who aren't so good think that you make photographs out of ideas. And they generally get only about halfway to the photograph and think that they're done.

This conversation with Chip made me reflect on my approach to photography and helped me learn a transformative lesson. We are all trying to converse in this visual language that we can never be fully fluent in, and it's the tension between *concept* and *description* that can be the most revealing. Chip believed the *world* was more interesting than any *concept* we can imagine, and he taught me how to help prove him right!

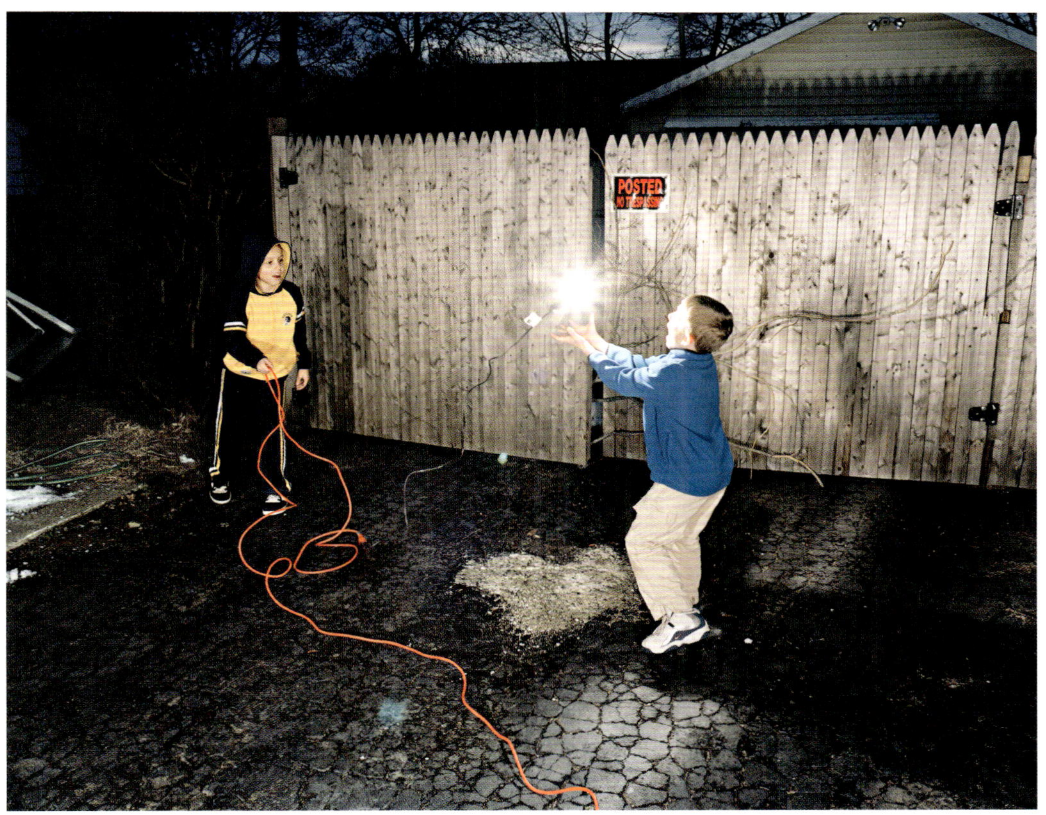

Untitled (boys throwing light bulb), 2008
Archival pigment print
24 × 30 in. (61 × 76.2 cm)

In 2006, the year after I graduated from Yale, I began working at Exhibition Prints, Joel Sternfeld's former lab on 29th Street in Manhattan. The lab had previously made only darkroom prints, and Sternfeld wanted to build out a digital wing. There were far fewer people who understood a digital workflow then than today, and by some stroke of luck, I found myself at the helm of the new enterprise. Chip had always advised finding jobs that put you close to the things you need for your own work. Professional printing had long done that for me.

At the time, I was just starting to work on my portrait series *The Gray Line*, which I had decided needed to be black and white. One peculiarity about my working practice is that I shoot on 4-by-5 color film and digitally translate that to black and white. I needed to make inkjet prints but absolutely hated the paper surfaces available at the time. I wanted a paper surface that looked like a gelatin-silver print. At a loss for options, I decided to fix unexposed gelatin-silver paper and run it through the printer. It worked, and it looked great! I wondered if it was stable, so I reached out to Chip and asked for his thoughts.

Chip's response is a classic example of his approach to photography, and it best encapsulates why those of us who were lucky enough to be around him learned so much more than technical skills. He set an example for how to approach our desire to describe the world clearly: with curiosity, inventiveness, humor, and a lack of preciousness.

I did end up taping a print to my window, and it held up just fine! The cost of printing that way was the major impediment, so I was relieved when paper manufacturers began producing baryta surfaces. Interestingly, I found a box of fixed paper in my studio recently and ran one through the newest Epson to make a print as I had done back then. To my surprise, the ink no longer holds to the surface of the paper. I can think of only one person who would be able to explain why.

Date: 8/03/06
Subject: Am I crazy?

Hi Chip,
So Joel Sternfeld has hired me on to facilitate his lab's move into digital scanning and printing. (good fringe benefits for me!). I am suddenly able to experiment with tons of cool new toys and surfaces. I have started printing on fixed black and white fiber paper. It looks really fantastic. Have you done this? What do you make of its stability?

Hope you and Barbara are enjoying your summer.
Kristine

Date: 8/03/06
Subject: Re: Am I crazy?

First of all, you are certainly not crazy-odd perhaps, but that is OK for artists like us.

I have never tried this, but there is no decent black and white gloss or semi-gloss paper out there, and if this does it then hooray. As to stability, I have no idea. The permanence of ink jet printing isn't just about pigment fading or not but is very complex in terms of chemical reaction to the support, sizing and pigment interaction. So-I would do this. make a print and cut it in half and tape it on a south facing window for a few weeks and see what happens. Also dangle a piece out a New York window, face down where it won't get wet (but not in any sort of container) to see what the vile NYC air does to it. Any fixed silver based paper has an inherent instability because hypo is the prime crude of the world, but a good fixing and washing should at least let these prints be as good as all the other silver prints that will eventually (long after we are gone) turn yellow and save the world from having too many bad pictures around.

Hope you are doing well - Chip

Untitled (from The Gray Line), 2009
Archival pigment print
25 × 20 in. (63.5 × 50.8 cm)

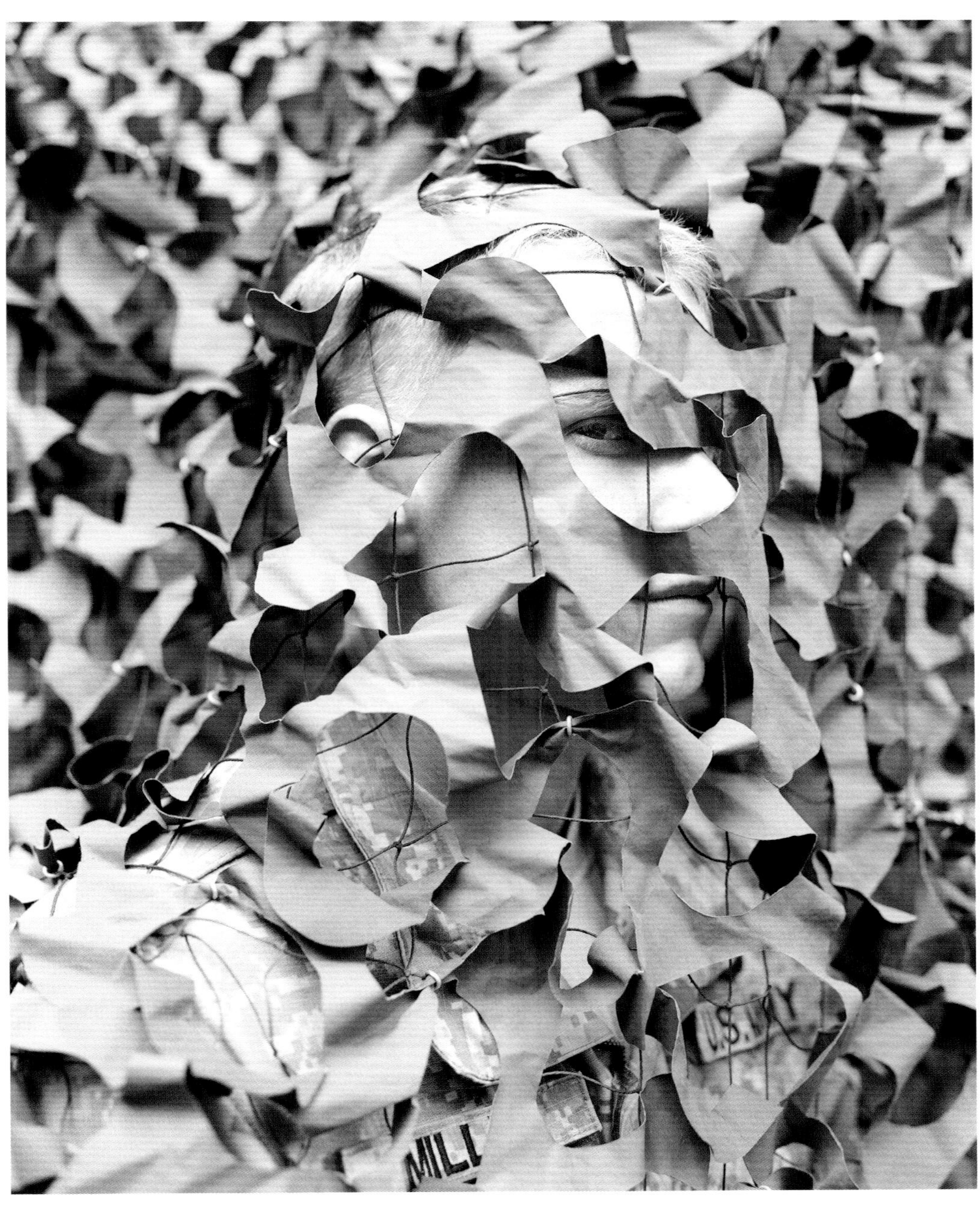

I remember the time Richard invited me and our entire MFA class to his home. He showed us his garden, his book collection, his studio where he made both photographs and clocks. I wasn't aware of Richard's interest in clocks until that day. It took me by surprise because I knew him only as Richard Benson, Master Printer and Photographer. As the ten of us stood in his studio facing a wall of clocks, surrounded by metal parts and plans drawn on scraps of paper, he said that clocks were the most complicated thing to build.

Richard was never intimidated by a challenge, and he followed his passion wherever it went. He had the ability to effortlessly flow from solving complex technical and artistic problems to the routine of his daily life—all while maintaining a contagious enthusiasm. As we sat down to lunch that day at his long kitchen table, Richard talked freely about his family, his children, and the adventures he had while traveling the country in his RV named Giraffe. Richard was authentically himself no matter what he did, and he made you love him for that.

As a student of Richard's, I internalized his generosity, his energy, his discipline, his character. He taught me to think about art in the context of life, and that no matter how particular and exacting your work is, the most important thing is to be authentically yourself in every aspect of your art and your life—especially when confronted with challenge.

In recent years, I have drawn upon the lessons absorbed during my time with Richard as I have needed to face and accept the uncomfortable and challenging shift in my identity from artist to artist-mother. I no longer have the same time and freedom to search for photographs as I had as a young artist and have needed to figure out a way to make important work while confined to the responsibilities of home. I often think about Richard and the fact that he never resisted challenge—how he could effortlessly weave the complexity of life into art. Rather than resisting the challenge of my situation, I am weaving the complexity of life into art by using photography and drawing—a new practice for me—to incorporate the constraints of the quotidian in an investigation of domesticity, routine, ritual, and play. In this work, *Scratch Drawings*, I photograph sunlight coming through the windows of my home as it shines onto colored paper. The overlaid shapes, created by etching into the photograph with thousands of minute X-Acto blade marks, are abstractions of photographs found, seen, and created in the everyday. Just as Richard would have expected of me, I've embraced the challenges I face to make work that is uniquely, authentically, and painstakingly my own.

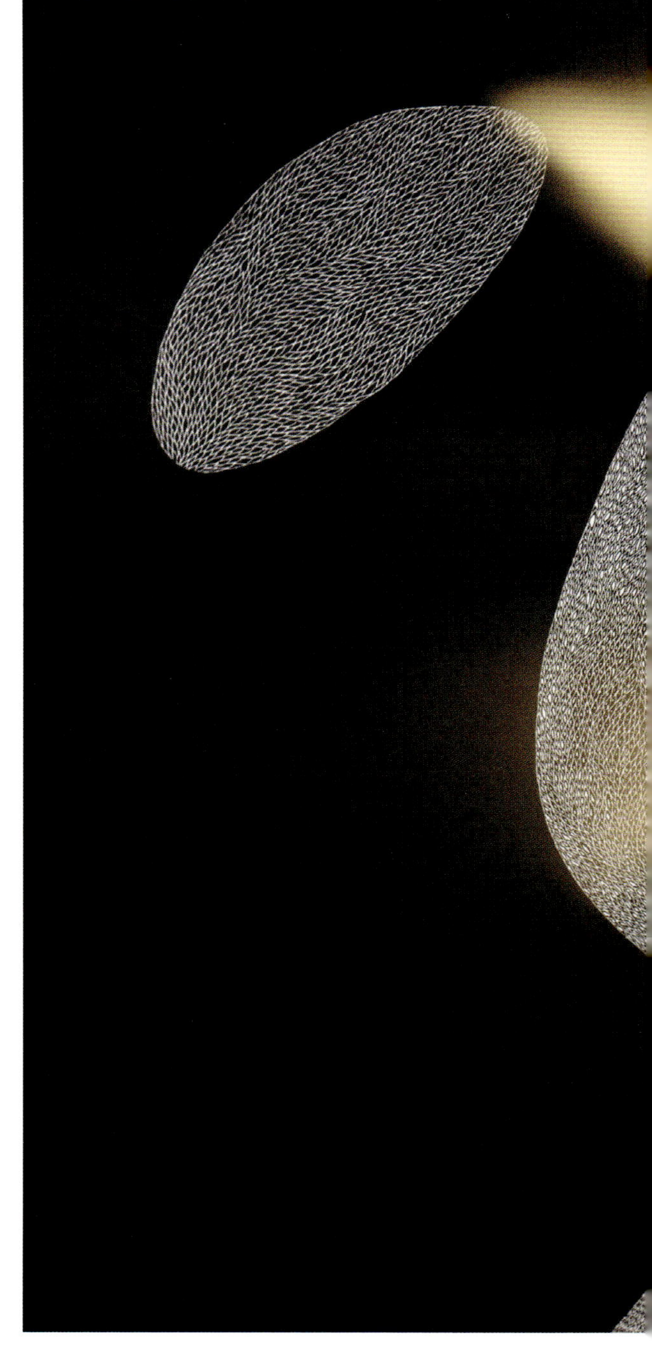

Into Yellow, 2021
X-Acto blade etching on a photographic pigment print
30 × 40 in. (76.2 × 101.6 cm)

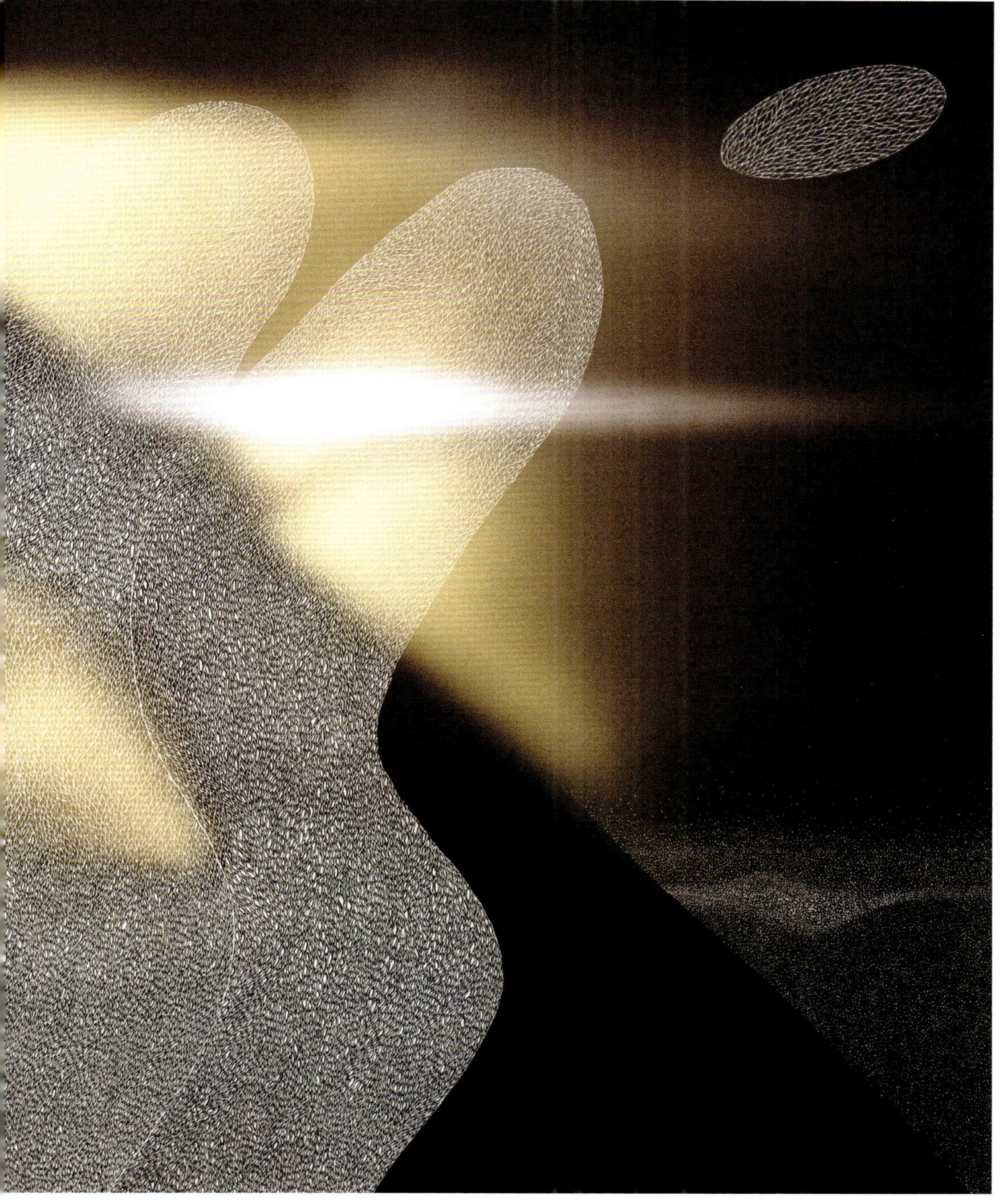

For someone born in an era before computers and digital cameras, the digital tsunami seems unbearable at times, especially as AI creeps closer and closer into our lives. The question of photography being an art form still haunts us.

Is the photographic print an art object, a valuable object, or—because of its ability to be reproduced hundreds of times—just a commercial object? If that is one of the questions and arguments for this medium, then where does the book fit? This democratic vehicle allows the public to own many images; the book is a constructed narrative and a final object made specifically to hold in one's hands and viewed in the privacy of one's chosen setting.

Richard Benson could be said to have reinvented or at least freed the book form from antiquated technical restraints. In 1981, Richard was asked to reproduce two hundred historical photographs from the massive private collection of the Gilman Paper Company. He convinced the company and the curator that to achieve the best possible results, the company should buy him a press to make individual offset reproductions of each image, since this way, he could exert maximum control over color and density. It was a project that took the best of four years. The outcome was a massive book like nothing that had ever been seen before: each reproduction breathed new life into the images.

Richard came from an old Yankee family from Newport. His father, a stone cutter, passed on a love for hard work and meticulous virtuosity of craft, and Richard considered himself an honest maker of objects.

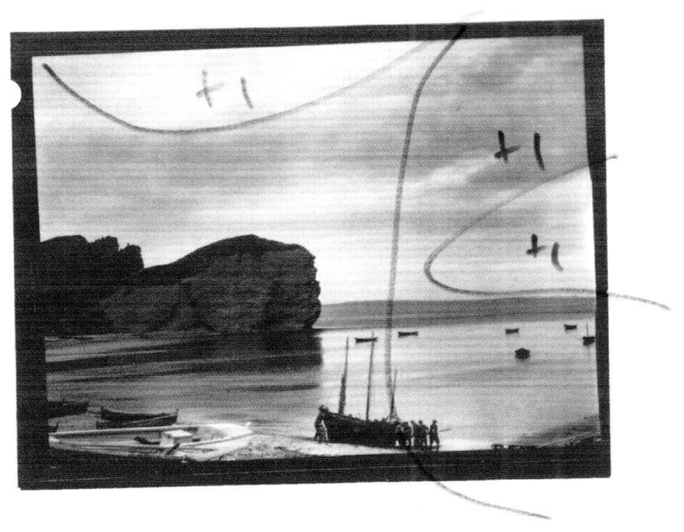

DATE:	5/10/16	ENLARGER:	II
CLIENT:	Paul Strand	LENS:	150
NAME OF IMAGE:	GSP-SEA NEGATIVE #: 3|6|17	F STOP:	8
PAPER:	Ad·x MCC ,12	CONTRAST:	5.5
PRINT SIZE: 8x10 IMAGE SIZE: 4x5		EXPOSURE:	8.8
NOTES/OTHER:		DENSITY: 0 OUTPUT POWER %: 77	
		DEVELOPER/TIME:	BW 65 1:1:5 3min
		TONING:	Gold 10min

Along the way, he learned how machines could reproduce, via mimesis, an exacting image of the world out there. This became the main focus in his life as a photographer, and his relentless fascination with mechanical objects became a way of giving back to the medium.

Richard had started at Yale a year before I entered the graduate program, and I was fortunate to have had him as one of my professors. His positive energy and optimism were addictive, and it seemed that whatever the subject, he knew something about it. By the clarity and quality of his observations, one would discern his intelligence. His life as a printer was one of problem-solving, and he was into the things we make physically—the object. In other words, his view was that "thought is only a piece of what makes the art."

When Richard was stepping down after ten years as dean, he was given a goodbye party at the home of one of his students. I had not seen him in a while—I had been busy running my photographic printing business in New York City and continuing to make pictures, shooting film with a handheld 4-by-5 view camera. To my delight, the first person I saw at the party was Richard, who came toward me and my wife with a big smile on his face. In his powerful voice, he declared, "Sergio! Film is dead!" Richard was not afraid to toss out the old and bring in the new, metaphorically speaking. Luckily for me, film is not quite dead—I am still processing it for myself and clients, still printing analog but taking advantage of digital technology to make analog negatives from digital files and pigment prints.

Gowanus Canal and 3rd Street, Brooklyn, 2012
Gelatin-silver print
20 × 24 in. (50.8 × 61 cm)

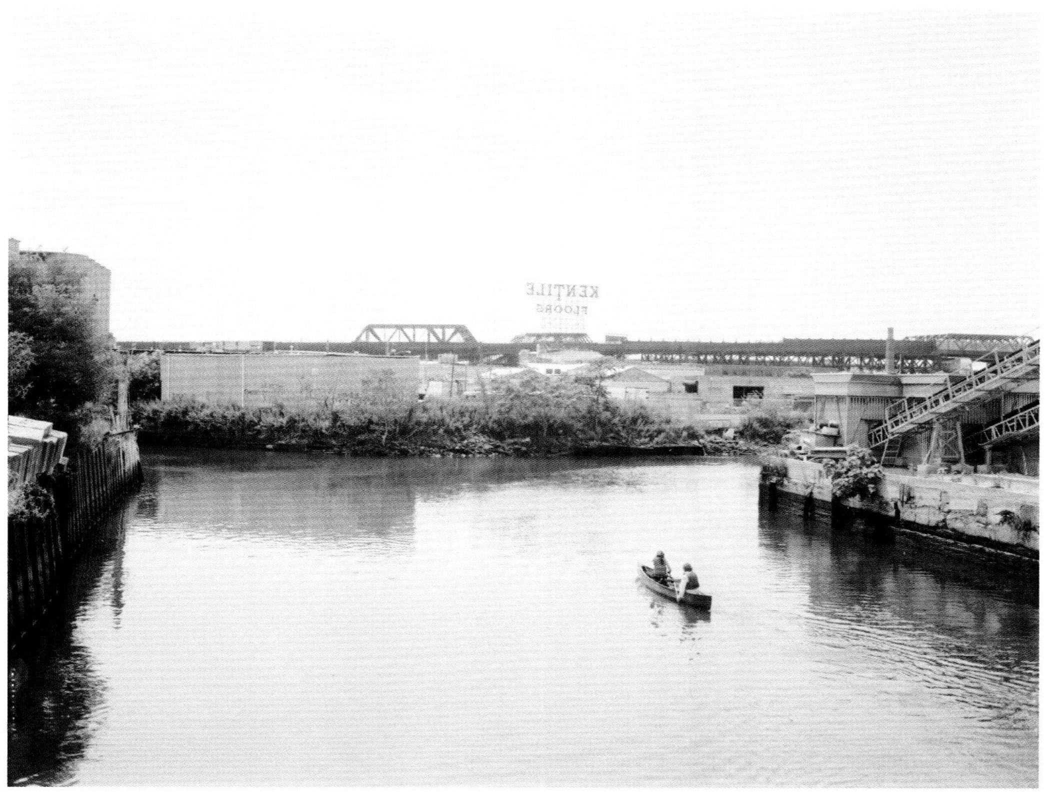

In 1999, GHP Media, my printing company, was working on color separations for Helen Levitt's book *Crosstown*. The color separation process in those days involved scanning Helen's C-prints, outputting film and making match-print proofs, adjusting the underlying digital files to improve the fidelity of the match prints to Helen's C-prints, and sending the results off to Helen for approval. Our judgments about the fidelity of our proofs to Helen's prints were made in the 5000 K lighting conditions used for decades as the standard in graphic arts lighting booths.

Chip Benson happened to be in my office on the day that Helen received our *Crosstown* proofs. Helen, then in her late eighties, called me to say that while our proofs looked pretty good, we needed to take yellow out of all of them. After getting off the phone, we struggled to make sense of Helen's comments. Finally, Chip realized that the problem was that Helen was looking at our proofs under a single incandescent lamp in her dark apartment. The warm light gave them a yellow cast. I called Helen back and put Chip on speakerphone with her. Chip confirmed the viewing conditions and explained that these were not ideal and why taking yellow out of our separations was a bad idea. Helen agreed with everything Chip said, thanked him profusely for explaining things to her, and told me that our color separations were approved as is.

Five minutes later, Helen called me back and asked if Chip was still in my office. When I told her he was not, she said, "Take the yellow out." When I told Chip about the call, he just smiled, and my company proceeded to do as Helen asked.

Nine years later, I was on press with Chip with his book *The Printed Picture*. We had already done extensive proofing of the color separations that Chip had made himself, and he approved the first two press forms we had printed in record time. As we were readying the next press form, Chip began walking press sheets around our printing plant and agonizing over them. The problem, he told me, was that the 5000 K lighting used in prepress and on-press viewing reduced the amount of red that most people, looking under standard fluorescent or incandescent bulbs, would see in his pictures. So he made the decision to run the magenta ink level on the rest of the book down 3 percent from where he had on the first two press forms. When I asked him if he wanted to reprint the first two forms, he said, "Of course not, no one else will ever notice."

We printed that book three times, and Chip was right: no one ever noticed the slight difference in inking that he decided in midstream was best for his book. Both Helen and Chip were accomplished masters who could make decisions about the reproduction of their work however they wished. In Helen's case, it was clear that she wanted reproductions to look good to her, regardless of how "standard" her viewing conditions were. In Chip's case, he decided to abandon the graphic arts viewing standard he had used for decades because he realized this standard had limitations, and he wanted his pictures to look good to others. Respecting tradition and turning it on its head was Chip's lifelong practice.

Cover (below) and press sheet from the cover (right) of *The Printed Picture* (New York: Museum of Modern Art, 2008)

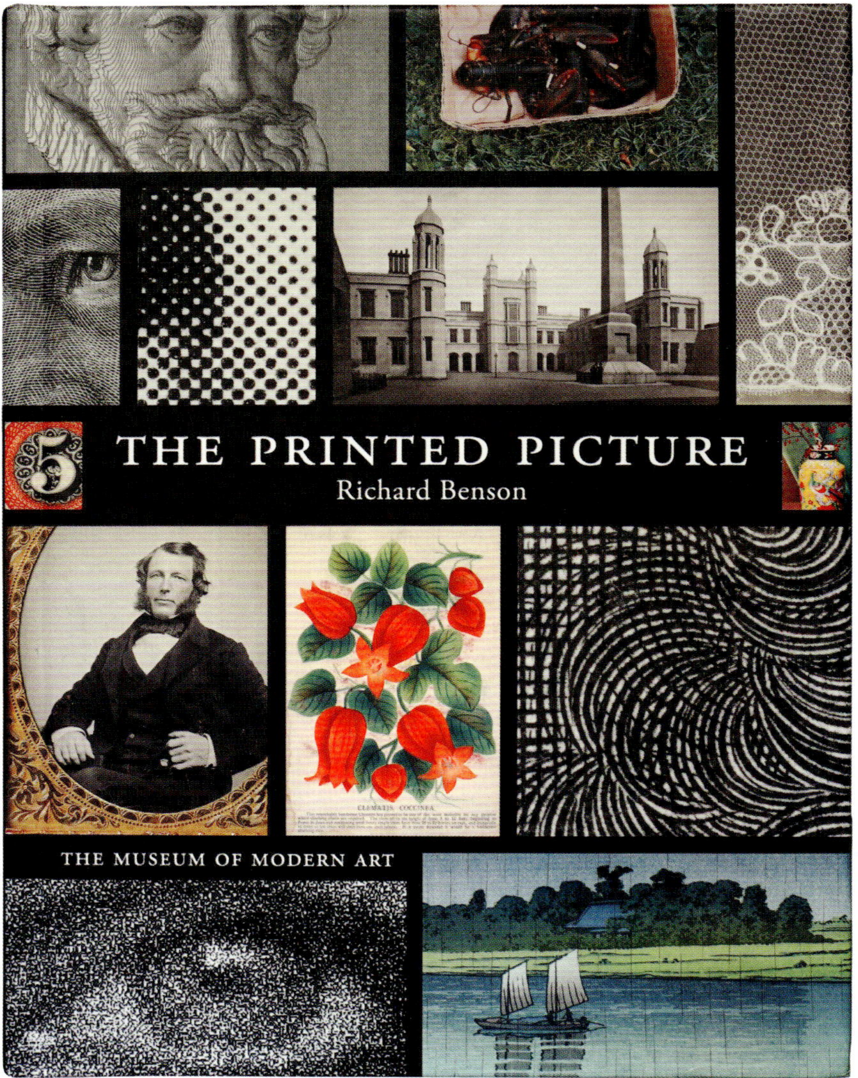

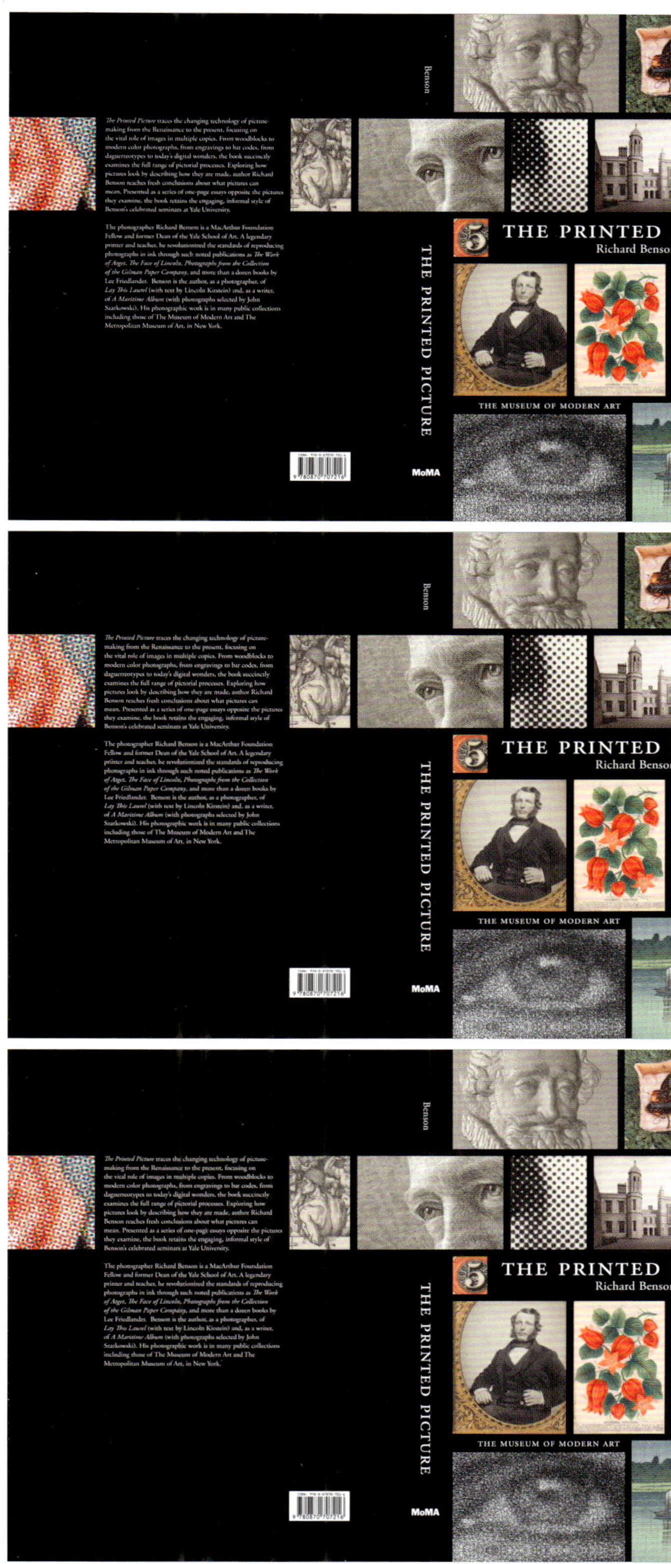

Benson
The Printed Picture traces the changing technology of picture-making from the Renaissance to the present, focusing on the vital role of images in multiple copies. From woodblocks to modern color photographs, from engravings to bar codes, from daguerreotypes to today's digital wonders, the book succinctly examines the full range of pictorial processes. Exploring how pictures look by describing how they are made, author Richard Benson reaches fresh conclusions about what pictures can mean. Presented as a series of one-page essays opposite the pictures they examine, the book retains the engaging, informal style of Benson's celebrated seminars at Yale University.
The photographer Richard Benson is a MacArthur Foundation Fellow and former Dean of the Yale School of Art. A legendary printer and teacher, he revolutionized the standards of reproducing photographs in ink through such noted publications as The Work of Atget, The Face of Lincoln, Photographs from the Collection of the Gilman Paper Company, and more than a dozen books by Lee Friedlander. Benson is the author, as a photographer, of Lay This Laurel (with text by Lincoln Kirstein) and, as a writer, of A Maritime Album (with photographs selected by John Szarkowski). His photographic work is in many public collections including those of The Museum of Modern Art and The Metropolitan Museum of Art, in New York.
THE PRINTED PICTURE
Richard Benson
THE PRINTED PICTURE
THE MUSEUM OF MODERN ART
MoMA

John Robinson

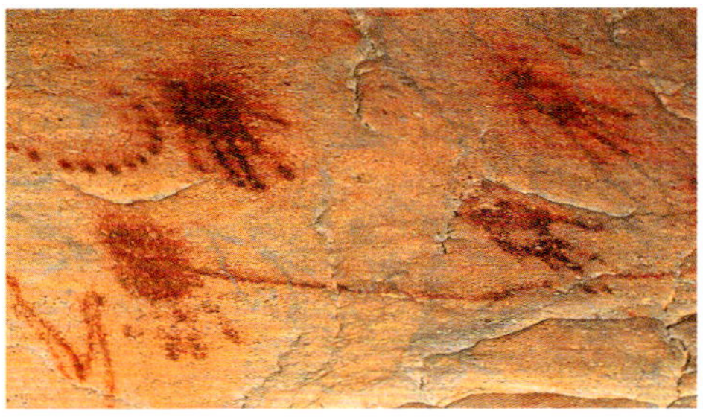

Pigment prints. Hands from the walls of the Chauvet cave, Ardèche, France. c. 30,000 B.C.

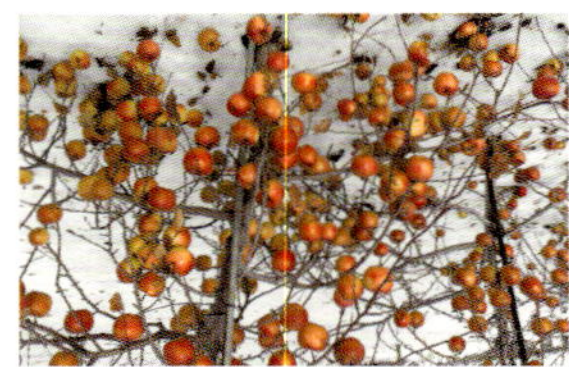

Relief printing

1.1 WOODCUT

This print was made in Europe in the late fifteenth century. The image is in ink — in this case black pigment that was held in oil — and is printed onto a paper support. That little scrap of paper is revolutionary in its technology: paper is cheap, light, flexible, and above all portable. Where the drawings on the stone walls of the caves are firmly stuck in their original location, this paper print could be made and passed on to users somewhere else. As soon as pictures were able to move, they assumed a new power, since in serving multiple users they could permeate society. Like language itself, the paper image spread throughout human culture. Pictures on stone, whether painted on cave walls or carved as monumental inscriptions, existed as single copies that were stuck in one location. Paper, in its capacity to move freely, completely overwhelmed these massive older forms of communication.

The picture has been made with a woodblock. The image is not a unique drawing but the visual record of a carving in a flat wooden plank. Those areas that were not intended to print were carved away, and the remaining surface of the wood, after being inked, transferred the image to a sheet of paper. There were probably multiple copies, and they may, at some earlier time, have been bound into a book. This particular copy now resides in Newport, Rhode Island, among the thousands of bits of paper that I have collected through the years. Fragile and small, this little object has managed, over the course of 500 years, to travel across the Atlantic, survive hundreds of wet and freezing winters and hot and humid summers, and still absolutely clear and legible. Because a few hundred or so might have been made, the odds have favored some remaining to this day. This safety in numbers is the same method used by some biological species that produce many offspring, increasing the likelihood that some will survive.

The design of the picture is fundamentally linear. The use of lines as descriptive tools, found as far back as the cave paintings, is perhaps the most remarkable innovation in the entire history of picture-making. While lines appear in nature in many forms — from blades of grass to winding rivers — in pictorial terms they are completely artificial. In life the leg and foot of the person we see here are soft and rounded; the lines that describe them in the picture are artificial, yet their meaning is absolutely clear. There must be some remarkable circuitry in our brains that we can so effortlessly see the lines and imagine the object.

THE PRINTED PICTURE

Richard Benson

THE MUSEUM OF MODERN ART · NEW YORK

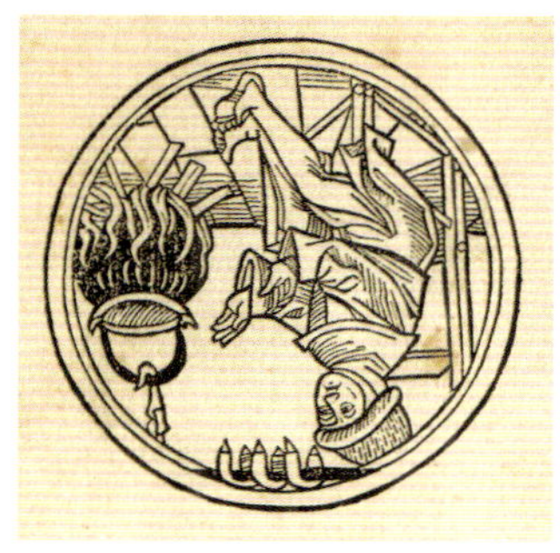

Woodcut. Artist unknown. *February* c. 1484. Print. Johannes Schönsperger, Augsburg. 3⅝ x 3½ in. (9.2 x 8.9 cm) From a German almanac.

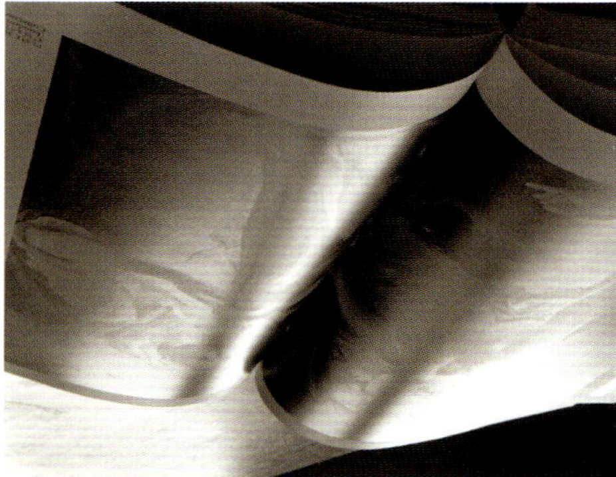

Gelatin silver print. Abelardo Morell. *Pietà by El Greco.* 1993. 18 x 22½ in. (45.7 x 57.2 cm)

Introduction

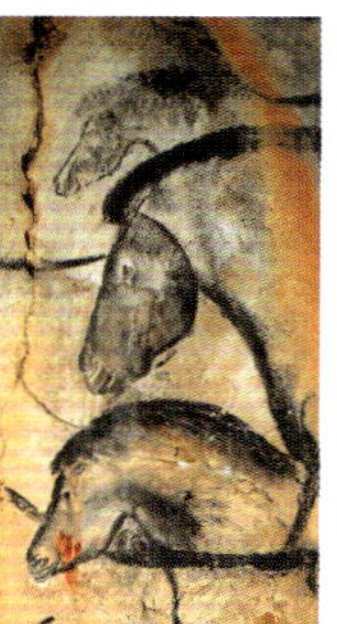

Horses from the walls of the Chauvet cave, Ardèche. France. c. 30,000 B.C.

The oldest pictures we know appear on cave walls in Europe. They were drawn with carbon black, derived from burned wood or bone, and with red ocher, a naturally occurring iron compound. The oldest of these pictures, dating back as far as 30,000 years, display fully evolved representational art. Linear description is handled magnificently, shading is used to render rounded forms, and picture structure is so well handled that these paintings rival anything made since. If we look at representational painting in the West for the thousand years preceding the Renaissance, we can only shake our heads in wonder at how much had been forgotten since the artists worked in the caves.

Mixed in with the hand-drawn pictures in the caves are clear examples of printing. The most common of these printed pictures are of the human hand. Sometimes the image is dark, obviously made by impressing a pigment-covered hand onto the wall, while in other cases the hand appears as a negative, clear but surrounded by colored material. As we go along in this book we shall be defining the basic types of printing, and the hands we find in prehistoric caves represent two of the fundamental forms. The positive images (those made by the hand itself carrying the pigment) are examples of relief printing, the system that underlies printing with moveable type or with wood or linoleum blocks. The negative images (those blank hands surrounded by colored pigment) are examples of stencil printing, in which image-bearing pigment is passed through or around some form that holds the picture information.

We can make an argument that printing has existed as long as people have been making pictures. While this book concentrates on pictures on paper, we should always remember that the practice of printing — of using an object to control the form of a repeated picture — has had a role in human culture from its earliest days. We should note as well that while most of the examples in this book are European or American, printing was in use in East Asia and in the Islamic world centuries before it became common in the West.

FOREWORD

It is impossible to conceive of modern visual culture apart from the very particular contributions of highly creative individual artists, and the preservation, display, and study of their work constitute the principal mission of The Museum of Modern Art. It is equally impossible to ignore the vast and ultimately anonymous transformations wrought by technological change. MoMA has grappled steadily with that very complex domain as well, without ever attempting a comprehensive program.

Richard Benson's book *The Printed Picture* is a major contribution to the latter tradition. Its marvelous illustrations include more than a handful of outstanding works of art, but the great bulk of the pictures are utterly commonplace. For Benson, these humble things are more important than their exquisite, rare, and sometimes very valuable cousins because their social function has been enormously more influential. That influence rests upon the capacity to multiply the image, and the book's essential subject is just how that physical capacity is created: the way pictures are made shapes the way they look and behave, and hence what they can mean.

Richard Benson is uniquely qualified to guide us through this sprawling territory, which today, with the advent of digital technologies, is once again expanding rapidly. A dedicated artist and teacher, he is also an inspired tinkerer, who four decades ago led a revolution in printing that would radically improve the quality of photographs in reproduction. He has himself made nearly all of the many kinds of pictures he discusses here, and that hands-on experience makes itself felt on every page.

The Museum is proud to present this landmark contribution to our understanding of the life of pictures in the modern world. We thank the excellent staff of the Department of Publications, led by Christopher Hudson, and we salute in particular David Frankel, who edited the book, and Marc Sapir, who collaborated with the author in producing it. Finally we are grateful to Robert B. Menschel and his fellow members of the Committee on Photography, who nearly twenty years ago generously established the John Szarkowski Publications Fund, whose support has been indispensable. Never was a name more rightly linked to a project, for John Szarkowski initiated and shared some of Richard Benson's most ambitious and fruitful experiments in offset lithography, notably the four-volume *The Work of Atget* (1981–85).

Glenn D. Lowry, Director
Peter Galassi, Chief Curator of Photography
The Museum of Modern Art

I became one of Richard Benson's many devoted followers in the fall of
1979, during my freshman year at college—not originally as his student
but as a curious, rather stunned nineteen-year-old observer. It started
in the gang darkroom in the pungent basement of the Yale graphic
design building. While I cannot recall why I was there, as I was not yet
enrolled in any studio art classes, I came across Chip instructing other
latent photographers on fascinating if arcane negative processing
methods, obscure printing techniques, and how and why small-format
cameras were just plain "lousy" for serious picture makers. His com-
mand of the complex language of photographic practice was brilliant.
To my eyes, he looked like a messianic Kentucky woodsman with wild
hair, an unkempt beard, and stained fingernails—not the New England
Yankee with a passion for optical precision and a genius for photomechanical printmaking that I soon learned he was.

A year later, I was his student. It seemed inevitable. With little
patience, Chip convinced me that my elegant 35 mm camera was a
mere child's toy that had to be replaced. Immediately. I needed, he
argued, to get an 8-by-10-inch view camera, just like one that Walker
Evans used in the 1930s, or Atget a generation earlier. One day he
brought to class a dusty old wooden Kodak 2D camera and on the spot,
sold it to me on an installment plan. It didn't have a lens or a tripod (he
would quickly help me find both), or film holders. By the spring of 1981,
I was a full-fledged Richard Benson acolyte, lugging an 8-by-10-inch
camera around New Haven. It must have been quite a sight.

Between 1979 and 1983, I had the distinct pleasure of watching Chip
teach alongside Tod Papageorge and numerous other talented faculty,

while also working on his own special projects. These included facsimile reproductions of a stunning book on the history of printed playing cards owned by the Beinecke Library and his early experiments reproducing photographic masterpieces from the Gilman Paper Company collection, a set of some 8,500 photographs, of which the Met is now the custodian.

I believe I may also have been the first and possibly only nonart major undergraduate for whom Chip served as a formal thesis advisor. Chip even introduced me to Alan Trachtenberg, who served as my principal academic advisor in the American Studies department. He also convinced Alan, then dean of undergraduate studies, to sell me his beloved 9½-inch Goerz Dagor lens. Alan, per Benson, would never have time to be more than a weekend photographer, so the lens would otherwise go to waste. I now had a supersharp lens.

My American Studies thesis, *Home Work*, examined the image of the home in American literature and photography, from Nathaniel Hawthorne to William Faulkner, and from Mathew B. Brady to Walker Evans and Wright Morris; it featured a long essay as well as my own photographs. These were carefully tipped into an oversized volume that Chip and I designed and constructed together, with a special pocket for my essay. Chip helped me select the correct paper stock, then cut, fold, and hand-sew it. The "book" remains a treasured reminder of my college years under the influence of one of photography's greatest advocates. In ways I am still discovering, Chip transformed a Missouri kid with an early childhood interest in pictures into a lifelong believer in the medium of photography. It sustains me today.

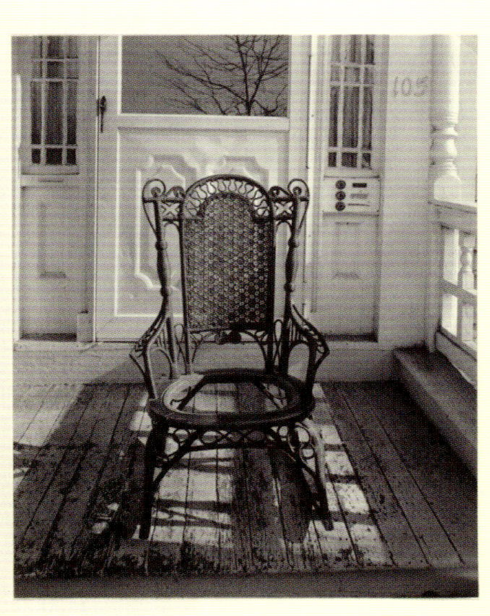

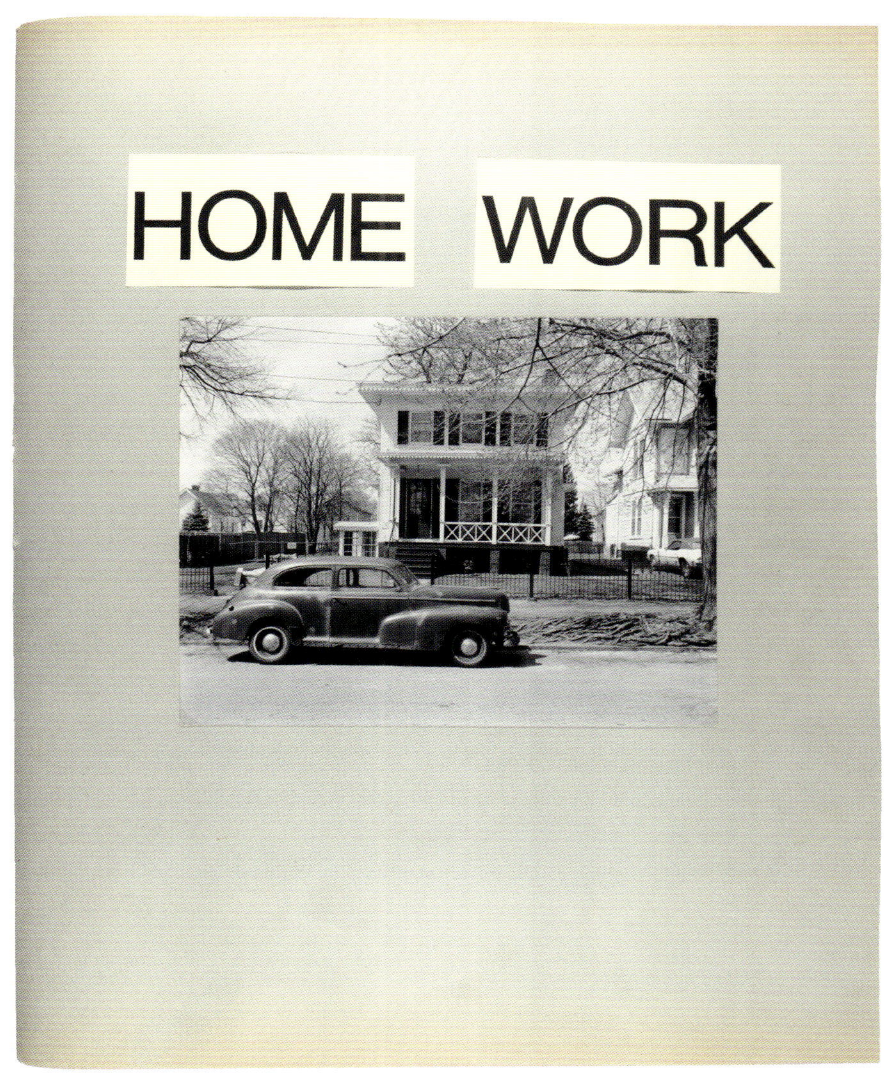
HOME WORK

In 2006, when I first arrived at "The Pool," home to the Yale MFA program, I didn't yet know just how much I didn't know. I saw myself as a committed documentarian, a purist who bristled at anything that felt like photographic contrivance. That hardened stance survived a semester of annihilating critiques, only to crumble after the discovery that (a) photographs can, in fact, be successfully staged, and (b) it is generally a more efficient way to engage in the medium. What once felt transgressive became my operative mode as my images increasingly took on exaggerated and baroque forms. As I was installing my MFA show, it occurred to me, momentarily, that these photographs might have been made by another artist. Though Chip's voice was not the primary one that permeated my psyche during my two years at Yale, his words and, more importantly, his relationship to his own practice clarified the stakes of being an artist and affirmed my own need to be submerged in the flux of the world when making photographs. During one of the last conversations that Chip and I had, in the week leading up to graduation, he told me that an artist needs to love their own pictures, even when they are terrible. Though I did not think much of that offhand advice at the time, it is the epitaph that has staved off a string of crises that have a way of getting the best of us. Estrangement, or disassociation from what one makes, is not an act of impersonation or inauthenticity but a necessary evolution. Giving value to one's worst experiments—in other words, "loving the terrible pictures"—is trusting that the work might sometimes know more than you do.

Range Rover, 2011
Pigment print
33 × 48 in. (83.8 × 121.9 cm)

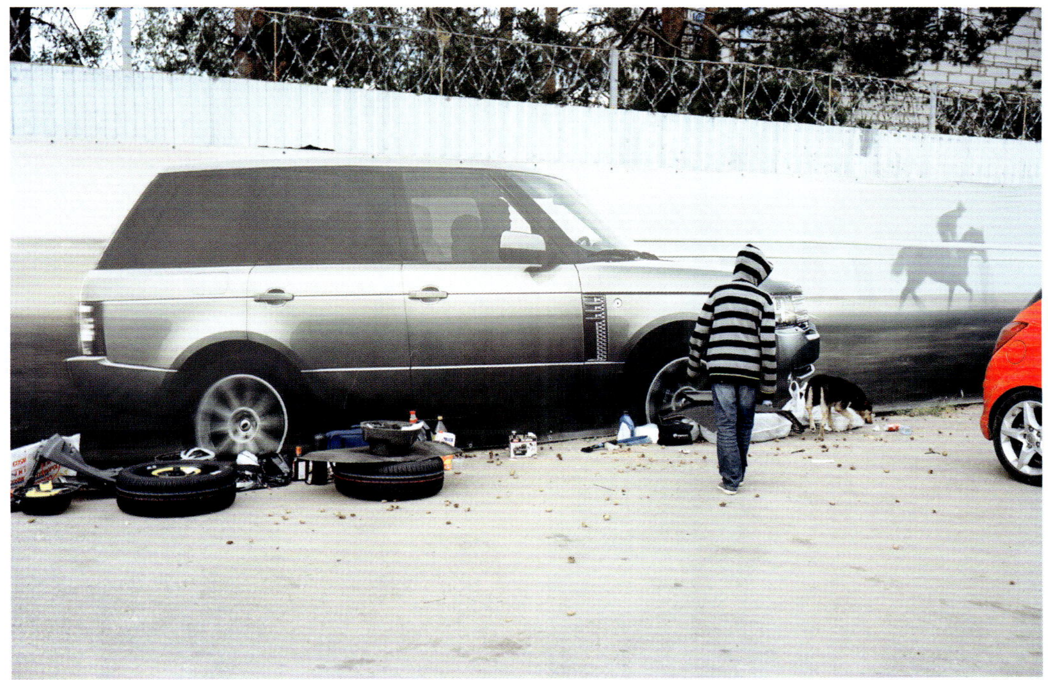

In 1992, I was approached to print the camera art for Madonna's book *Sex*. I turned it down several times because of the frightening penalties in the nondisclosure agreement. When it was finally revealed to me that Richard Benson would be making the separations, I could not resist. There is always translation in reproduction; Benson doing the separations gave me the unique opportunity to have a dialogue with the master print separator through the prints I produced. We never actually spoke. I challenged him with eccentric print tonalities so he would have the widest range of possibilities to interpret. The final book affirmed my decisions. This experience gave me the confidence that I could always maximize the potential of reproductions on press.

In preparing my 2005 book *Nudes*, I received unacceptable proofs from an Italian press's scans. Jeff Hirsch of Foto Care insisted I speak to Richard Benson. I was shy of Benson but I called. We reminisced about *Sex*; he was incredibly generous and lovely. I told him I had been producing print guides from scans made by Tom Hurley of Laumont Photographics and sending the prints to Italy to match, without success. Benson simply replied: "You made your scans, you like the prints you've made from your files, why would you not simply send your final files to the press to print the book?" Go figure. It was just that simple.

In this exchange, we also talked about his book and exhibition *The Printed Picture*, which opened that year at Yale's Jonathan Edwards College (and was further developed for a 2008 MoMA exhibition). He affirmed for me pigmented ink printing as the most controllable and least fugitive form of reproduction. This marked the beginning of my making pigmented ink prints for exhibition, and moving away from exclusively analog processes.

Benson's great legacy was his great ability to teach.

Madonna, *Sex* (New York: Warner Books, Maverick, and Callaway, 1992)

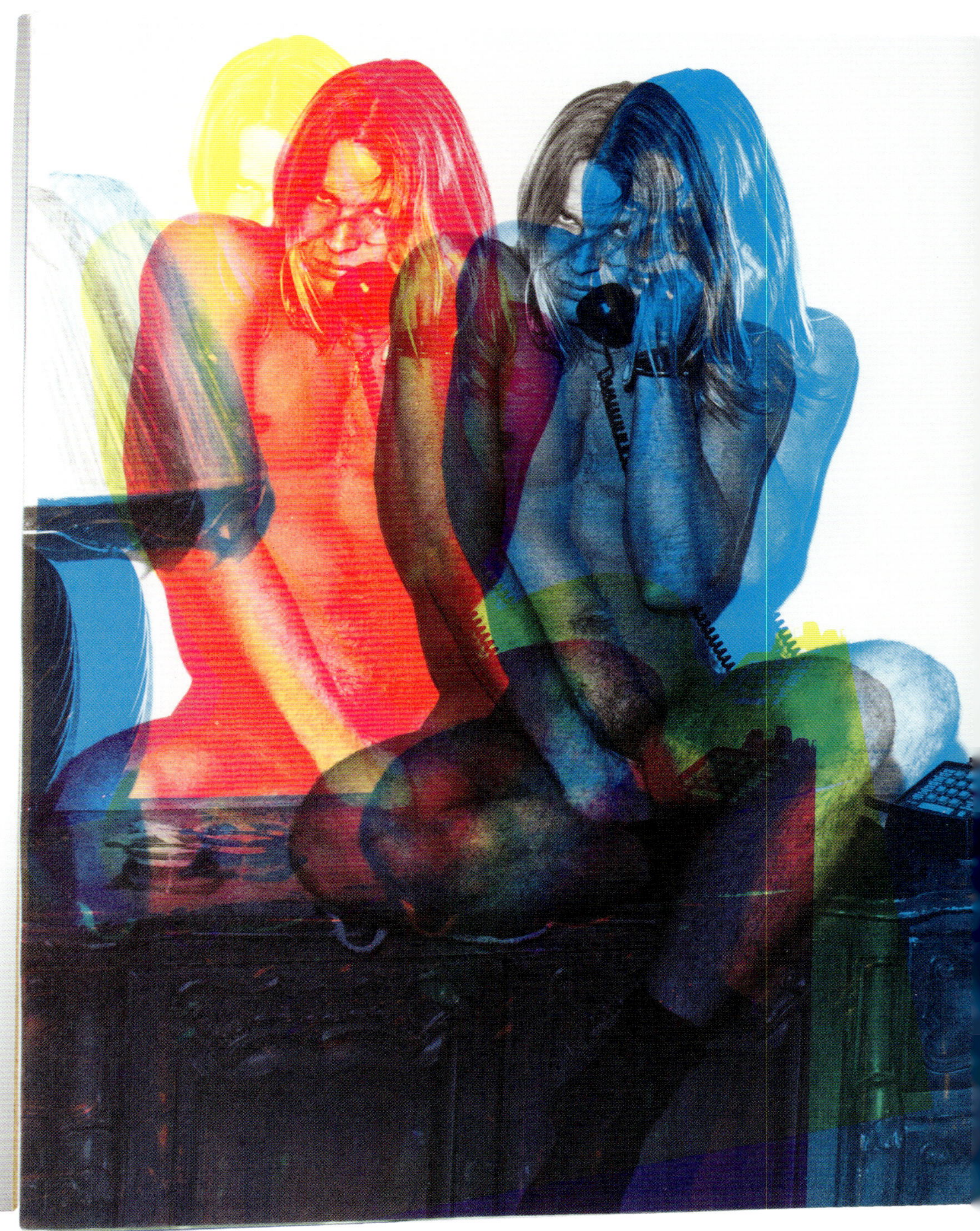

Madonna, *Sex* (New York: Warner Books, Maverick, and Callaway, 1992)

Pillow Talk? Some people do it really well. Some people do it so badly that you break up laughing and you just can't go through with it. I had a boyfriend who laughed every time he came. Some people know how to talk and some people don't. With some people it's an affectation and they think that's what you want, that you need that. Other people know how to do it and it just clicks. It's like phone sex. Some people know how to do it and some don't. Phone sex can be excellent. It's an absolute necessity if you're separated from somebody you love. Thank God for Ma Bell. Screaming and loud noise making really annoys me. I hate it when guys come and don't make any noise and you can't tell if they came or not. But one time I was fucking this guy and every time he came he was so loud I finally had to smack him. I was sure the whole neighborhood could hear us.

The first time I think I caught Chip's attention was in his famous printing class, which I took while pursuing my master's at Yale in 2006. Chip was teaching about processes, and I was making a joke to another classmate. She burst out laughing, and Chip said, "Shut the fuck up, David!" I'll never forget it, nor will I forget him or his class. I eventually shut up and listened to Chip.

I couldn't have gotten through those foggy, somewhat tortured and traumatic two years without Chip's support and guidance. I had arrived just as digital technology had taken over; most students were printing, and some were shooting digitally. I took it upon myself to do the opposite and spent my days and nights in the color darkroom, mostly because I wanted to find something new in the medium before the color-processing machines became relics. I shot my work on large-format color film and began manipulating it in the darkroom, using unorthodox techniques. Chip saw the works I was making and seemed intrigued. I think rebellion in a controlled setting, much like Chip's own printing techniques, was something he appreciated and took seriously. When I'd present in critiques, Chip helped me develop the language for my work by describing what I was doing as an alternative process. He understood my desire to print in a tactile way and why I was drawn to the methodical and physical approach of using a large-format camera. When I began printing in vibrant monochromes, he guided me toward historical photographs and printing techniques that I could align myself with. This was a revelation for me, and I immediately took his teachings to heart. I probably wouldn't have pursued the work that I've been immersed in for the last fifteen years if it wasn't for Chip. He lit a fire under me to push boundaries.

I'm grateful to have had him as a guide on this journey, as someone who understood the essence of my work and process from its origins to this day. Every time I make a print or a book, I think about Chip and his love for photography, printing, and most importantly, breaking rules to find new meaning.

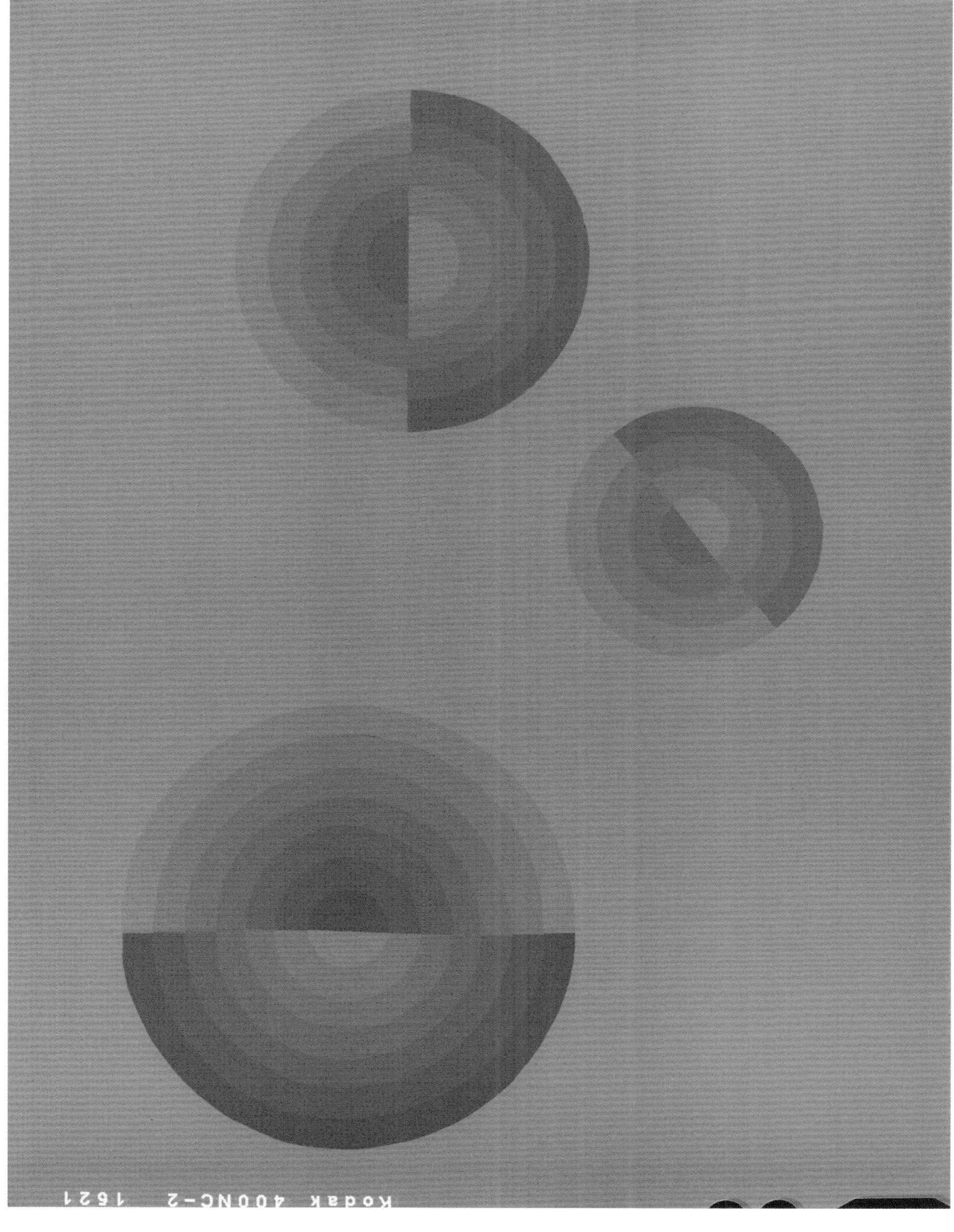

In my last year at Yale, we were lucky enough to have an artist visit with Robert Frank. We were all starstruck and afraid to ask any questions. Richard was always worried about how students would make a living after graduation and would often ask guest artists for advice on our behalf. Toward the end of the lecture, Richard asked Robert what he would do if he were a younger person who had just graduated, where would he go to find work and culture and to make art? Robert replied, without hesitation, "I would go to Los Angeles." So, three months later, I moved to LA. *Rivers of Los Angeles* was my first serious work after leaving New Haven. This project had a rocky start. I discovered that I really disliked Los Angeles and had a difficult time making work, mostly because I was afraid to make bad work. I had just graduated from Yale and was now supposed to be a talented artist. I felt lost no longer being part of a crit group, but as I plowed forward, Richard Benson's gravelly voice came to mind, giving me a much needed kick in the butt while I wandered the catacombs and wastelands of LA. In school Richard had said so many things that initially seemed at odds with what I thought I knew about photography. But now, as I forced myself to make bad photographs while I worked through my fear of failure, he suddenly started to make sense. Observations like: The world is a much more interesting subject than any artist's idea. A photograph has to be simple before it can be complex. Photographs explain a lot and at the same time are confounding, and this is what is great about photography.

When teaching, Richard would often humorously state what was wrong with the world. What's wrong with the world is coated paper. Or: What's wrong with the world is graphic designers. These were great introductory, inflammatory statements for a discussion topic that would be wonky at first, and then, after Richard finished his explana-tion, you would be in complete agreement and would never forget what you learned. Channeling Richard's voice helped me learn to get over myself and find joy in making work. What's wrong with the world is the way people in Los Angeles . . .

Richard's voice is still in my head, and his example continually reminds me of what is really important, whether it is teaching, making art, or striving to be a good person. What is wrong with the world is that it desperately needs more Richard Bensons.

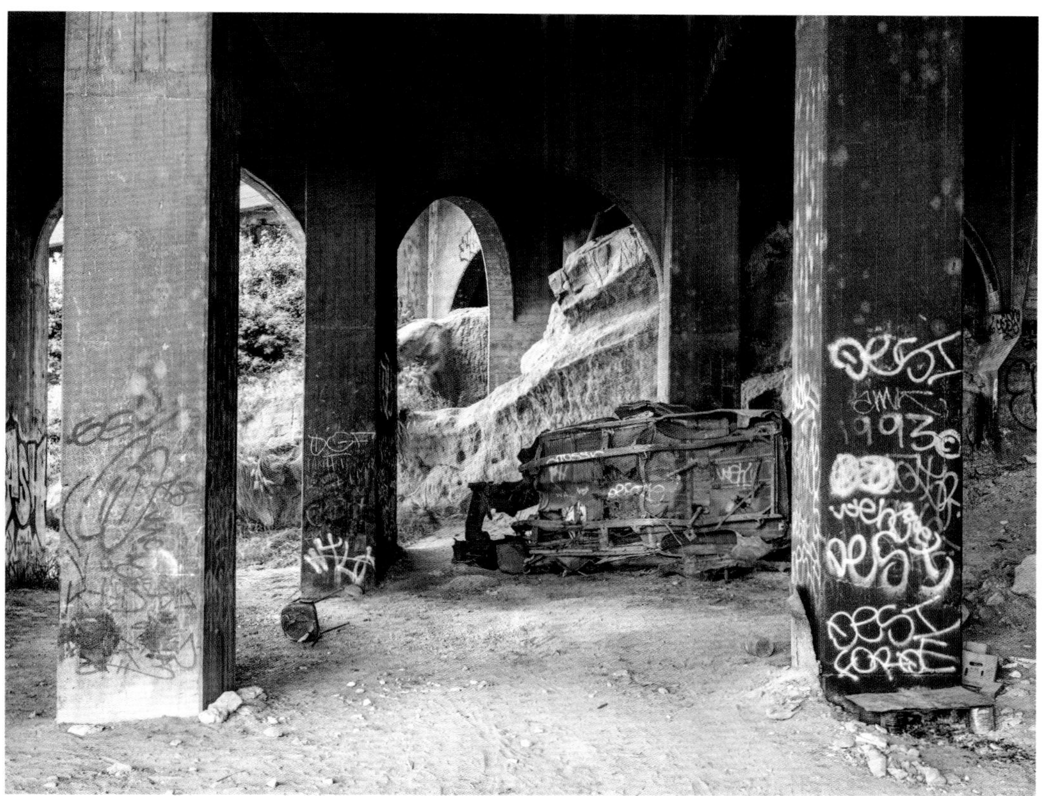

Under the 5 Freeway Adjacent to the LA River, 1994
Gelatin-silver print
11 × 14 in. (27.9 × 35.6 cm)

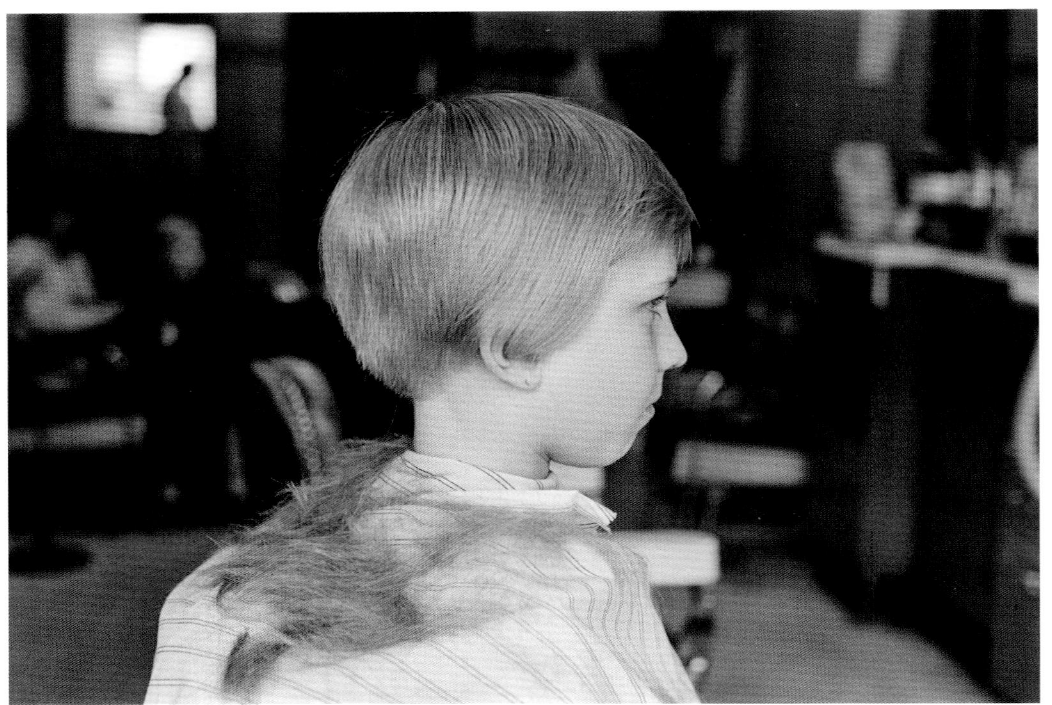

Ansonia, Connecticut (Haircut), 1985
Gelatin-silver print
20 × 24 in. (50.8 × 61 cm)

This took place in 1985 during a darkroom class held in the basement of the old Art and Architecture Building: not prompted by anything I can remember, Richard turned to me and said, "This is something you'll need to know," and he wrote something down on a slip of paper that he handed to me. The note read: "There is no relationship between quality and financial success." I've found that line to be comforting from time to time.

During my two years at Yale, Chip and I discussed many things: digital printers and how to get our own for the photo department, Robert Frank's groundbreaking book *The Americans*, tattoos, Abraham Lincoln, and much more. He spoke about the necessity for our practice—the thing we spend so much time working and thinking on—to be a part of our whole life. Not something we went and did. It had to be in our home, in our work, and most important, be a part of our whole selves, which includes your family. When my Lincoln was born and I became a mother, this idea sunk in: I could be an artist and a mother at the same time; they are inseparable.

We opened TILT (formerly the Philadelphia Photographic Arts Center) a year before Lincoln was born, then came my daughter, Madie. They have both slept next to the printers, cried through count-less openings, followed along artists who came to Philadelphia to shoot, flipped through photobooks, made their own pictures, sat for me to take theirs, and to this day are surrounded by photographs. I asked Lincoln the other day, when will he come work with me? He declined, but he walks into TILT like it's his second home and always asks me what I am working on.

I think of Frank's 1956 picture of his wife and two children in their car in Del Rio, Texas, and Chip's stories of traveling to photograph with his beloved family in an RV. I know my work has always come from what I know best, and that my practice has shifted and changed and will continue to do so, but my passion and love for this medium will always sit firmly in my home with my family.

New London, Connecticut, 2007
Archival inkjet print
23 × 28 in. (58.4 × 71.1 cm)

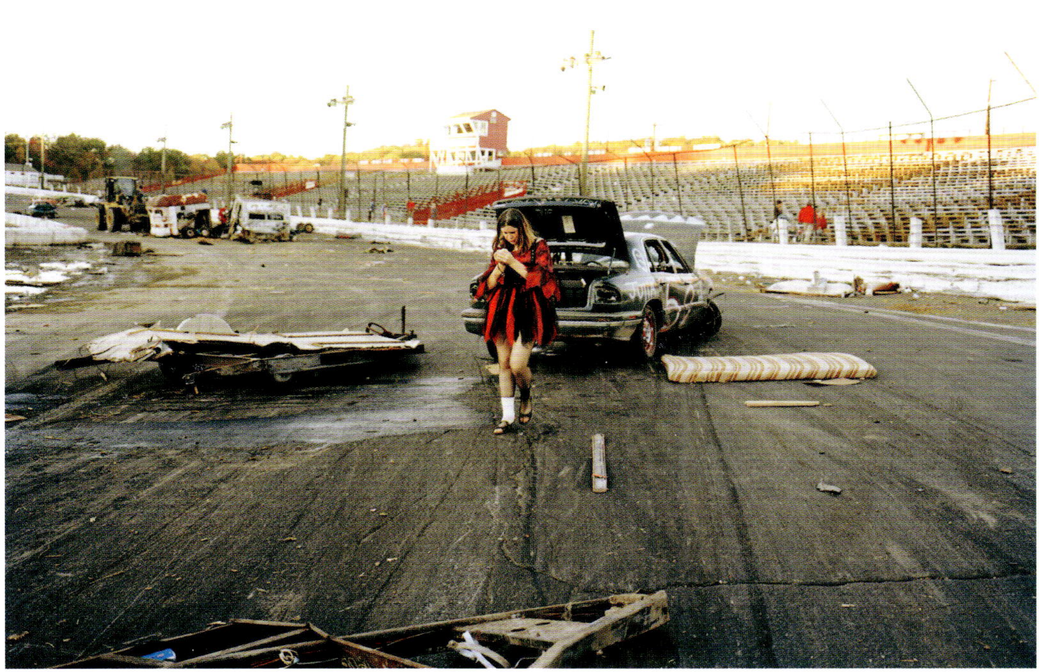

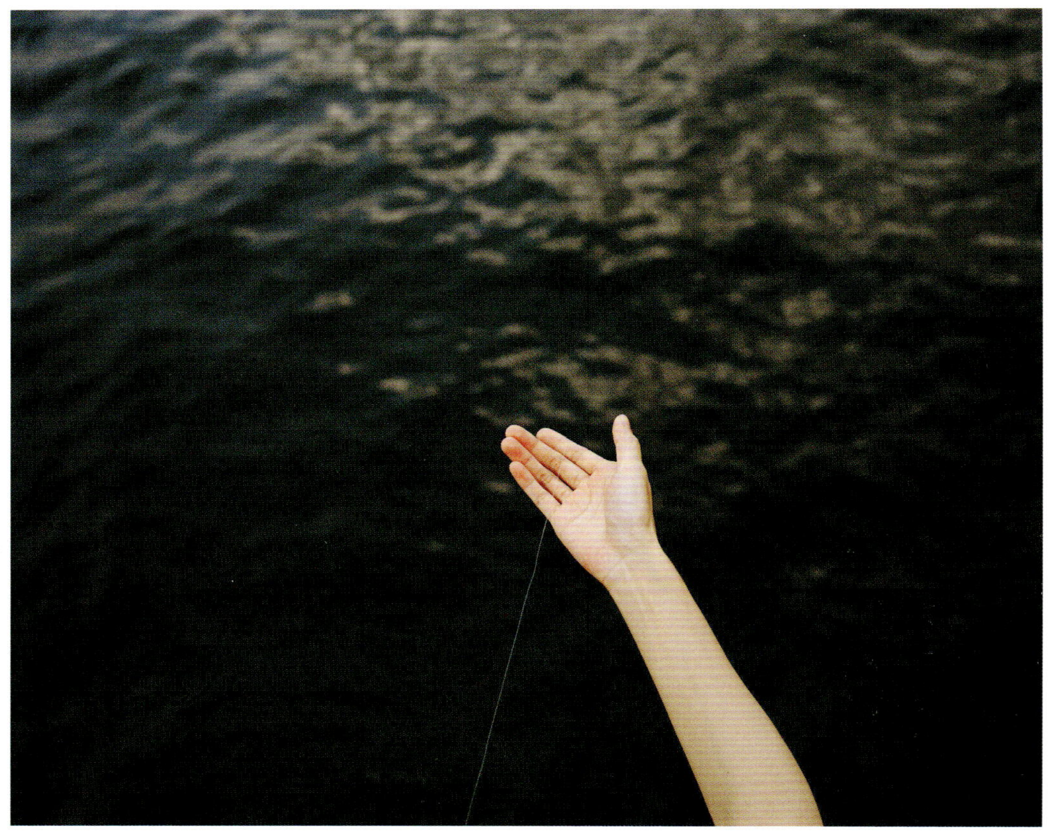

A.

When I went on press for my own book, I channeled Chip as best
I could, even down to bringing a press sheet into the bathroom.
Chip used to say, "If it looks good in the crappy bathroom light, it
means it's good!"

B.

Hardship . . .
Chip would drive down from Rhode Island in the early morning, and
we would start as early as 9:00 a.m. and go until the end of the day. He
would bring prints, physical objects—a focus on the materiality of work.
He would take us out to lunch at Zaroka, the restaurant behind the
school. At the end of our final semester, knowing we had all run out of
money, he took us out one last time to feed us. His tone shifted to
something more serious, and he said to us: "It's not about doing what
you want when you feel like it, being an artist for the long haul means
getting up and going to work even if you feel like crap and if it is raining." For me, the lessons would be the pictures I have made after
school, when I was feeling like shit—physically in pain, or had the worst
cramps, or when it was raining. But if you were to look at the pictures,
one would have no idea. None of this is an attempt to valorize the
endeavor of art-making. Rather, it's the opposite. The measure of an
artist is in those other immeasurable moments, no heroics or myth-
making here—just getting to work even when you don't feel like it.

To that lesson of working through hardship, I would also add that
the most I thought about materiality was during some of the most
challenging moments of my life: when I was protesting in Hong Kong in
the summer of 2019, before our baby was born. The transformation of
everyday materials—steel barricades, bricks repurposed to stop traffic,
cardboard, plastic bottles, Saran Wrap, umbrellas transformed into
shields and armor, traffic cones to trap tear gas—is something I still
think about. That, and the effort it took to work together as strangers,
through hand signals and telegrams, sharing food, looking out for each
other. That summer, when I wasn't protesting or crying literally every
day, I would leave the center of the city and head to an outlying island,
to the water. I would sometimes do this alone and sometimes with
friends. Watching people fish with nothing but a line, just hands tossing

into the water, somehow matched what I felt: a sense of loss and searching. Of course, that was before the political situation got from bad to worse, to the quiet horror that is today as I write in 2021. And it was before the baby was born. These two events are forever linked: a world that was being torn apart while a new being was coming into it.

Back to my second year of graduate school, ten years before these water pictures: Chip had lent me his camera, a full-frame digital SLR, so that I could experiment with video. (They were still hard to get ahold of then.) What would it look like if I made some work off-tripod, with a smaller camera, he had asked. I had been stuck on 4-by-5 film and video work that was on a tripod, and the work felt pre-prescribed, preconceived, and without surprise. That spring, Chip had lent another student his UV printer so that she could make platinum prints; I lent her my hot-water heater (a dorm-room gadget best for tea and late-night ramen). Chip had taught us that you should steam the paper beforehand so that it doesn't crack. He was supportive in that way, lending us his own tools, driving them down from Newport, getting us to push and experiment and help each other. Chip wasn't a video artist, but he was the kind of educator who would truly see you, and the you that you would grow into. (This is what I've learned as a teacher.) All this was conveyed without judgment, without him ever wanting to mold you into his form, or any form. The video I ended up making—off-tripod—is still something I'm proud of. *As you sweep the room imagine that the broom is someone that you love, or Sport* was made at the British Art Gallery, and it is inspired by my own days of working as a guard at the Metropolitan Museum. It is about work and labor but also play, imagination, and who gets to end up on those walls, anyway?

Now, going back, or forward, to 2019, the images of hands casting into the water, the non-protest pictures that were about the protests—those were also about movement and freedom . . .

A ties in to B, and to this past year somehow—thinking about context—while being in the thick of crap! What makes you is how you are or what you do or how you respond given the circumstances you are in.

Untitled, Hong Kong, 2019
Archival inkjet print

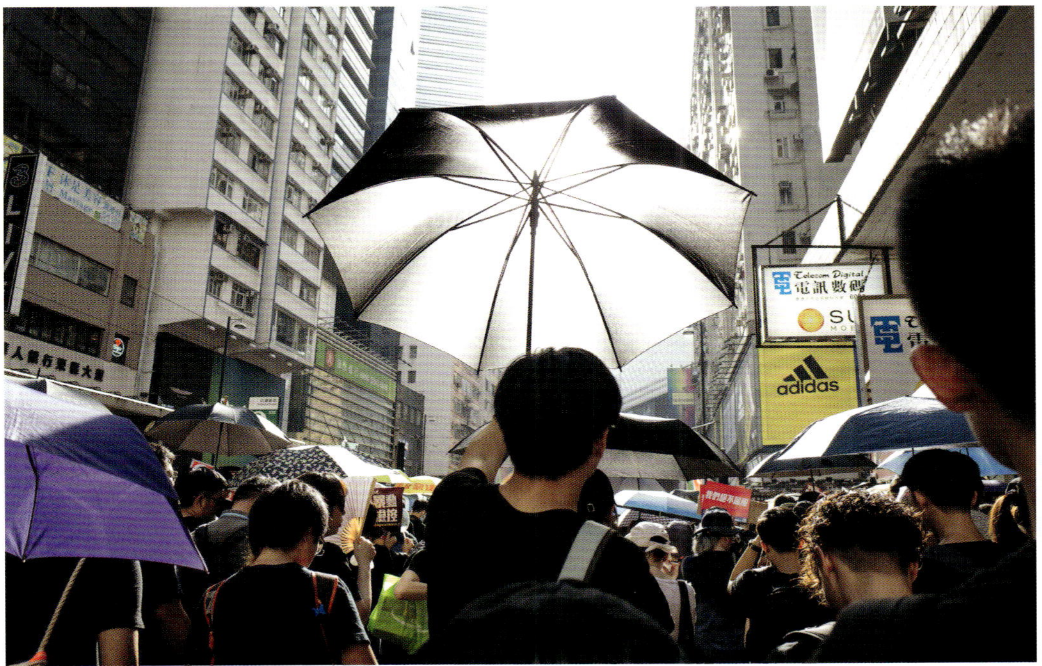

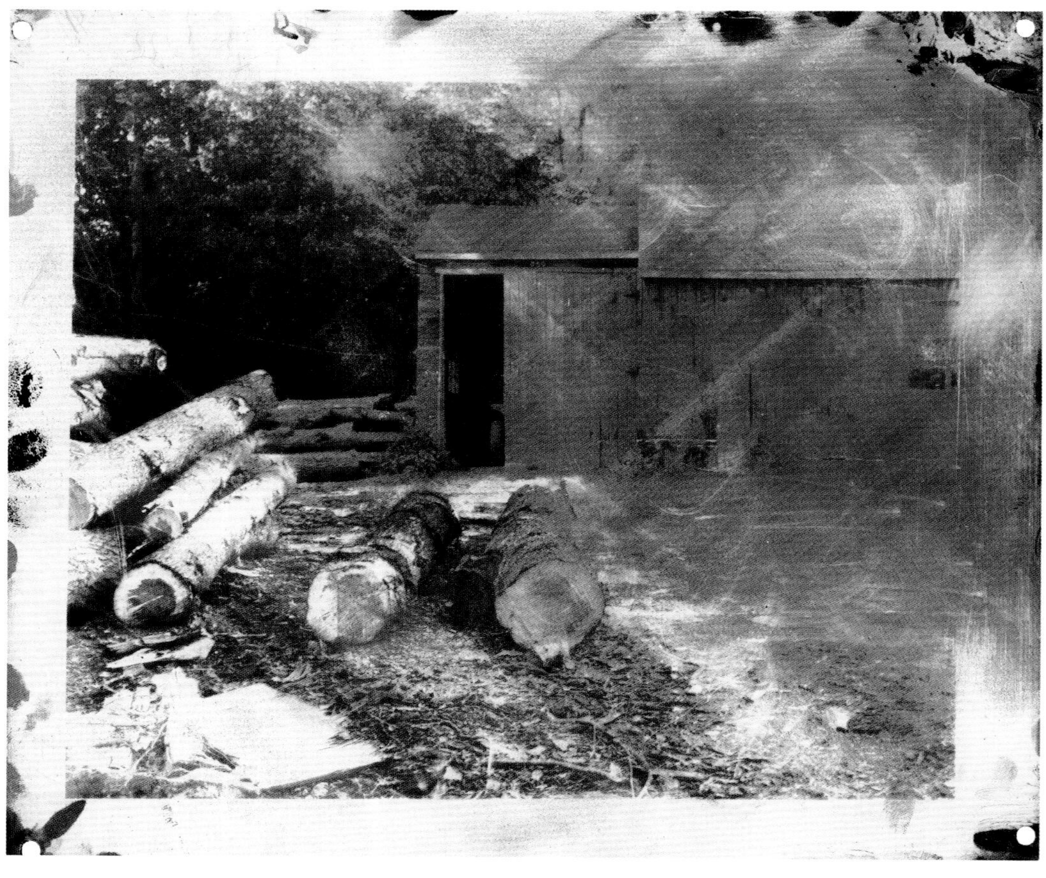

In 1990, I read Calvin Tomkins's *New Yorker* profile on Richard Benson. I was familiar with the portfolios Benson printed for Paul Strand and the books he created for fine-art publishers, but I was not aware of the outlaw process he invented for printing photographs in acrylic paint. A few years after reading the piece, I saw a gallery show of these arresting works and I naively set out to make some myself.

I followed Tomkins's description in the *New Yorker* as best as I could, but finally I had to telephone Benson, who was generous enough to share the component formulae and materials list with me. At the same time, he tried to dissuade me from making these photographs, claiming that the process was too daunting for those lacking photo-mechanical experience. I would soon discover he was right.

Following Benson's instructions, I coated a sheet of thin aluminum with gelatin and potassium dichromate. I then exposed this emulsion through a piece of halftone film using ultraviolet light. The exposure hardened areas of the plate not protected by the halftone dots, leaving the areas under the halftones soft, which I washed away using a tray of tepid water. Then I coated the plate with a special mix of diluted acrylic paint, dried it, and under a stream of warm water, gently abraded the entire plate. This crucial last step removed the acrylic paint sitting on the emulsion "resist," leaving paint adhering to the areas under the halftone dots. A faint positive resulted, and after many cycles of re-exposing and recoating, a tonally rich photograph appeared. Complicating things enormously, every step of the process required unerring control. I struggled for months before I managed a few badly made prints.

In the late 1990s, I visited Benson in his backyard, where we looked at his acrylic photographs. The saturated colors glistened in the sunlight, and I was able to make out the layers of paint by slightly angling the plate. Benson told me that some of the pictures received more than forty coats of acrylic (I had only managed six coats in my failed pictures). After carefully studying Benson's pictures, I turned them over to inspect the skinny fingers of cyan, magenta, yellow, green, black, and white paint running in all directions across bare aluminum. How perversely exciting it must have been to make color photographs in a darkroom sink filled with trays of pigment.

Despite my failures, I never abandoned my goal to make acrylic photographs, and after a twenty-year interval, I tried the process again, but with significant modifications. Since the labs that produced halftone film had disappeared, and I never quite mastered Benson's formula for mixing the acrylic paint, I used conventional film and aniline dyes. I ended up with 240 dichromated gelatin and dye prints in a kaleidoscope of colors (*Julia Mamaea*, 2018–19).

After *Julia Mamaea*, I decided to stop using dichromate emulsions, which are carcinogenic. I Googled nontoxic printmaking and discovered a simple process that uses a laser printer to produce lithographic plates. With this technology, I created a body of work (*Cento*, 2019–21), and this experience offered me an insight into how Benson might have concocted his photographs in acrylic paint. The offset lithography plates Benson worked with are beautiful, precision-made objects. Part of the plate attracts ink; part repels it. Part of the plate is bare metal; part is emulsion. Looking at an offset lithography plate, Benson might have intuited that the emulsion could be made to resist ink rather than attract it. With this insight, he'd have glimpsed the exquisite elegance of what he would eventually create, a photograph in acrylic paint, something absolutely unprecedented. The difficult work would be to determine the steps necessary to remove the resist and retain the acrylic, all the while aligning the dozens of layers in perfect register. After decades solving gritty problems in offset printing, this would be a minor challenge for Benson, who seemed to live by George Santayana's maxim, "The difficult we do immediately; the impossible takes a little longer."

Julia Mamaea, 2018
Dichromated gelatin and aniline dye on polypropylene
14 × 11 in. (35.6 × 27.9 cm) each

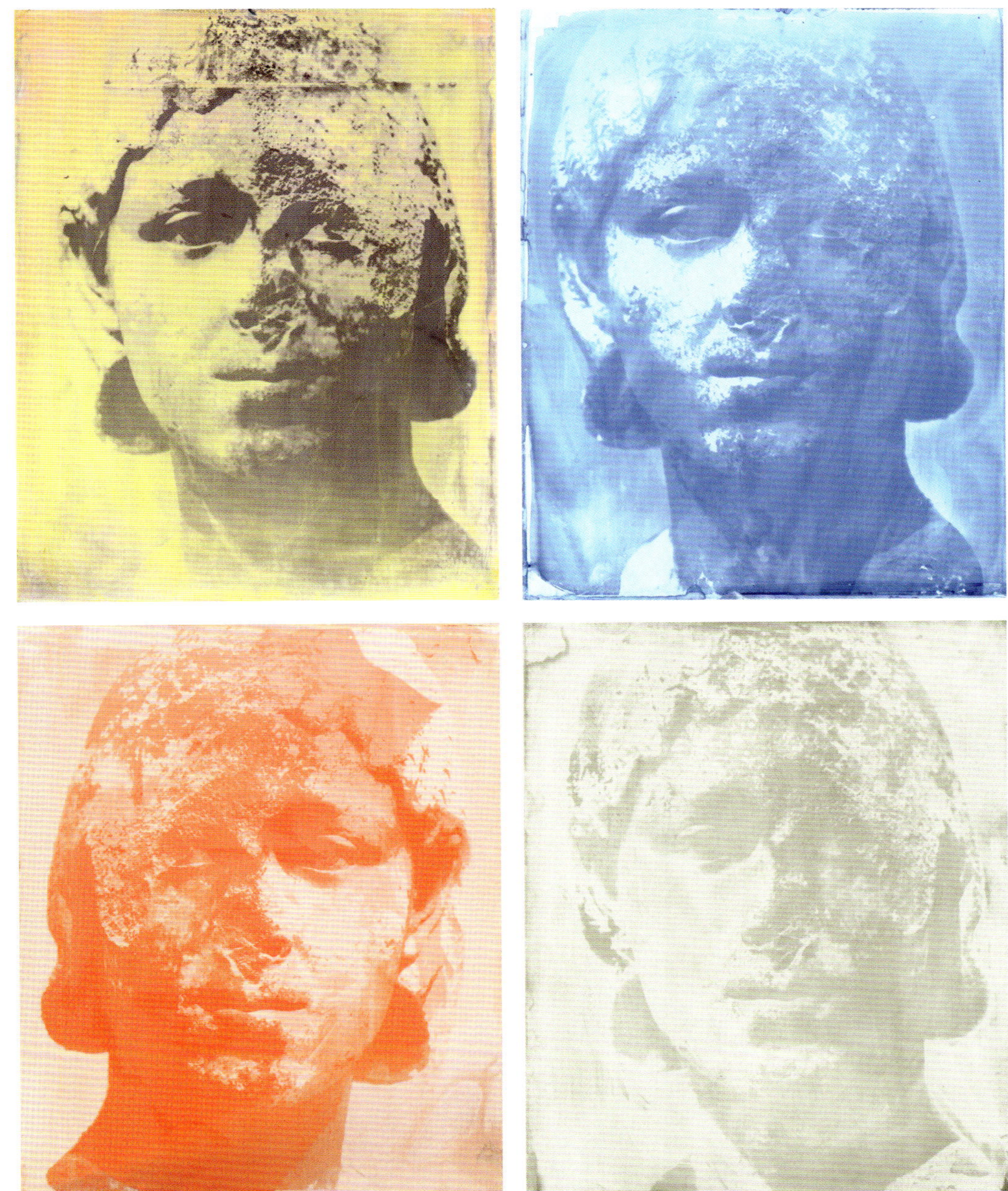

When I came to Yale, I decided to change everything. I bought a used view camera from eBay to coin my new artistic persona. I hadn't known Chip, then the dean, for long before I realized my camera was broken. After being prodded by my other professors and second-year students to "ask Chip," I reluctantly showed him my terrible camera. He took one glance at it and told me to meet him at six in the morning at his house so he could fix it.

He answered the door in the dark of morning and hollered back to his wife, Barbara, "He actually showed up." That made me both proud that I got out of bed so early and embarrassed that he may have been expecting to have a leisurely morning. I was not yet aware of his aversion to leisure; in fact, he had been up for two hours and had probably already built a clock and a steam engine. He fixed me a cup of coffee, and I followed him down a narrow, awkward staircase into the basement.

There were machines and bits of machines everywhere, but the main focus of the room was an industrial milling machine. It was a hulking mass of oiled metal, with its spindles, dials, and levers arranged like planets orbiting a giant engine, encased in a grayish-blue body of forged steel. The basement was like a catacomb, and I looked around to find the opening through which the team of riggers moved this goliath in place. All I could figure was that they must have built the house around the machine. I found myself hoping my camera was broken enough to require Chip to fire up this thing and make something. But it wasn't. What it needed was tiny.

Chip pulled the camera apart with tools that were loosely organized on the workbench, all within his reach. A cog on a shaft was slipping. The shaft was bent, so he put it on an axle press (that he had made) and started striking it with a hammer.

"How much did you pay for this camera?" he asked.

I told him.

"You got ripped off. But it will work."

He then took a gear puller (that he had made) to pull the cog, which was the size of a lentil, from the shaft. With the tiniest drill bit I'd ever seen, he made a hole between the teeth of the cog and another in the round shaft. He found a 1/64-inch pin in one of his tool sets, and with three swift and sure strikes from a slim hammer, the pin was set. He filed off the ends of the pin, his hands flying.

We chatted the whole time, and his hands never hesitated to make the next move. It was like watching a musician play a memorized score. His fingers had their own brains. His mind was in a state of delight—not with me but with improvising on a machine, making things fit and, as he said, "correcting bad design."

I was making work about bridges and infrastructure in New Jersey when I got the news that Richard had passed. Scores of 3-inch-diameter steel rivets fitted by striking hammers have held up the Lower Trenton Bridge since 1917. I can't speculate if the rivets were pounded into the drilled holes in a fit of human delight, like the kind that Chip took in building and fixing, but I imagined him feeling a similar sense of awe knowing how ingeniously the built world fits together.

What I gained in two years under Richard Benson's tutelage were feelings I had forgotten about in my art practice: wonder, awe, excitement, amazement. I think it is natural for an art photographer to analyze and critique cultural systems, to be critically introspective, to look at the world with a dose of cynicism. Chip appreciated our energetic endeavors in trying to point out and correct our society's bad design, but what stands out to me is how much delight he took in human ingenuity. His humility and generosity, as evidenced by a man of his position repairing a student's cheap eBay camera, was born from his sense of awe of the world. He didn't teach us that; he modeled it.

Tomorrow Drivers, 2016
Selenium-toned gelatin-silver contact print
(composite of twelve negatives)
40 × 41 in. (101.6 × 104.1 cm)

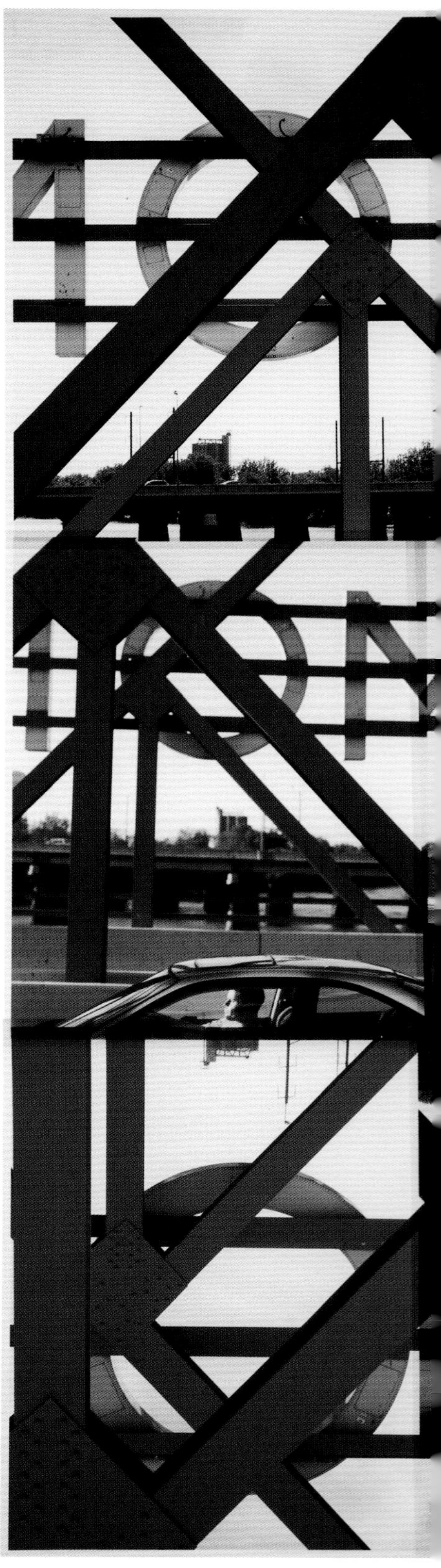

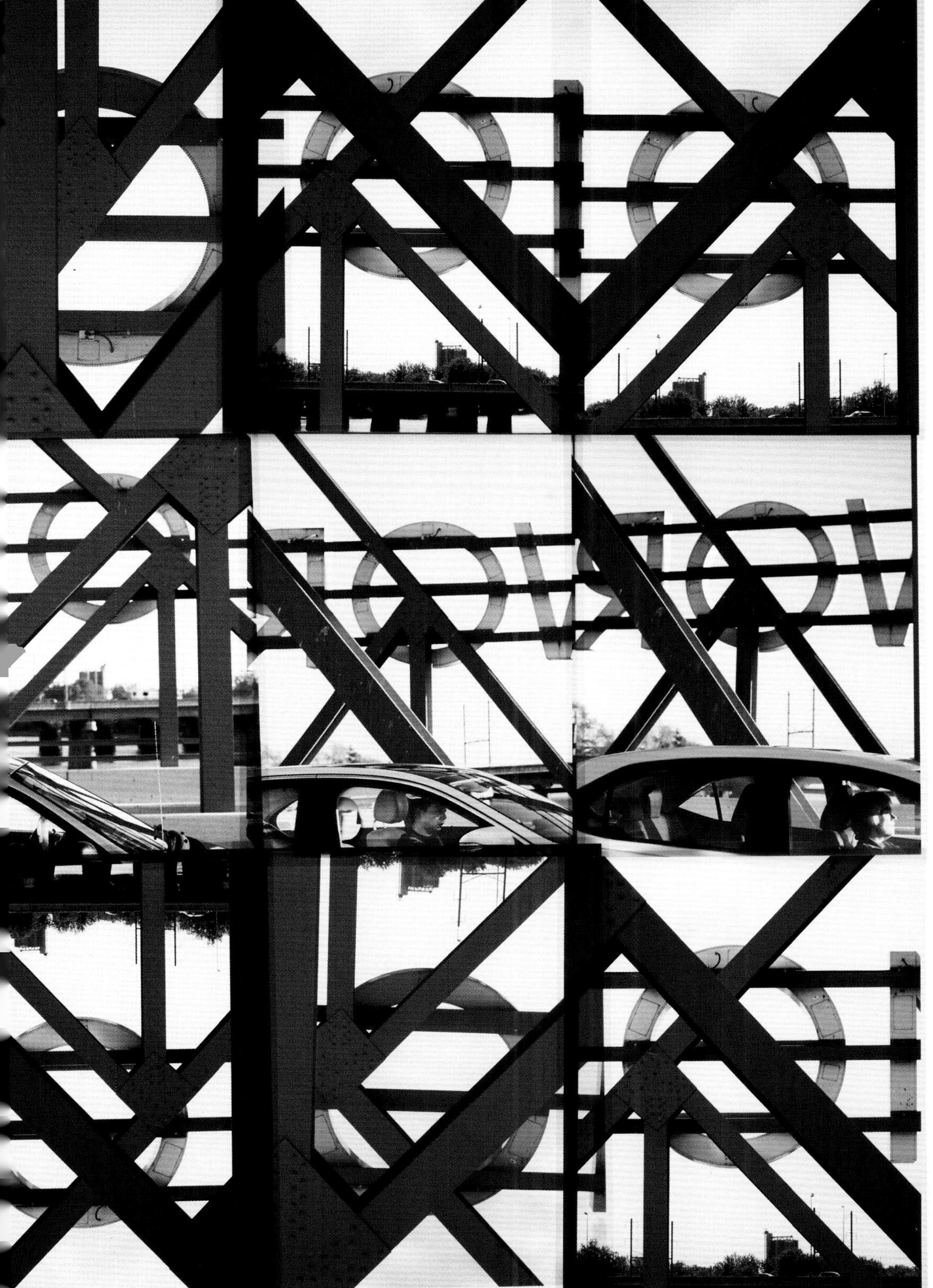

Conversations and Writings

In conversation

I had the privilege of meeting Richard Benson sometime in the 1970s, either at the Museum of Modern Art or at LIGHT Gallery, where I worked. Over the years, we got to know each other better through our mutual friend John Szarkowski, and, after John died, I believe we became quite close through a deepening friendship and through the act of representing Richard's work in our gallery. (I must admit that the idea of representing Richard's work is a bit of a laughing matter, for how could one ever seek to define the scope of it?)

Through numerous visits to the Benson home in Newport, I met Barbara and grew close to her too. How could one spend time with Barbara and not become close? We'd often sit and visit when Richard was otherwise occupied. Her generosity with her time, words, and enlightening thoughts always lifted me. She was, with Richard, at the head of Team Benson. A teacher of piano and music, Barbara ran the Benson "business" and that included the books, the household, judgment of character, and joint decision-making.   Peter MacGill

---

Peter MacGill   The idea here is to try to talk about—and maybe this is an incorrect label—a community that circled through or cycled in and out of your house of friends, of students, and generally inquisitive people. What's clear is that it wasn't just Richard, it was the two of you. It was the sense of home you had with your children, the sense of family, and the sense that people could show up feeling one way and leave feeling another. We just talked about the domino falling—the idea that people would show up and a domino would fall, creating a chain reaction to self-realization, the development of an idea, or the solution to a problem. I don't think anybody ever walked into your house without hoping the domino would fall.

Benson   I was talking to a friend after Chip died, after his memorial at Yale. And she asked, "How did the memorial go?" I said fine. "Who was there?" I said, "An awful lot of Chip's students." She asked, "How many of them did you know?" And I said, "I knew all of them." She said, "What?" I said, "I knew all of them. They came to our house—my kids knew all of them."

She said, "You went to college, right?" And I said yes. "How many of your professors' families did you know?" I said, "Well, none, actually." And she said, "Did you know their husbands or wives?" (In my case, wives, because all of my professors were men.) I said no. "Did you know their children?" No. "Did you ever go to their house?" No. "And you know all of Chip's students?" And I said, "Well, yes." [*laughs*]

That says a lot, you know? It's just true.

I never thought of it as peculiar. Chip had never taught before he started teaching at Yale, except at Marlborough College, but that was a one-on-one or one-on-two situation. He wasn't a formal teacher. He hadn't been trained in teaching. He believed his job was to impart his knowledge to his students, and he felt he could do that best in his studio, so the kids came up to our house from Yale.

And while they were there, they found out you could be an artist and have a regular, ordinary, ho-hum family. But he didn't invite them there to teach them that lesson. He wanted them to see his shop and his work in the shop.

MacGill   The first visit I made to your home was a mindboggling experience. It was a parade of people stopping by. This idea of wanting to share your home, meals, ideas, or answers—was that something you talked about, or did it just happen?

Benson   Just happened. It was a sharing community. There was nothing proprietary about anything.

MacGill   Why did Richard feel that he didn't need to be proprietary about things?

Benson   He didn't give two shits about money. It was not a part of his DNA. He did what he did because he liked doing it, not because it put food on the table. That was not a concern of his. That's where I came in [*laughs*].

MacGill   Not unlike Eleanor Callahan. Harry could work making pictures. Eleanor worked in an office.

Benson   Made sure the lights were on the next day.

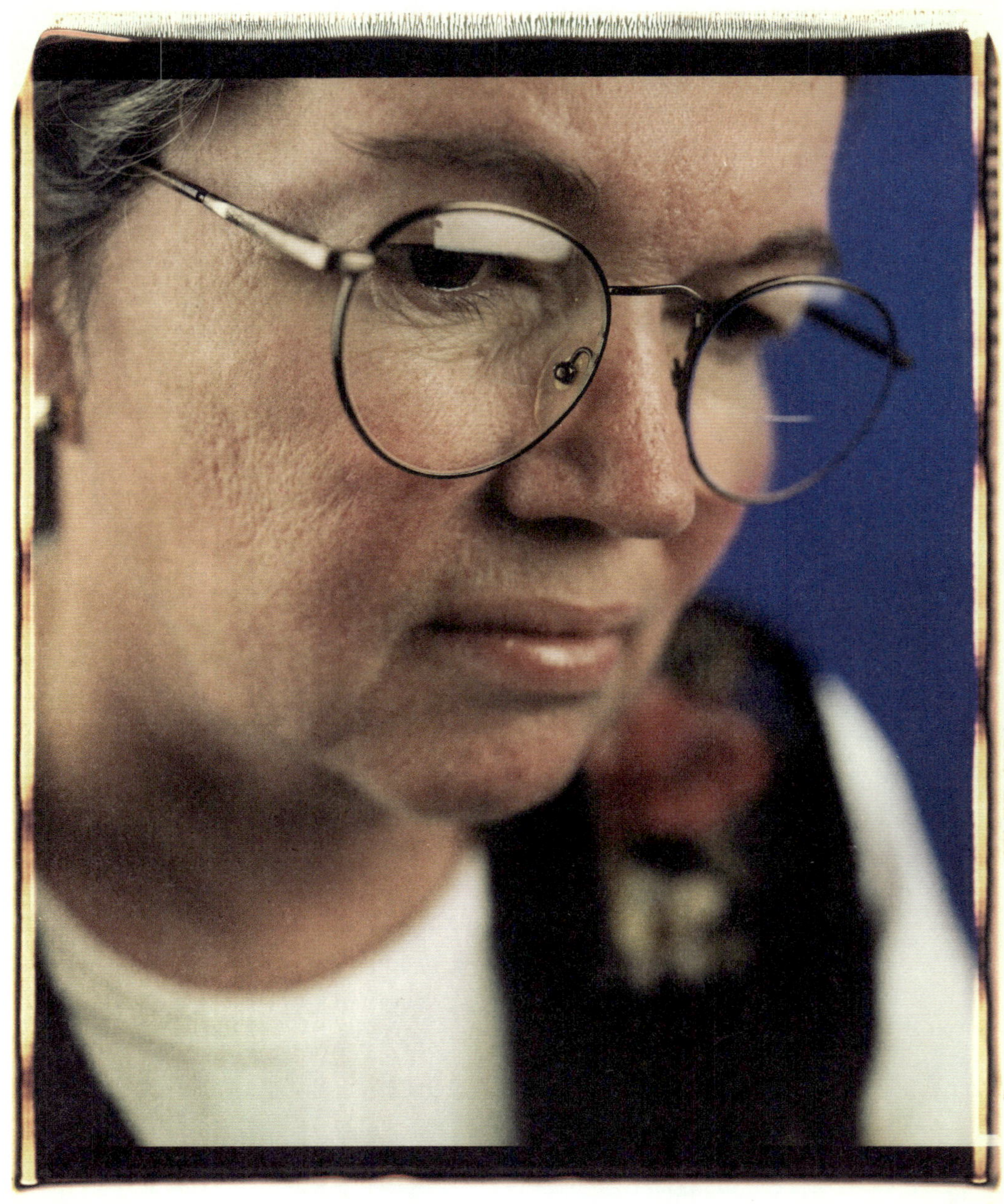

Dawoud Bey, *Barbara and Richard Benson*, 1999
Two instant color prints
28¾ × 21⅞ in. (73 × 55.5 cm) each

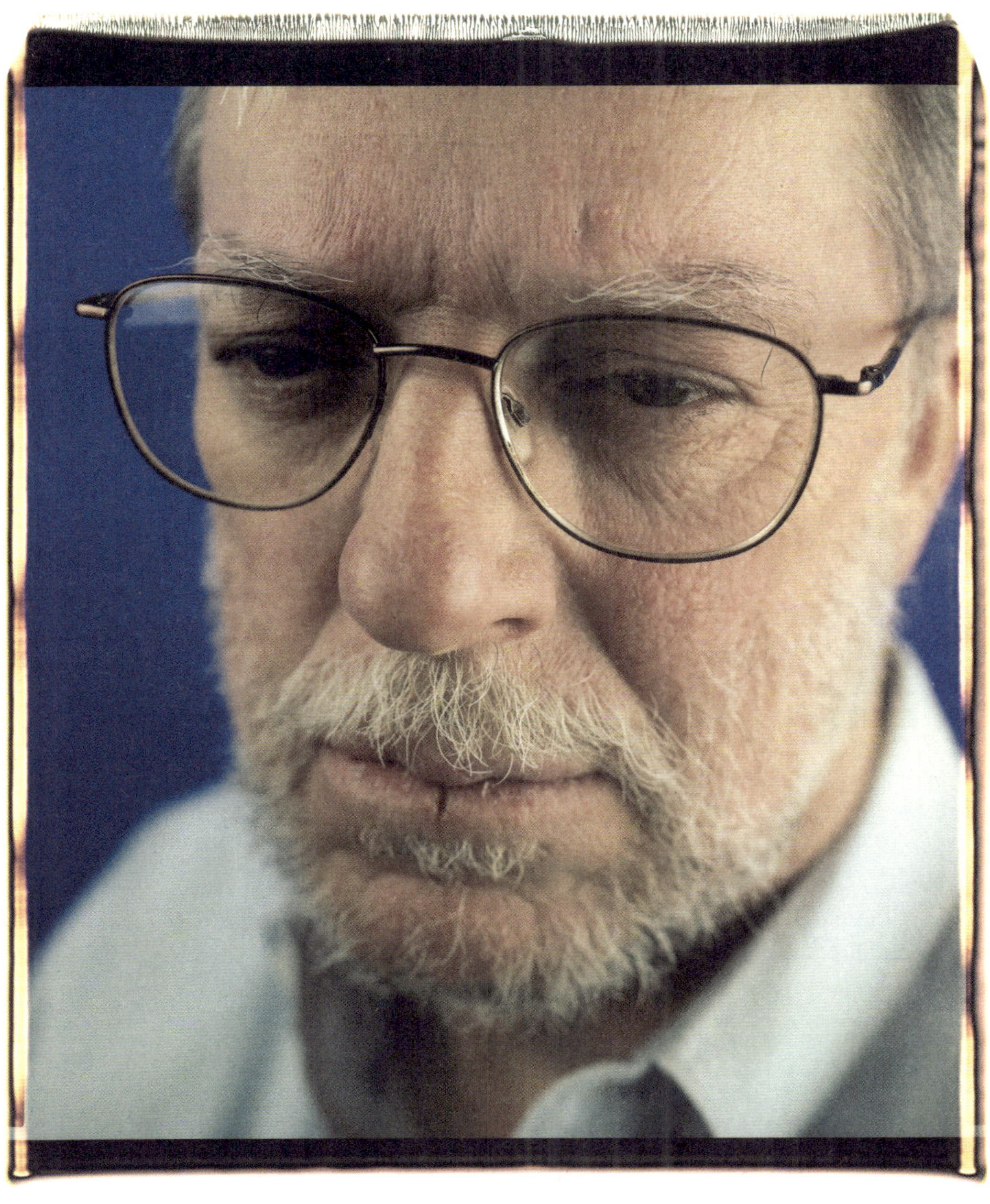

MacGill   Exactly. But as you said, it just came naturally to your family. So when Richard's students would graduate, did they go away, or did they keep coming back?

Benson   Only some of them came back. Some students came and went on, and we never saw or heard from them again. Maybe Chip did professionally, but there were others who really felt comfortable, and who continue to return to this day.

MacGill   Was it a responsibility to the students that you all felt, or was it just your way of doing things?

Benson   It was just the way. It was his way of teaching.

MacGill   What would happen if somebody showed up who wanted to talk about a specific problem about what they would call "their practice"?

Benson   He didn't use that kind of terminology.

MacGill   But if they showed up and they wanted to do something with photography, be enlightened, or have their photo domino kicked while Richard was figuring out how they built the pyramids, for example, would he drop the project of figuring out how they built the pyramids and help the students with their specific questions, or would he share what he was doing at the moment?

Benson   Well, you have to understand that the visits from his students were group visits. It was a class. It didn't happen in New Haven. It happened in Newport. He just said, "Show up." (How they got there was not Chip's problem—and he wanted them there on time, which never happened and used to piss him off.) That was not the venue for one student to solve a vexing problem. That would have meant somebody staying afterwards or making a different trip.

MacGill   His generosity was to teach what he knew.

Benson   To give it away. People used to ask, Don't you think you should copyright that? Don't you think you should patent that? He looked into patenting a number of things and just said, I can't deal with patent attorneys. They don't know as much as I do, and I'm not going to teach them how to know what I know so that they can write me a patent. Forget it. I'm not going to patent that.

MacGill   He would have had a lot of patents.

Benson   He would have had a lot of patents. But he was more interested in what he was going to come up with next than he was in cashing in on what he'd already come up with. He taught people how to make photographs by applying multiple layers of latex paint. Yet nobody did it, could do it.

MacGill   As with his multi-pass inkjet printing—anybody and everybody was welcome to come learn it. I know four people he taught his process to, and everybody would go home, try it, and say, I can't do this.

Benson   It sounds good, but you have to be Chip in order to do it [*laughs*]. He just didn't know that. He really thought everybody could do it.

MacGill   That's probably at the root of his generosity and belief in people.

Benson   Yes. He was never mercenary in any way. His father also taught a lot of people how to carve stone over the years.

MacGill   But not many could do it.

Benson   And those who could came back and worked for him.

MacGill   Something that Thomas Palmer brings up intermittently is that Richard would go down a path such as the multi-pass printing, which was unlike anything anybody had ever done or seen before, and eventually renounce it, believing more fully in a new path or process. Single-pass printing with his Espon printer just wasn't enough. He remade his printer so that he, not the software, told it what to do. This enabled him to print the same piece of paper, the same print, through the machine more than once. The results were astounding.

Benson   Yes, but the inkjet process that you're talking about was an extension of what he'd been doing since Meriden Gravure in '66.

MacGill   On press, yes, that's right. But with the modified inkjet printer sitting in his studio, it was more dexterous.

Benson   It wasn't that. It was that he had developed a technique, and he always credited Sid Rapoport . . .

MacGill   I believe it's called "stonetone."[1]

Benson   Sid always claimed that he had invented tritone. And Chip always credited him, even though he felt he had invented it too. I think they invented it at the same time. But Chip took that knowledge from his time at Meriden to his private jobs at other presses and to the photographs in paint.

Chip was a frustrated painter, and he hated the fact that in photography, you went into the darkroom, turned off all the lights, made a print, looked at it, and, if it wasn't right, you threw it away and started all over again. He wanted everything to be additive.

He'd make a print and say, It's not right, what can we do to fix it? Put on another layer, the way you would with a painting. He figured, why not do that on the inkjet? He re-engineered the printer to make it do what he wanted it to do. The store-bought printer was a one-shot deal: in, out, done. "In, out, done" always frustrated Chip (so he said). He manipulated the machine so it could do what he wanted.

That's just what Chip did with everything, from start to finish. But it was all because of this painterly desire that he had to figure out how to use additional passes. He called it "additive thinking" in order to produce whatever you hold in your hand. He was big on this idea: We're only going to talk about what you're holding in your hand. I don't care how long it took you to get there or how you did it. What matters is what's on the wall.

Early on, in his crits, the students would stand with their photograph on the wall, and they would talk about the emotions they had when they made the negative. And Chip would say, That is bullshit. I don't want to know what you were thinking when you made the photograph. I don't care what your feelings were. Let's look at the photograph. What does the photograph say? That's the only thing that matters. And he was consistent in that attitude, from beginning to end.

MacGill   When Richard had his first show at the gallery in 2008, it was astounding for people to see his pictures and what was on the wall. They had never seen anything like them. The richness and clarity had never been achieved before. The prints were much closer to what our eye actually sees than traditional analog or single-pass inkjet prints. Thomas Palmer walked in and said, "He'll change his mind about this whole thing soon, don't worry about it."

Benson   He never arrived and said, Eureka, my life is over, I've succeeded. It was always, What's next? People said to me, when I was a teenager, "Why are you interested in him?" And I said, "Listen, I'll never be bored." And that was really important to me, and let me tell you, I was never bored.

MacGill   When he made *The Printed Picture*, he was convinced he could use a single file from which everything could be printed, from the prints on the wall to the reproductions in his book. But then when he was on press, he said, "No, that's wrong." He had to adjust all the files, which for him, was not a problem. He realized that the ink he used in his Epson printer was one thing, and the ink used on press was another. Of course they don't work. And then he was off in another direction.

Benson   Chip didn't get up in the morning and say, Okay, I'm done with that, what will I do now? He woke up in the morning with an idea, and he just got out of bed and went and started doing whatever that idea was. These things just kept coming, you know?

MacGill   How did he decide that he was going to try to figure out how the pyramids were made? Where did that come from?

Benson   You know, the John Stevens Shop[2] moved stones. You don't think of them as stone movers. You think of them as stone carvers. Let me tell you, moving stones is part of the job. You've got to get the stone into the shop, and then when you're done, you have to get it out of the shop. You have to deliver it and install it at the site. Moving stone is something that was in their family forever. Chip's father, John Howard Benson, was also intrigued by the pyramids. I can imagine Chip saying one day to Fud [his brother], Well, let's figure it out. And Fud would say,

Well, they did this, and they used this, and Chip would say, Let's try it. They tried using poles as levers, like all the books tell you they did. In trying it out, they realized that's not how they did it. They believed the Egyptian builders were smarter than that, you know? They were always respectful of the people doing the work. They wanted to figure out how it was done. The blocks of stone that they were experimenting with got bigger and bigger [*laughs*]. I still have them in the backyard. Hunks of granite twelve inches around or more. I can't get anybody to move them.

MacGill   What's interesting is that their experimentation grew out of what the family did for a living, but also what you talk about is a respect for the maker, the doer. The two of them wanted to figure out how they actually did it. And that's a different approach. That's a humanistic approach.

Benson   Yes, exactly. They moved a whole lot of stone! So they had respect for the guys who built the pyramids. There was some satisfaction at the end when they'd figured it out. I'm not clear just what they figured out. Because of course the next day, he had another theory, you know [*laughs*]?

MacGill   Speaking of always moving forward, how did Richard go from the multi-pass inkjet printing, which changed our small world, to denouncing printing entirely, choosing to display his images on a 4K monitor through a self-written computer program? He called this "the contraption." The screen was now the thing.

Benson   First of all, he bought into the digital camera and the computer world early on, without reservation. He just dove right in. But nothing he made ever satisfied him. He was always saying, Well, I like that, but that's not quite what I had in mind. So he'd go on to the next thing. When he had gotten to the endpoint of experimenting with inkjets, he still wasn't satisfied with the thing he held in his hand. And he really came to believe that the best way to view his photographs was on the computer screen. That was more satisfying to him aesthetically, as an artist. He loved his images on the contraption's screen. That satisfied him. He didn't think that it was going to satisfy him for the rest of his life, but it was another step.

MacGill   A stop on the journey.

Benson   Making it to one stop on the journey was more satisfying than anything he could hold in his hand.

MacGill   His attendant work moved the contraption on to its different iterations.

Benson   Yes, but more of it was the screen's format, because before he really got sick, he was writing. He was putting together words and images. He had printed some of those out with the inkjet earlier, but he really liked that idea on the screen too. He had something to say. It's kind of interesting, because he always felt that the thing you held in your hand was what you were saying to the public, whatever that means. But then he wanted to put the image and words together. I thought, Hmm, that's a change. He started with straight images on the computer, then started putting words with those too.

MacGill   Putting words with pictures was a change for him because it was the thing on the wall that was important. Putting words with pictures was a generous act. He simply gave more to the viewer with this work by showing his picture along with his encyclopedic knowledge about the stuff seen in it.
   One thing I could never believe was that when he made subsequent Epson prints from a file, he didn't just go back to the same file.

Benson   Oh—push a button and out it would come? No, no.

MacGill   To reprint it, he'd make totally new files. No two were the same.

Benson   Yes. But that's because he liked to work. That's *how* he liked to work.

MacGill   Do you remember when Emmet [Gowin] came up to visit you? He and Richard made a multi-pass print together, and it was all very good, but it was like Yale playing Princeton in football. Here were the two opposing coaches, and they were not about to give each other any tips on what offense was going to happen on the field or what defense was needed to deal with the offense.
   Their approaches, their teaching methodologies were . . .

Benson   Totally different. And not right or wrong, just different.

MacGill   The thing that bound them or linked them was their—and I'm sorry to use that word again—exceeding generosity and knowledge.

Benson   They were teachers. Teaching is giving. You share your knowledge and your expertise with your students. That's what they hire you for, right? That's kind of basic.

MacGill   That's the community you and Richard nurtured, fostered. You know, you lived with it. You contributed to that whole culture.

Benson   It's our norm. Don't you understand that about families?

MacGill   Yes.

Benson   Emmet was like that too. Nothing remarkable there.

MacGill   What would you consider to be Richard's greatest legacy contributions and why?

Benson   Professionally? I can't speak to professionally except to point out that he was always looking forward to the next discovery, the next camera, the next printer, et cetera. He had left behind the conception of an image printed on some sort of substrate and was experimenting with images solely on the computer screen. The contraption. Who knows where he would have gone next?

---

1.   Stonetone is the process through which a halftone screen is created and then used to apply multiple passes of ink to produce a duotone or tritone reproduction.
2.   The John Stevens Shop, founded in 1705, specializes in the creation of inscriptions in stone, including architectural and memorial lettering such as that found on the Vietnam Veterans Memorial and the Franklin Delano Roosevelt Memorial in Washington, DC. Richard Benson's father, John Howard Benson, worked at the shop, as did Richard's brother, John Everett Benson. Today, Richard Benson's nephew Nick Benson is the owner and creative director.

Richard Benson, *Photographs from the Collection of the Gilman Paper Company* (Meriden, CT: White Oak Press, 1985)

In conversation with Lesley A. Martin and Miko McGinty

Lesley A. Martin   I wanted to start with a very simple question: Can each of you summarize concretely what you learned by working with Chip Benson?

Thomas Palmer   Everything. Everything that I know. Chip didn't believe that if you were just told something, you could learn it. You had to do it. There was no practicing. When I first started working with Chip, we worked together making halftone separations. And the first halftones that I made were used in the book that we were working on then. He believed that you have to figure it out. He had little patience for people whose work was largely done by other people. He might respect it, but thought it was sort of a different thing. The only way you could do something is to do it, and do it, and get it right.

Paul Messier   Creative restlessness—it's a good thing. You can't just rest on prior accomplishments. You have to constantly push forward. If you're not creating, you're not innovating, and if you're not learning, you're not doing your job properly. These ideas were very inspirational. Also—materials are important. I think they're vital, and clearly Benson took craft seriously. But for me, it's not as much the nouns but the verbs, the making, the process. I think Benson took process to a new level. The process of making something, and its context—it's very connected to past practices, to his printing and his bookmaking. He was absolutely fluent in the material history of the medium. But it's not just a sort of virtuosity. I don't think he would have been satisfied with just that. It was having that fluency to be a virtuoso, a virtuoso performer, and then the courage to tear it up and make something new. To give himself the license to not know what the heck he was doing, yet the confidence and the security that, through process, he could see something through and make it new and important.

Palmer   That's pretty much the way I see it. I guess I always thought of Chip as a materialist, for lack of a better word. For him, the art existed through the materials. Art didn't exist outside of them. The Gilman Paper Company book is an example of that. When he started, he was trying to understand how a reproduction in ink, on paper, as a multiple, could carry the eccentricity and emotion of a unique object created forty to one hundred forty years ago.

We think of craftsmen as these people in beautiful studios who are very precisely going about their work, everything is in the right place. Chip, with all the reproduction work, was a printer. He was no longer working in a printing plant, but he viewed himself as a printer, just a guy making halftones. We can all imagine what he might say if we said, Oh, you're an amazing craftsman. He would understand that and like that, but at the same time, he would be like, Bah, I'm just a printer. Somebody asked him one time what we are doing—we were in the middle of the Gilman book. He said, "We're just a couple of guys trying to make a buck."

Messier   He would have been fine with the idea, the notion that you guys didn't know what you were doing when you were making the Gilman book. But to say we're just trying to make a buck, just trying to make a book, is not quite . . .

Palmer   Well, that's what he would say. Chip was never afraid of failing and making a mistake. Often, he would finish something and then decide that he had taken off in the wrong direction, and he had to go back and redo everything. We all make mistakes. We generally like to keep them somewhat hidden, but he would be the first person to say, I totally fucked up, and I have to do it again. He never hemmed and hawed.

The first thing you have to do is say there's something wrong, then you can go and fix it. That allowed him to do a lot, having that sort of fearless approach: A, I can do it, and B, I'm going to screw up and I'll correct it, and it'll be better. He was more than willing to accept the blame and just try and figure out what needed to be fixed, and how to fix it, and then tell people that, whatever it was, that it was the best book that had ever been done, no matter what it looked like at the end. It was very charming.

Martin   Paul, you had mentioned earlier: it is not so much about materials, it's about process, and Thomas, you're saying, he is a materialist, but maybe those two things are inextricable.

Palmer   You could make that case for everybody: you take a picture and make a print. So it's material. But most of us are satisfied with buying the material off the shelf. If we don't like it, we buy something else.

But, with Chip, it was about the whole process. If he didn't like the result he was getting, he threw out everything on the shelf, tore out the shelf, and then the room that the shelf was in, and then rebuilt everything from the ground up.

Messier   It's not an either-or. These are things that are fundamentally intertwined. Process is not just isolated to being on press. There are all these other factors that have influence. Being able to effectively synthesize those factors and come out with a great product at the end—that's the talent. That's good management and good process. But then to always push, push that process, push those materials— that's the fundamental denominator. To do something unique, to commit to yourself that you're going to do something, that you're going to take those opportunities and do something special with it—that's the process.

Miko McGinty   Paul, you were about to embark on talking about the Gilman book, and how that exemplifies this process. Can you tell us more about that?

Messier   I'd be really interested to hear what Thomas has to say about this, but the Gilman book is an absolute tour de force of analog printing. The Gilman book came out in 1985. The first Mac, the 128K Mac, came out in early '84. The ground was ready to shift under everybody's feet, fundamentally. And to me, thanks to that book, the analog printing era could have ended with a period, but instead, it ended with an exclamation mark.

McGinty   Has it ended?

Messier   Well, not entirely, and its true there are echoes of the analog in contemporary printing. Maybe I'm taking artistic license by marking the end of analog with the introduction of first generation digital tools, but we have to think about certain works that are definitional in the pivot from analog to digital, from a purely analog visual culture to a purely digital visual culture. The Gilman book is going to be right there in that conversation.

PLATE 41
PHOTOGRAPHER UNKNOWN
[illegible]

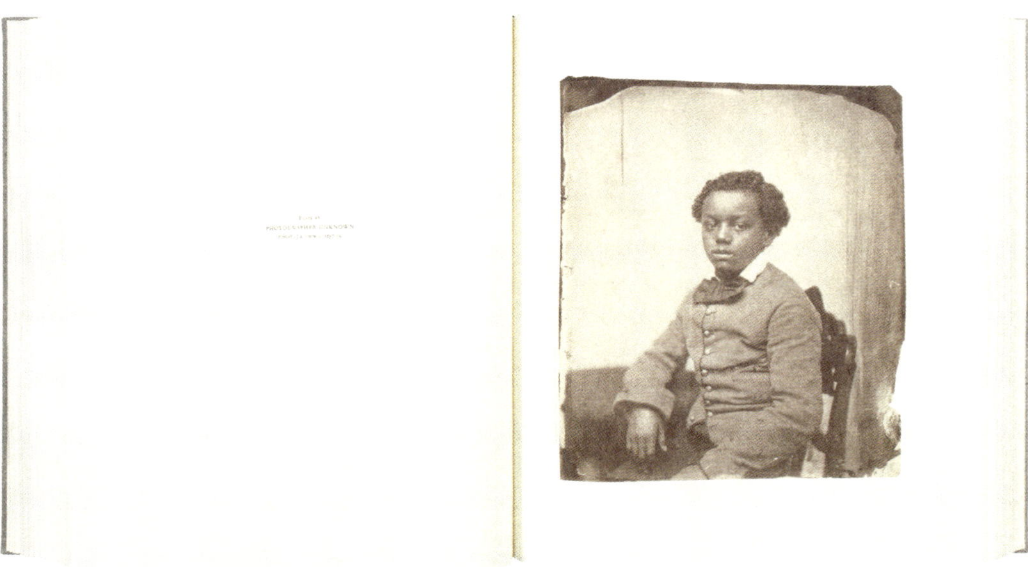

PLATE 42
PAUL STRAND
[illegible]

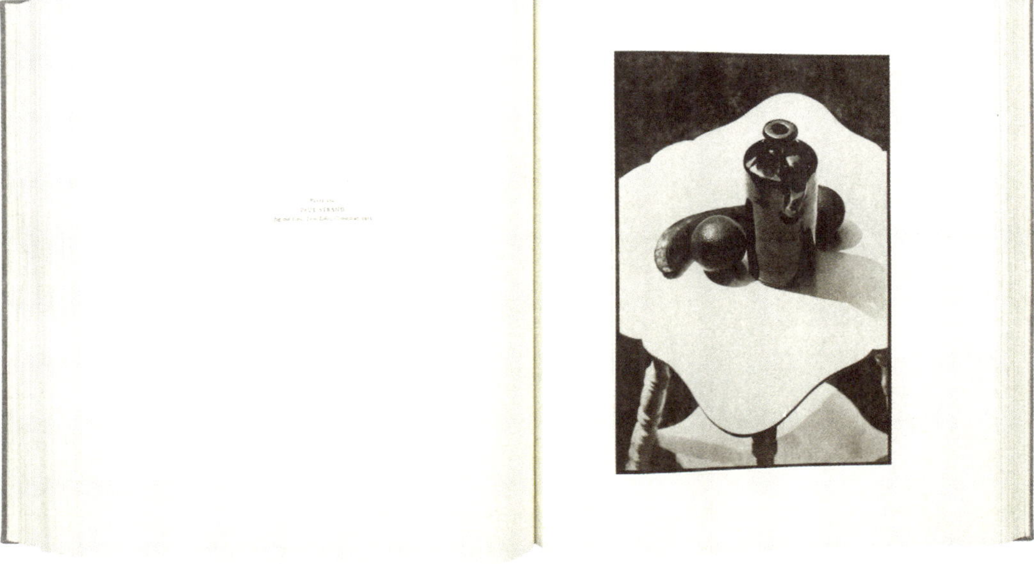

Palmer   This conversation has been underway since Jock Reynolds started burnishing the great myth of the Gilman book. I ask myself: How many people saw the Gilman book, ever?

Messier   This is an excellent point. It requires a particular type of literacy. If you show somebody the Gilman book today, somebody who's been embedded in the publishing world, and ask them to put into words what's special about it, I think people would have a bit of a hard time. They'll come up with words that almost mean nothing, like, "Oh, it's beautiful." Okay, it's beautiful.

Palmer   It weighs a lot.

Martin   It's almost a conceptual object in that regard because you have to know the process and the intention behind its creation. I often ask myself the same question about *New Topographics*. How many people saw that exhibition? There wasn't a great, best-selling catalogue, and yet it had this oversized impact and created a whole genre of photography. So it's a similar question of the Gilman book because it does have a mythic presence. Paul, you may be right in that it both summarizes the history of analog printing and puts a capstone on it. And yet, clearly Richard was looking into the future.

Messier   My personal understanding of the basic ethos of the Gilman book is to be true, to be faithful, to the medium of photography—to represent the material history of photography that no one had really challenged themselves to do before. To me, it's very much embedded in the material history of photography and rendering of images in ink. That goes to back to Talbot, and goes back to the entire visual understanding of art history being based on the printed photograph in the '20s, '30s, '40s, to the '70s. As a conservator I worry about the loss of that literacy and fluency—and the kind of deeply faithful effort that was made in the Gilman book to the medium of photography, a devotion to the medium of photography. I don't know if that language has value anymore.

Palmer   In the 1970s, it boiled down to: if the photographs were twentieth-century they were gray, and if they were nineteenth-century, they were brown. That was it. Mostly because people were reproducing everything as duotones. So you used either brown ink or gray ink.

We were happy with catalogues and the representation of those pictures as a memory device, really. Back then, people were happy if the two rectangles were in register, and it looked like the original picture. The Gilman Paper Company had a photography collection, and they needed to reproduce some of the photographs in this collection so they could put them up on the wall. Chip said, Well, the way to do that is to print them in ink. He was going to use the printing press: initially the idea was, you only needed to print one or two copies, basically, and they could put them up on the wall.

And then it morphed into, well, if you're printing one or two, you could get a sheet of paper and you could print two at a time, and then you could fold it, and you could sew them, and you have a book. Eventually, it morphed into the behemoth that it became. One of the ideas behind it was, okay, so you've got the Gilman book, now this can go to a library or any kind of a public place, and somebody who does not have access to the originals, who has been looking at reproductions that are either all-brown or all-gray, can all of a sudden see that there's this vast variation in photography. It might not be 100 percent accurate to the originals, but you would get the idea. That was one of the rationales that Benson used to sell the whole thing to Howard Gilman.

McGinty   I want to know how you guys did it.

Palmer   Chip had already done *Flowers and Trees* (1981) for Friedlander at Meriden, which was printed as tritone—the first tritone he did—essentially a monochromatic reproduction. And then he started working on the MoMA Atget books which were tritones with a lot of color. I think other printers were also experimenting with tritones or making duotones with a tint and calling it a tritone. So Chip had that basic knowledge. I don't know exactly how he made the leap to say, Okay, we can do anything, in terms of number of ink layers, screen angles and that sort of thing. But he—how can I say it . . . let me just back up and go into it from a different direction. So one of the things that Chip thought was a failing of printing was that, Paul, let's say, would go to Meriden Gravure with his exciting book idea, and he'd talk to sales, and then he'd drop his prints and design off. And the salesman would take them to the darkroom and say, "Here's the idea," and the guy in the darkroom would make the duotones, or whatever he was making. And then he would give the film to the strippers, and then the strippers would give the flats to the platemakers, and the platemakers would give the plates to the pressman, and the pressmen never saw the originals. They didn't know. So it was this sort of telephone game. And the excitement was gone. And you got the book, and it looked like a book that was printed at Meriden Gravure or at Rapoport.

So Chip's idea was, what if one guy runs the whole show? He decided he had to move a press, a single color Miehle 29, into his basement and print the reproductions by himself. So he did that. Eventually he realized he didn't want to carry all that paper by himself so he hired me.

Chip made the halftone negatives directly from the originals. The simplest images required three negatives and the most complex, seven or eight. He gave me instructions on how the film was to be stripped, and how the plates were to be exposed and developed. We mixed custom inks for the different plates and passes as we went. Most of the inks were made up of red, blue, and yellow, with an extender for transparency. We didn't keep careful notes. Chip was quite proud of the fact that the only instrumentation used were the timers in the darkroom; in the plate room, a scale for weighing the inks; and the impression counter on the press. Each pass built on and modified what came before. That was a major breakthrough for Chip, and he used it in most of the subsequent printing techniques he developed: paint on aluminum, multi-pass inkjet printing. The idea that you could build up a photograph, step by step, making adjustments as you went, until the print was finished. We printed all the images, and then everything went to Stamperia Valdonega in Verona, Italy, for the letterpress printing, tipping-in of all the images, and binding. Extraordinary Italian craftsmanship.

Martin   The object—as it exists now—has developed a mythology around it. But what are the lasting contributions to the field that we can learn from Richard and carry on today?

Palmer   There were a number of books that emerged from the thinking behind the Gilman book, namely, that monochromatic photographs were inherently colorful and should be reproduced as such. For example, Jeffrey Fraenkel published a book in which all the pictures were tritones or quad-tones—we used seventeen different ink colors in the book, probably a few more than Jeffrey thought necessary. It was a survey book of photographs of sculpture, *The Kiss of Apollo*. The originals were gorgeous—silver prints, salt prints, platinum and palladium, albumens, you name it. The innovative thinking behind the Gilman book—that you could have different inks for different kinds of pictures in the same book—shows up in other books as well. Keith Davis was responsible for a number of books first for the Hallmark Collection and then the Nelson-Atkins Museum that used a stripped down version of multiple colors printed in one pass on a six-color press. And Irving Penn's *Passage* benefited from Chip's development of the quadtone, usually using two blacks, two grays, and a varnish. People will say, "Yeah, well, if we had that much money, we could do that too." But I think they would be extremely surprised by how little it cost to do that. And nobody, as far as I know, got rich doing that book. Chip was still working on other projects to make ends meet—working doing halftones for Aperture, for MoMA, working on Leslie Katz's *O, Write My Name*. He put everything back into what he was doing.

Messier   I was thinking about this question about lasting contributions, and I would rather think about the example of learning—this kind of insatiable curiosity, and Chip's understanding and respect for what came before, yet not being content to replicate that. He was not content that there was a final word on anything. It's about having the courage to recognize where there were new opportunities and work to be done. To just keep moving forward.

Palmer   At one point, Chip announced that paper was dead. Nobody was ever going to print on a piece of paper ever again, and if they were, they were idiots. He believed that 4K monitors were where it was at. At the very end of his life, he was trying to figure out how to combine the best attributes of the screen—the beauty of the projected image, the immense storage capacity, the flexibility of software, and the user interfaces of the computer—with the rigorous editing process, artistic control, and our cultural familiarity with the bound book.

Messier   I was on a panel discussion with him at MoMA, and we were fake-sparring like the whole time. I was talking about silver-gelatin, black-and-white, and material history. And he was like, "Kid, you know, you're wasting your time with that silly sentiment. Look to the future." Nobody in the room left thinking about photography the same way.

Palmer   One thing we shouldn't forget either is that his own photography was about the physical, objective world. Whatever camera, whatever technology, however messy or complex the process, the result had to be clear and precise and articulate and beautiful and engaging, and, in a sense, useful. Chip was all about trying to show you the world.

In conversation with Miko McGinty

As an undergraduate in the early 1990s, I felt the influence of Richard Benson mainly through other professors: namely Lois Conner, the beloved photography teacher of many of my friends, and graphic designer John Gambell, an important mentor to me as a young letterpress printer in my residential college Jonathan Edwards, where Gambell is a fellow. When I returned to Yale School of Art for my MFA in graphic design, Gambell continued to be an important influence and Benson was my dean. This conversation evidences the influence a printer can have on a graphic designer.

Acclaimed chemical engineering professor Gary Haller was master of Jonathan Edwards College from 1997 to the end of 2008, and his personal interest in art led him to Richard Benson, who had by then been the dean of the art school for a year. Haller had begun curating and organizing art exhibitions in the Jonathan Edwards College house, including publishing booklets about the exhibitions, and this conversation explains some of the curatorial work that Benson was able to pursue with Haller.

Throughout our conversation I was struck by the familiar themes that resonate with my education in letterpress and design, and with my current work overseeing printing. Gambell and Haller's longtime connections with Benson, and the intersection of photography, printing, and graphic design within these relationships is part of the legacy of the era when printing and photography began to incorporate the digital processes we use today.   Miko McGinty

Miko McGinty   John, how did Richard Benson influence your work?

John Gambell   Right from the beginning, anything that had to do with printing had to do with Chip. I'd get a design assignment for the Yale University Art Gallery, and I'd always go over the images with him to talk about how to optimize them. In those days there were many opportunities to economize and, in most Yale settings, I was trying to do as much as I could for a reasonable amount of money. So I often consulted with Chip.

In the summer of 1980, Chip set me up at Eastern Press in New Haven to work with Hazel Strand on Aperture's edition of *Time in New*

England [1980] by Paul Strand. This was the culmination of a time that I spent figuring out what I was going to do in my life. I worked doing printing for Chip—real photographic printing, coating paper, varying the different chemistries to create different levels of contrast, that sort of thing.

One of the things he was trying, in having me do it, was to see whether palladium prints printed as halftones were as foolproof as he thought that might be. Because when something's a halftone, it's either essentially fully pigmented or not, and your gradations are created by the percent of the dot that's either white or black or, in this case, a kind of dark, wonderful brown.

Paul Strand had just passed away. Chip had been printing with him near Paris. Strand was approving things. And, unfortunately, Paul had terrible, painful bone cancer that affected his back and shoulder. Chip was helping Hazel through all this and was with Strand when he died. When it came time to print *Time in New England*, Chip said to me, "You're doing all the press checks on it."

So Hazel and I would go down to Eastern Press. That was at a time when we used film shot on the copy camera. Everything, even the type, was full of little spots and dots and holes and missing letters, and who knows what. There was a lot of work for a press checker to do at that point, not to mention making it look like a Paul Strand, whose work was rich and dark. Chip always said Strand did that to make sure everyone knew it was art.

I had been in school for a year by then, and this gave me confidence around that aspect of graphic design and printing supervision that I would not otherwise have had.

McGinty   Gary, how did you start working with Richard Benson?

Gary Haller   I ran into Chip on Cross Campus [Yale's main quad], and he said, "*O, Write My Name* would be a good idea for one of your Jonathan Edwards exhibitions."

The portfolio *O, Write My Name: American Portraits of Harlem Heroes* included photographs from the Carl Van Vechten portraits of African American cultural figures, twenty-five men and twenty-five women. There were one hundred copies printed, and one is in the Beinecke. And at first, I thought I had to get them on loan. I went to Chip and he said, "Oh, you don't have to do that. I have a copy." And of course he brings it over. The exhibition took place in 1998.

McGinty John, do you remember that exhibition?

Gambell I do. Right after I graduated from the School of Art, Chip had started the project *O, Write My Name* with Leslie Katz at Eakins, and they purchased a big beautiful American French Tool Company etching press, which they had installed in my studio in Erector Square in New Haven. Chip printed some of the proofs, and then I printed a complete set, which Chip ended up approving. It became clear to me that I was not going to be able to pursue my life as a graphic designer if I didn't stop working with Chip. So at that point, the press and the project got transferred to Thomas Palmer. All of the pictures were shot by Chip in his shop in Newport and turned into gravures. He used film positives, aquatint, and a photo resist that went over the aqua. This was born out of Chip's fascination with hand-pulled gravure, which gave you the greatest tonal range from the lightest lights to the darkest darks. You can build up a visible layer of pigment on a piece of etching paper. And he was fascinated with this. It's a marvelous case of Chip having a visual/technical interest that he then translated into a project that constitutes probably the best rendition of Van Vechten's mission to record these incredibly influential people.

McGinty The next exhibition of Chip's was *The Face of Lincoln* [1999].

Haller He had a book with that title, and he gave me the proof prints for the book, which was part of the exhibition. There were also a number of Master's Teas—events for students and fellows at the Jonathan Edwards house to gather for a discussion and a reception—and one was "The Changing Face of Abraham Lincoln: Richard Benson and Alan Trachtenberg in Conversation."

Gambell The Lincoln book was printed well before he was dean, in the '70s with Jay Mellon. And I remember his son, Daniel Benson, who's now forty-something, was there during those early meetings. And at one point, I remember Barbara and Chip having a huge laugh because it turned out that Daniel thought that the word "Lincoln" meant "photograph." I've done another Lincoln. Hey, look at this Lincoln.

McGinty   Gary, those are both interesting examples of printing projects that became exhibitions many years later, in which Benson presented subjects of great interest in the wider academic community: Carl Van Vechten and the Harlem Renaissance, and Abraham Lincoln. As time went on, it seems like Benson began to curate exhibitions in Jonathan Edwards that were more closely related to his contemporaneous practice. I think that Benson got asked to work on a book for the tercentennial celebration of Yale in 2001.

Haller   Yes, he did a book called *A Yale Album: The Third Century* [2000]. And immediately following that, he did a version as an exhibition in Jonathan Edwards. And again, there was a Master's Tea he gave: "Process and Context of Picture Books by Richard Benson."

For the exhibition announcement, we used a picture of Jonathan Edwards College under construction. It announces the Master's Tea with Richard Benson and John Gambell: "Issues in the Presentation and Representation of Yale in Photographs and Photography Books: Richard Benson and John Gambell." Do you remember that, John?

Gambell   I was so nervous about making that presentation with Chip that I wrote the whole damn thing down. Chip did his usual offhand remarks, and he introduced me, and I started reading. He said, "John, just stop that," and he laughed. "This isn't the place for that."

Haller   And everybody was at that tea. I sent out invitations quite widely, and we always had an opening dinner at Union League. The Jonathan Edwards fellows were invited to those dinners, and they were quite faithful in coming.

Gambell   And the students too. There was a good smattering of interested students, design students, for example.

Haller   The students participated in all of those events; that was why we were doing it, of course.

McGinty   These exhibitions and the Master's Teas brought together Benson's practice as a photographer and art professor with the university, and that's where we can really see him interacting with more people, more scholars throughout Yale.

Gambell   They were bridges, too, from his core profession of printer. The exhibitions *O, Write My Name* and *Lincoln* seemed to make him more and more confident about thinking even more broadly than just as a printer and photographer. He came to understand how articulate he could be about what a picture conveyed, not only in terms of what it showed but how it was made, when it was made, why it was distinctive for that time or why it was conventional in that time. In *A Maritime Album: 100 Photographs and Their Stories* and *A Yale Album: The Third Century*, which he put together himself, he moved past the pictures themselves and contextualized them.

McGinty   Gary, in 2003 you and Benson put on the Walker Evans exhibition, and it's such an impressive exhibition especially with the addition of the speakers and the teas. It's like you were running an art museum.

Haller   The opening reception tea was "Walker Evans, His Process and Wit: Richard Benson and Jerry Thompson." Other teas included "Books and Translations: Alan Trachtenberg and John Hill" and "Recollections of a Friend: John Szarkowski," the emeritus curator of photography at the Museum of Modern Art. From the very beginning, Chip was always all-in, but the idea that I could borrow things from the Yale Art Gallery came later. For the Walker Evans show, I was told that I could choose what I wanted because Chip Benson recommended that the gallery should do so.

McGinty   Which brings us to *The Physical Print: A Brief Survey of the Photographic Process* exhibition in 2005.

Haller   John, you and Chip also made the accompanying catalogue, right?

Gambell   I did the typography and layout, and he made the digital files of the images.

Haller   This was the fifth exhibition catalogue I made with Chip. He said, "I'll help you with the catalogue." I made the mistake of saying, "Chip, you can just do whatever you want," and I meant that literally. When I got the cost quote for printing the catalogue, then I realized that I was in trouble, because he wasn't even done. Chip kept adding things. I remember that it was not three colors and black. There were four shades of gray and three or four varnishes to try to get the prints to look like photographs. He also proposed that we make it spiral binding, saying, "That's going to be so much better. It will lie flat. It will be nice for teaching." I'm glad it happened, but I just didn't know what I was talking about when I said, "You can do whatever you want."

Gambell   The printing is incredible. It's like an extension of the Gilman Paper Company book, because his approach there was to take each picture and optimize the printing of it so that each one would look as close to the original as possible.

Haller   He was just starting to conceptualize *The Printed Picture* exhibition for MoMA at that time, and I think he was using this catalogue and exhibition to begin to work out what that project would become. In the JE exhibition, I wanted to put fancy frames around each of the printed images. Chip was not having any of that. He said: We're just going to slap them together with the little clips, and that's the way they're going to be. So that's the way they were exhibited.

McGinty   John, I always wondered about the Wire-O binding. Now I understand it. Were sheets printed with different inks and then shuffled in the book?

Gambell   Chip and John Robinson figured out most of the logistics around the sheets. Some pictures don't have any varnish on them for a particular reason; others would have a matte or gloss varnish. They printed the ones that were going to be matte varnished together and the gloss varnish together. It was a real production.

The Physical Print is printed with the grain going in the wrong direction to the binding edge, and it actually makes the pages easier to turn, because they're a little boardy and not so floppy. So Chip was right about it being a really, really handy book. He was very kind to me about the bright orange of the inside covers that I thought would be terrific because it was a reference, in my designer's mind, to the old Kodak color-film boxes like the ones Chip would store prints in. So I thought of that as a container.

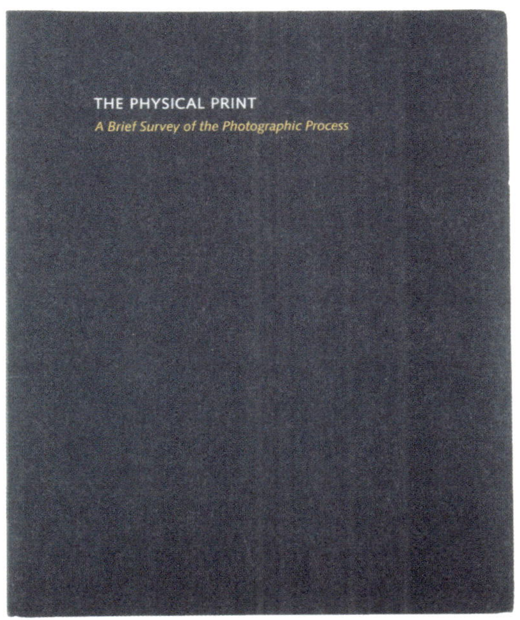

7

William Henry Fox Talbot, *A Scene in a Library*, 1844
Lithographic reproduction of a salt print, from *Photographs from the Collection of the Gilman Paper Company*

In this reproduction we can see the brush strokes that applied the coating to the photographic paper. The negative, also on paper, was trimmed to a rectangle, and we can see the paper edge of that negative. The process used to make the original print was called "salt printing." The image-forming material is silver, and its light-sensitive state, prior to exposure, was silver chloride. Silver chloride is an insoluble compound, and it was almost impossible to coat it evenly on a sheet of paper. The early workers in photography learned to coat a sheet of paper with a simple salt solution – often just table salt dissolved in water with a little gelatin added – and this coated salt, once dried, could be converted to silver chloride by brushing on a second coating of silver nitrate dissolved in water. The silver nitrate and sodium chloride, both easy to dissolve and apply with a brush, reacted together to make a perfect coating of the impossibly difficult silver chloride.

This picture is from a book made by Fox Talbot, called *The Pencil of Nature*. He never completed it, but it is exciting to recognize that, at its very inception, photography was understood by its inventor as a medium that should live on the pages of books. Today we have millions of books and magazines containing even more millions of photographs made in ink on printing presses. The original chemical prints that we cherish are unimportant, near vestigial objects, existing in a small number of copies and seen only by the advantaged few who can go to museums and galleries. Even in our homes, the family albums of original prints are only seen by a few viewers. Billions of photographs in books, embedded in the multiple editions of the printing press, have become primary structural elements of our society.

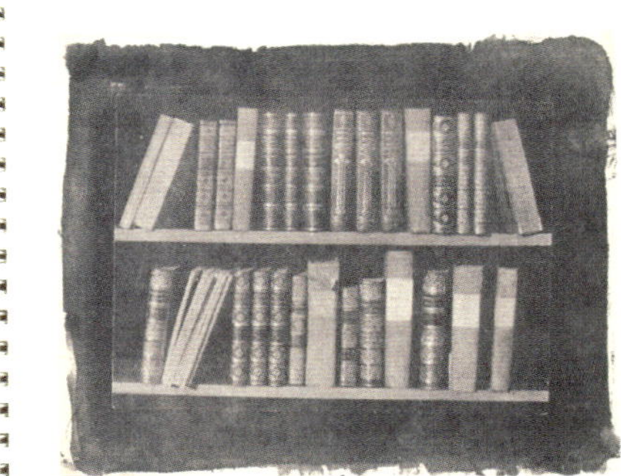

McGinty   Were you working with him regularly at that time?

Gambell   He came to me now and then with these things. He had a certain fairly lighthearted contempt for graphic design. He felt that it involved asserting an ego over content, and he always pushed me, pushed me to be invisible, especially when it came to picture placement: to keep the images in proportional size to one another. You don't want a little picture very big, and you don't want a big one very small, but you also don't want to have a huge contrast in sizes. I developed a system around Chip's strong desire to let the picture and the content come forward. Chip always wanted the picture to be unobtrusively framed on the page. Centered so that there was no design feeling about it, that it was just framed. And that seemed to make a lot of sense.

McGinty   John, do you have any thoughts or comments about his deanship? You were teaching then, and I was a grad student when he was dean, so I remember him. I was curious if you had any thoughts about his thinking while he was dean.

Gambell   Chip was all about making things. He didn't take the approach of coming up with a great idea and then trying it out like a designer does. He started from making. He didn't work things out in minute detail in advance. In his own work, he would make something, he'd look at it, think that it's not good in this way, make it again, make it again, make it again. He thought like a painter. His photographic painting process, where he put layer after layer of resist down, spraying paint down through the resist, removing those, putting new ones down, building it like a painting—it was all about making. Making and judging, but very little about matching a concept to a form as a starting point.

McGinty   We had all that incredible equipment in the art school because of Chip's contacts in technology. For example, those brand new HP printers that we had when I was in school.

Gambell   One of the first things I remember him saying was, "Remember, John, the computer is the enemy." Computers were just coming into printing, and I think he said this in conjunction with printing and creating direct-to-plate printing. Instead of going through negatives, you'd make a thing on a screen and then render that. But Chip meant that in the deepest way. He thought computers were the root of all evil. He didn't mince words. Later, I would joke around with him about it: "So now you're the most adept person with Photoshop in the world? What's this about?"

McGinty   When did that happen?

Gambell   He got interested in it very early. Adobe contacted him to be one of the people consulting on Photoshop when it was first being developed. He certainly was interested in it. His really clear thinking about how you create tonal range, how you mix different elements—his whole life's craft was about the layering of actual materials and techniques to modify what you've made, to make it better.

For example, in the developer bath, a negative could be left to sit without agitation for a certain amount of time to build acutance, or sharpness. According to Chip, still development created a kind of chemical turbulence that amplified the contrast just along those edges. Functions like this are absolutely incorporated into Photoshop's algorithms and interfaces. So he moved from physical to digital. He was so facile at thinking around technology. He was much more interested in that conceptual thinking around technology than around art.

Chip's final kind of print was "the contraption." It was basically a big catalogue of his pictures displayed on high-density screens. He got to the point where he said, No point in printing anymore, this stuff's just so much better. He could do all the manipulations that were so challenging on paper or another substrate. It was the complete evolution from, remember, the computer is your enemy. He was a remarkable craftsman in the physical realm, and then he got really, really good at dealing with the digital.

It was no secret that Richard Benson had been working for many years on a taxonomy of tools. On his untimely death, in 2017, the project's countless iterations had reached the stage of a manuscript titled *Tooltax: a classification of all the things we make.* I am grateful to Barbara Benson for letting me read it. The first part is indeed a taxonomy, well developed but unfinished, probably unfinishable. The second part is an extended essay, which explains and analyzes the taxonomy—and a great deal more. No doubt Benson would have continued to work on the essay, but it seems complete and coherent as it stands, and I hope it eventually may be published.

The essay is written in Benson's beguiling matter-of-fact voice. It isn't terribly long; there are no notes. But it certainly is ambitious: I'd summarize it as a sketch for a history of the universe, from the Big Bang to the fast-approaching era when machines will leave human beings by the wayside.

Benson's unwavering good humor and charm, his utter lack of pretention, his talent for fooling us into half-believing that we were collaborating with him on the task at hand—all of that allowed us to think of him simply as an exceptional master of photography and printing. We knew about the telescopes and the clocks, the boats and steam engines and the Model T, but we flattered ourselves that Benson was essentially an outstanding expert in *our* field. (About the boats: if you haven't read Benson's *A Maritime Album: 100 Photographs and Their Stories* (2017), a treat awaits you.) *Tooltax* demolishes that parochial fantasy. It proves, hands down, that Benson would have been exceptionally good at whatever he chose—maybe something we'd never even heard of, or something that hadn't yet been named.

Instead, Benson gave the best years of his youth to the curiously confounding problem of reproducing a monochrome photograph in ink on paper. Today, thanks to him and the professional cohort that he led, and to the digital revolution that followed, the problem has more or less evaporated. Throw a Lee Friedlander photograph on a hundred-dollar home printer and hit "copy," and nine times out of ten, you get a distinctly better image than the reproductions Benson made at Meriden Gravure half a century ago for Friedlander's first book, *Self Portrait*. Offset lithography was just then emerging as the dominant technology for reproducing photographs, and the challenge of improving on the plates in *Self Portrait* nourished Benson's genius for the next two decades.

He relished calling those plates "dog-shit duotones," though he didn't use that particular term in "Working with Lee," his essay for the book that accompanied Friedlander's retrospective at the Museum of Modern Art in 2005. It was an ideal introduction to Dalia Azim's comprehensive catalogue of Friedlander's publications and portfolios: Remarkably, all of Friedlander's books, from *Self Portrait* in 1970 through *The Jazz People of New Orleans* in 1992, were printed from halftone separations by Benson. Now, however, I suspect that the text is most valuable because it constitutes, in Benson's words, "a miniature history of my efforts to solve the puzzle of turning millions of tiny dots into recognizable photographs."

Attempting to paraphrase Benson is a fool's errand: effortless clarity invariably congeals into mud. And there is no need in this case, since the text is reprinted here. Please note, though, how deftly Benson moves from the concrete to the abstract and back again, or from what may at first seem like a charming anecdote to a stark articulation of bedrock principle.

The essay concludes with an explanation of how digital technology swept away the "host of variables" that had bedeviled analog offset lithography. Appropriately, the focus remains on Friedlander's books, so there is no hint of the wide horizon that digital technology was opening up for Benson's own art. Even as he abandoned monochrome imagery, offset printing, and eventually the paper support itself to embrace the ephemeral image on the screen, Benson exploited the lessons he had learned in the analog era: the heart of the matter remained the alchemy that can be wrought by taking the image apart and putting it back together. (Benson's digital experiments did fold back into the realm of offset once, in 2011, for *North South East West*, surely the only four-color book of photographs that ever went through the press twice—or ever will.)

The advent of digital technology enabled Benson to keep exploring photographic imagery as a wild frontier, but it was the nagging puzzle of analog offset lithography that had launched the adventure. That's what lured Richard Benson's multivalent magic into our world.

Working with Lee

I met Lee Friedlander in 1969, when he visited the Meriden Gravure Company in Meriden, Connecticut, where I then worked. Lee wanted to publish a book of his photographs, and he had money available from the proceeds of a portfolio he had done with the artist Jim Dine. In typical Lee fashion, he didn't go to a publisher to have the new book made but instead decided to do the whole thing himself. Meriden Gravure had a good reputation through the careful printing it did for museums and academic presses. Lee went to Meriden to get an esti-mate for a book of self-portraits.

It was a ritual at Meriden that visitors were given a tour, and I met Lee when he was brought into my new camera room, which had been created for the express purpose of doing research on the task of prop-erly reproducing black-and-white photographs. This strange man—tall and pale-eyed, with a Leica around his neck—said hello, completed the tour, then escaped from his handler and came back to the camera room declaring that he thought I was the only normal person in the place. On his next visit Lee came home to stay with Barbara and me while we proofed his book, and we have all been fast friends ever since.

No printing task is more difficult than reproducing a monochro-matic photograph. Prints and drawings—most of which are generated by hand—are coarse enough that the flaws in the printing tend not to show. But a photographic gelatin-silver print—Lee's stock-in-trade—contains smooth and perfect fields of gray tone, and ink has a terrible time emulating them: shading becomes rough, shadow detail disap-pears, and delicate highlight values are blown out. The folks at Meriden had given me one day a week to work on these problems, and a book like Lee's was the perfect guinea pig for my trials.

Fifty years ago nearly all printing, whether for books, newspapers, or advertising, was done by letterpress. Photogravure and offset

Originally published in *Friedlander*
(New York: Museum of Modern Art, 2005)

lithography, two completely different processes, hovered at the periphery: gravure had its place producing beautiful but expensive illustrated books, while offset lithography was confined to labels, for cans and other mundane objects. For centuries letterpress printers had printed words with cases, or forms, of heavy lead type, and pictures with carved wooden blocks. With the advent of photography they began to replace the wooden blocks with zinc or copper plates, which were mounted on wood and locked up in the forms with the lead type, making it possible to print words and pictures in a single pass through the press. By the mid-twentieth century these older devices—type and block—were routinely converted into lightweight plates that could be wrapped around cylinders and printed from at high speeds. Pictures made with letterpress never looked very good, but they were adequate for newspapers, magazines, and most books. Letterpress was inexpensive, and just good enough, and it dominated the printing trades.

By 1980 all this had changed. Photo offset lithography had usurped virtually the entire territory held by letterpress, and the older machinery had gone to the junk heap. The innovation was the offset blanket, a tough yet versatile rubber intermediary that received the ink image from the plate and transferred it to the paper. The new presses could perfectly register images made in multiple impressions, and do this with a thin photopolymer plate that cost only a few dollars yet could print ten thousand copies with ease. Offset killed letterpress, and even sent lovely photogravure into its final decline.

The system for printing pictures, in both old letterpress and modern offset, was based upon the halftone. In halftone reproduction the picture to be reproduced is photographed through a screen, which breaks up the image into a grid of equally spaced opaque dots that vary in size to emulate tone. The printing ink used is black, but the press has no capability to print black ink in shades of gray; if the halftone dots are small enough, however, the eye sees them as blended together, and the illusion of tone is created. Tiny dots produce a light value, midsized ones (which usually form a checkerboard pattern) show a mid-tone, and very large dots combine to leave a black field, checkered with small white dots (the paper itself), that appears as a dark value. Only through clever and precise manipulation can the halftone dot pattern end up looking like a photograph.

Lee's books are a miniature history of my efforts to solve the puzzle of turning millions of tiny dots into recognizable photographs.[1] Many people worked on these problems, but I was lucky enough to work at an inspired company that recognized the importance of fine printing, and to have Lee come on the scene with a lifetime of books in the wings that could present ever growing challenges for the printer.

When I began working with Lee, it was easy to see where the halftone process of the day failed in making reproductions. The tonal steps portrayed, going from black to white, appeared to have smooth transitions in the film that held the dots, but the prints made in ink from these negatives failed in five specific areas, generally arising from practical issues of ink, press, and paper:

1. The inability to produce a dense black

The inability to produce a dense black derived entirely from the challenge of holding detail in the dark areas of the print. In halftone reproduction, the areas printed with ink and the nonprinted spaces between the tiny dots were distinguished from each other by a film of water on the plate, which repelled the ink; but if the separation between the dots was very fine, any excess of ink would plug those spaces and ruin the printing. At the same time, heavy ink was needed to print a rich black. An offset plate could carry a heavy ink layer, which the blanket could easily transfer, but at all stages along the way—on plate, blanket, and paper—this heavy layer could bury the information held in the halftone dot pattern. Printers printed weakly to preserve that information, particularly in the shadows.

2. A loss of detail in the shadow areas of the picture

Loss of detail in the shadows was directly linked to the weight of the ink layer, but it also derived from the nature of the photographic scale in the halftone image. Halftone screens never produced an accurate rendition of a photograph's tone, and most screens had a dot structure that did not accurately transmit the variable intensity of the light passing through them. In the flexible, film-based screens used to produce halftone images at the time (replacements for the cumbersome glass screens of earlier years), the individual dot images were soft, possessing high density in the center and tapering off to clear film at the edges. As more light passed through the fringes of the dot, the film emulsion, developed with a high-contrast developer, produced a larger solid dot. In a coarse screen the tonal curve of the dots was more accurate than in a fine screen; in the 300-line screens made by Eastman Kodak, and used at Meriden—the finest made, with 300 dots to the linear inch—the dot structure was, to put it mildly, atrocious. In practical terms this meant that any halftone negative holding accurate shadow information had to be so heavily exposed that all other values in the negative became inaccurate.

3. A jump in the transition from dark to light mid-tones
A jump in the mid-tones was a break in the smooth transition through the middle-gray values. In a photograph such as a portrait, the light passing across the curved surface of skin might show a hard transitional line where the description moved out of shadow into fully illuminated areas. This break occurred because the halftone screen was inherently inaccurate in the area where the dot changed from a black dot on a white ground to a white dot on a black ground. It was difficult to determine exactly why this occurred, but the two dominant reasons were probably a doubling of the latent image in these areas of dot overlap and a jump in the intensity of the ink film when it became continuous on the printing plate. Whatever the exact reason, halftones always failed severely at the mid-tones.

4. Weakness in the light-gray values
Weakness of the light-gray values stemmed directly from the need to overexpose the halftone to render adequate shadow detail. Thus problems 2 and 4 were mirror images of each other. When light values were accurately portrayed (which could occur in a reproduction of a picture without dense blacks) there remained a secondary problem: the screen, ink, and paper combination tended to produce a rough description from the mid-tones on up to the light grays. This roughness varied

tremendously according to the condition of the blanket, the quality of the paper, and the care of the presswork.

5. The inability to accurately portray a white value
If a photograph contained pure white areas the printer had to make a decision either to drop out the halftone dots in that area or to retain them at the smallest possible size. Two difficulties occurred if the dots were dropped out. First, the transition from dot to no dot, as a very light gray moved to a white tone, tended to be rough. Second (and much more critically), if the dots dropped out in an area at the picture's edge, the border disappeared. Original photographs had the edges of the trimmed print itself, or the window of the protective overmat, to define the picture's borders. The printer had no such aid on the white page.

Because the printer might underink to retain information in the shadows, the single impression was often weak. The solution that evolved was to print each picture twice, from two different plates. The first plate printed with black ink and the second impression was with a gray ink, produced by cutting the ink with an extender. The gray ink layer went over the black. Both ink layers could be relatively weak, yet they joined to make a strong reproduction.

The first Friedlander book I worked on—*Self Portrait* (1970)—I made using duotone printing. The folks at Meriden had used those 300-line screens from Eastman Kodak with great success in museum work because the fineness of the pattern made the dots virtually invisible to the naked eye. The result was a print with a sharpness and smoothness surpassing anything that letterpress could produce. When used to reproduce photographs, however, this fineness became a liability: the separation between dots was *so* fine that any excess of ink plugged the spaces and ruined the printing. Detail in the shadows disappeared much more easily with these screens. So I decided to make the halftones for *Self Portrait* with duotone printing. My techniques were those used at the time, but I had not really thought the process out to produce the best results. Printers everywhere used duotones for their best work, but the scale of the two halftone images was not precisely defined. There was a vague notion that the black image might be a bit contrasty and the gray one a bit soft. Lee's book was made this way, and the reproductions, while adequate at the time, are actually awful. I had done the best I knew how, but the result is still terrible.

I was quite disappointed in the little *Self Portrait* book—not in the pictures but in the printing. A number of years passed before I worked on another book for Lee, and in the meantime I did a project for the Eakins Press Foundation, using my own photographs of the *Memorial to Robert Gould Shaw and the Massachusetts Fifty-fourth Regiment*—a great bronze by Augustus Saint-Gaudens, which stands on the edge of Boston Common, opposite the entrance to the State House. The pictures went into a small book called *Lay This Laurel*, which derived entirely from the inspiration of Leslie George Katz of Eakins Press, an extraordinary man who whipped me into a frenzy of interest in Shaw and his role in American history.

Leslie was simply crazy about printing. He collected books, and hammered at me, in the sweetest possible way, about how marvelous the printing of old was and how mediocre the contemporary work by comparison. Showing me gravure prints and even top-grade old letterpress illustrations, Leslie would bemoan the weak and muddy offset prints that were being produced on the new presses. I even remember getting a note from him one day in which he said he wanted the blacks in his next book to look like the black borders surrounding the designs in the wings of a monarch butterfly. Between Leslie and Lincoln Kirstein, who wrote the essay for *Lay This Laurel*, I was being battered to figure out better ways to use the halftone. Their influence was tremendous, and it built upon that of Doris Bry, who pushed me to reproduce Georgia O'Keeffe drawings and Alfred Stieglitz photographs, and John Szarkowski of the Museum of Modern Art, who was dragging me into an extended project on Eugène Atget. I had no choice but to try to understand just how the halftone worked.

Leslie had deep interests in America and in sculpture, and Lee had been traveling the country with his camera and photographing the thousands of memorial sculptures that appear in town squares and civic nooks and crannies across the nation. These monuments yielded an almost unthinkable number of original and brilliant pictures, and at some point Lee and Leslie met, decided to do a book, and brought me on board to make the halftones and oversee the printing. By this time I had quit the Meriden Gravure Company (where we worked six days a week for minimal pay) and had set up a copy camera with money lent by Doris, Lincoln, and Leslie. The new book, tentatively called *The American Monument* and eventually published in 1976, loomed large on the horizon, and Leslie's talk of butterfly wings led me to think that we should try a book on uncoated paper.

Printing paper in the past was beautiful stuff, made out of cloth fibers and sized with delicate coatings of vegetable or animal glue. With the rise of the steam-driven presses of the nineteenth century this old paper, made by hand, gave way to mass-produced sheets, manufactured in continuous rolls and later cut down into absolutely regular sheets to be used in the printing press. The new paper was made from wood rather than cloth, and it was smooth and consistent—by that measure far better than the older handmade papers. Even so, it presented problems in the printing of illustrated books. When text is printed the area covered by ink is relatively small, and moderate pressure will make a good impression. But an illustration, printed by any ink process, requires that a large area of the printing plate be impressed onto the paper; and if the paper is not absolutely smooth, the pressure must be high to generate a smooth print. Meanwhile, however, the speed of the presses increased, requiring that the printing pressure be light. This contradiction was addressed by sheathing the papers in a smooth, thin clay coating, giving them a still more even surface than they already had. Coated paper became the standard for printed illustrations—but while it supported pictures beautifully, this paper was awful in terms of permanence. The wood pulp from which the paper was made was acidic and soon became brittle, and the clay coatings usually contained chemical additives, which behaved unpredictably as they aged. Late nineteenth- and early twentieth-century papers worked well when they were printed, but left a legacy of crumbling books that still plague librarians, the keepers of our printed history.

Offset printing is based upon the principle of placing an intermediary between plate and paper. The process is rotary by nature, and this intermediary is a new, third cylinder (the old presses had two cylinders—one for the plate, another for the paper) holding a rubber-coated cloth blanket. The image ink goes from plate to blanket and then from blanket to paper. One of the miracles of offset printing is that this blanket, having a more flexible surface than the metal plate, can print beautifully on rough surfaces. Offset buried letterpress, and part of the reason was that it allowed the use of a new breed of uncoated paper called offset stock, which could be cheaply produced yet took printing more smoothly than letterpress. Leslie had published books of prose and poems on offset stock, and we had made *Lay This Laurel* on it. The paper surface, and the matte ink used, reminded him of rotogravure, and between the three of us (Leslie, Lee, and me) we decided to produce the huge *American Monument* book on this new paper. There were, by that time, fine coated papers that printed beautifully and were also relatively permanent, but the allure of a new style of printing was irresistible.

By the time we did *The American Monument* I had finally understood the five discrete problems that cropped up in halftone printing. It seemed to me that this new book, to be done on offset stock, required some special technique, so I adapted the old printer's trick of printing the same plate twice to make the reproductions. The two impressions cannot both be with black ink, because that would produce an extremely heavy result, but if the first pass is black and the second gray, a strong but quite beautiful result can occur. Of the five problems we face in printing, two are immediately solved: both the density of the black and the weak light values are strengthened. The other three difficulties, however, persist or may even get worse.

It seemed to me that these three remaining difficulties could be avoided by changing the tonal scale of the halftone film. For *The American Monument* I did this in two ways. First, I heavily exposed each halftone negative, developing it so that the shadow values were exaggerated (that is, made more dense in the negative). This took care of problem 2 (the loss of detail in the shadows), producing a negative that recorded the shadows in the right way—but on the other hand one that left the highlights of the image too thin on the negative, so they would print too dark. I then made a second negative of the picture (rotating the screen 30 degrees to avoid a moiré pattern). This second negative was just lightly exposed and overdeveloped, so that it only recorded the lightest values in the picture. When the time came to expose the printing plate, I taped the second negative on top of the first. Acting as a mask, this second negative worked to block the exposing light from about three-fourths of the highlight dots in the main negative. This had the effect of greatly brightening the lightest values in the print, providing a solution to problem 5 (the flatness of the white values in the reproduction).

There is an extremely interesting point here. The cumulative effect of the steps in offset printing—film, plate, blanket, and paper—dictates that there is a minimum size of highlight dot that can be held on press. If the tone becomes lighter, so that the dot size is smaller than this minimum, the dots start to break up randomly and values in the reproduction become rough. This limit in the fineness of the dot is the same for all screens: a 150-line screen produces the same-size highlight dot, under ideal conditions, as a 300-line screen. Yet the halftone with 300 dots per inch contains four times as many dots in any given area as the coarser one (four times as many because we are talking about area, not just the linear measure by which we designate screen rulings). This means that the brightest image we can practically produce with the finer screen is inherently darker than that which can be produced by the coarser one. Our wonderful 300-line screen, its dots so closely spaced that we cannot see them with the unaided eye, thus produces an inherently darker image in the lightest parts of any reproduction. The net result is that most fine-screen work is tonally inferior to that with a coarser screen, even as its resolution is higher. The nice effect of the mask used to print *The American Monument* was that in blocking out a lot of highlight dots, it effectively eliminated this problem inherent to the fine screen. The whites became light and lively, not because the dots were finer but because the dot count had been reduced.

Lee, Leslie, and I had an entertaining moment in the preliminary work for *The American Monument* when we proofed some sample plates at Meriden. The notion of using uncoated offset stock in a photographic book was then so radical that we decided to do a press proof on the more traditional coated stock as well—and the reproductions on the coated paper turned out to be far superior to those on the uncoated paper. They were clearer, held more detail, and simply looked better when set beside the prints on the offset stock. This put us in a quandary, since the whole goal was to translate Lee's pictures into matte-surface reproductions. Leslie's butterfly wing was hovering in the back of our minds, though, and when we separated the two sheets—rather than comparing them to each other—we saw that on the coated sheet the matte blackness we wanted had simply flown away, while remaining there on the uncoated. We decided to print on the uncoated sheet and simply forget what the coated one looked like. I learned a great lesson here: when evaluating press sheets, the worst thing to do is to compare one to another. Each must be viewed as a thing in itself, and a judgment made by the impressions it leaves in the mind rather than those on the paper. I think this lesson applies to many more things than pictures in ink.

The next book we worked on together was the blue book—*Lee Friedlander: Photographs* (1978). It was published by Haywire Press, Lee's private imprint, and he had arranged a prepurchase of a number of copies to finance the project. We decided to make a duotone book on coated paper, like *Self Portrait*, but with a better tonal scale. I had a new notion of how to achieve this, which Lee was willing to try. By this time I had realized that the scale of each halftone used in a duotone had to be carefully thought out and precisely rendered. As in *The American Monument*, I wanted to heavily expose the black negative and to underexpose the gray negative. This had a series of beneficial effects: the highlight dot in the black negative could be dropped out, so the only dot present in the lightest tones was printed with gray ink, thus solving the difficulty of the fine screen and its flat highlights. The light grays—those between the middle tone and the lightest values—could come in at the right place through a careful adjustment of the weight of the gray ink layer. The excellent shadow detail present in the black negative remained visible even after being overprinted by a heavy layer of the gray ink, since the transparency of this ink allowed the dark values to show through.

This kind of duotone could be made with either a slight difference or an extreme difference between the black and the gray negatives. For the blue book I chose an extreme difference. The gray negative was very underexposed. The halftone dot existed in it from the mid-tones on up, but for every value below 50 percent, the negative was clear. The result was that it printed a solid of gray over all tonal values darker than the mid-tones. This solid layer sat beneath the tones of the pictures, and it was a true gray—smooth and featureless, but articulated by the black negative, which carried the dark information in the picture. (I say it sat "beneath" the image, but this was the visual impression, not the actual location of the gray layer. A primary lesson of printing is that the dark values must be laid down first, since ink transfers best when it goes down on bare paper, rather than on a sheet already printed. If black is overprinted on gray, it tends to be weak. When gray is over-printed on black, though, the black dominates, and appears on top to the eye.)

The blue-book plates were very satisfying, if difficult to run on press. The solid layer needed to be laid down precisely—if too heavy, the print shifted easily to darkness, if too light, it went the other way. But the book was plated by Frank Poll and Bob Dewey, and printed by Willie Vincenti, and they were so good that it turned out very well. There was a great lesson for me in the blue book: the radical difference between the black and the gray negatives opened the door to a clearer understanding of what multiple impressions could accomplish. I need to diverge a bit to explain this.

Because the black negative was so bright—overexposed, and weak in the light values, but still strong on the blackest areas of the print—it began to act as a skeleton upon which the lighter values of the print were hung. As we printed, it became obvious that a change in the weight of the black ink layer could change the shadow areas of the reproduction without affecting the lighter values; in like manner, a shift in the weight of the gray layer could alter the light values without substantially affecting the shadows. If the gray was run heavier the print immediately became dark, but the shadow detail did not disappear—it remained visible despite the gray overprinting. If Lee asked for a bit more in the highlights, we could adjust the gray, and the light values would come down, but the shadow detail remained. Before this we had been stuck with reproductions that behaved like a darkroom print; more exposure made the whole thing darker, less exposure, lighter. Now, on press, we could dicker with different parts of the tonal scale independently. Furthermore, the gray layer, being so heavy in the light values, set the color for the print. If the gray ink was warm in tone, the printed picture shifted that way; if cool, then that was the appearance the picture took. In either case the shadows, dominated by the black negative, remained neutral. The reproductions took on a two-color look, and were capable of emulating the behavior of a gelatin-silver print (which, except for those on the fastest bromide papers, is almost always a different color in the light values and in the shadows). The duotone became an astonishing tool on press, opening up terrific new possibilities. We still couldn't make absolutely accurate reproductions, but the new control of tone let us do things on press that we couldn't achieve in the darkroom. The book plates became a thing in themselves, rather than simply echoes of Lee's originals.

The next book was a crazy one. *Flowers and Trees* came about because Lee, as usual, had a complete book hovering in the wings, and I was so excited by the blue book that I wanted to take the duotone another step and turn it into a three-negative process. We decided to do the book in three impressions, and to print it on uncoated paper again. The notion also came up that if we spiral-bound it (I think this was Lee's idea) the presswork could be more efficient. In a normal book in which we want every picture on the right side of a spread to be faced by a blank page on the left, we must print both sides of the sheet, putting half the pictures and half the blanks in a careful arrangement on one side and the rest on the other. Then the sheet is folded and cut, and ends up in the arrangement of pages we want. By spiral-binding the book, though, we could print pictures on every page area on one side of the sheet, leave the back blank, cut the printed sheets up afterwards, hand-collate them into the right order, and assemble them on a spiral binding. The cost of printing was cut in half. At the same time, we were trying a three-impression book, which increased the cost by half again. We obviously weren't in it for the money.

Flowers and Trees, made in 1981, was a tough book to do, since I hadn't thoroughly thought out the tritone (as it later became named). We used a heavy paper stock, and it was extremely hard to superimpose the three impressions exactly—out-of-register sheets are scattered throughout the edition. In many cases the plates are weak in the shadows yet terrific in the highlights, reflecting my imperfect negatives. But the tritone turned out to be a great tool. Looking at *Flowers and Trees* now, I love it. It is a nutty book, not only in the marvelous freshness with which Lee sticks his camera into bushes and plants but also in the eccentric yet complex grayness of the printing.

Our next project was *Factory Valleys* (1982). Commissioned to photograph in the industrial states of the Midwest, Lee had taken pictures of the towns and people who worked and lived there. We decided to produce another book on uncoated paper, but I was given the task of figuring out a halftone system that was relatively cheap (duotone, not tritone, to save money on the presswork) but that achieved a clear reproduction, holding all detail in the photograph— and this on the soft, beautiful surface of uncoated paper. After much experiment we did print the book as a duotone, but the gray printing plate was exposed to a sandwich of two negatives instead of one. A flat negative that would have made a very gray reproduction in the highlights was taped together with a highlight mask (like the one used on *American Monument*), and this composite was used to expose the gray printer. The black printer was a single negative, but, as before, it was very heavily exposed to produce great openness in the shadows. This odd combination produced a very beautiful reproduction, which held all the detail in spite of the tendency of the soft paper surface to muddy the printing.

Factory Valleys was published by Callaway Editions, a small publishing company run by Nicholas Callaway, who had long been obsessed with fine printing. Nicholas had hired Christopher Green to oversee the printing of the book. For all Lee's books in the past, he and I had stayed on press for the hours of makeready needed before the ink is balanced, the plates are registered, and the sheet looks good, and then to approve every sheet and look in on the run as it progressed. Christopher Green hadn't done much work on press before but he immediately understood just how the printing should be done and he was able to push the pressmen to get the precise ink levels required after Lee and I had left the press. Not only did we have his good judgment at work, we were also printing on a superb lot of Mohawk Superfine Eggshell paper. This matte-surface sheet held ink beautifully, and the batch that Meriden Gravure received for the book was absolutely terrific. The pictures, film, plating, paper, and presswork all combined to make *Factory Valleys* the most beautiful duotone book I have ever worked on. *Lee Friedlander: Portraits* was produced in 1985 using the same technology as *Factory Valleys*, but was not as good, and the differences came from a subtle change in the paper, the lack of

Green beating up the pressmen, and perhaps slight differences in the negatives. I tried to do the two books exactly the same way, but it just didn't work out.

After *Factory Valleys* and the portrait book, everything changed. All of the earlier books had varied in their techniques and details— duotone, tritone, coated, uncoated, big, small, spiral-bound, hardbound. The books that followed tended to be tritone books on coated paper. This was true of all the projects Lee brought to me until the advent of computer-generated halftones in the mid-'90s. The tritone process we used was one I developed for the series of books on Atget produced for the Museum of Modern Art in the early '80s. Those books, four volumes produced in four successive years, were produced using knowledge I had accumulated working with Bry and O'Keeffe on the task of reproducing the photographs of Stieglitz.

It is important to note here that all through this period I was being educated, and pushed, by a group of unconnected people who were all convinced of the importance of fine printing in the establishment of photography as the central art form of our time. Books were the obvious means through which photographs were to be widely seen, and to the minds of these people, no sin was greater than making a book that didn't at least try to render the beauty of a fine photographic print in ink. Doris Bry was pushing me in work on Stieglitz, John Szarkowski was just as driven for Atget, Leslie Katz kept dreaming of the perfect book on soft paper, and Lee and I kept trying to regurgitate this knowledge into his books.

The tritone consisted of three plated negatives, printed in succession on the sheet. The first down was done with black ink, the second with a dark gray, and the third with a light gray. By properly balancing the negatives and the ink colors, a superb reproduction could be made. All five of the problems of the halftone could be overcome. Shadow strength could be superb because three ink layers were used. Shadow detail was held because the black printer could be almost skeletal yet could maintain great detail in the darker areas. The jump in tone at the mid-tone break, inherent to the halftone pattern, was reduced because it occurred in different tonal locations in each negative. Highlight detail was preserved because the light-gray ink could be run quite heavily without affecting shadow detail. Bright white values were possible because the lightest parts of the picture could be dropped out in the black and dark-gray printers and preserved in the light-gray printer, where a fine dot could hold the picture edge yet be extremely light in tone.

The tritone had two other extraordinary benefits. The first was that the light-gray printer could be made in such a way that it put down a solid layer of ink covering all tonalities of the picture except the lighter ones. (This was an extension of the design of the gray printer used in *Lee Friedlander: Photographs*.) This uninterrupted film of ink acted as a tonal platform underlying most of the picture, and because it was solid, it had terrific smoothness. Any halftone dot pattern tends to produce some roughness, but this solid layer, with no dots present, was smooth, heavy, and luscious to look at. An uninterrupted gray sheet, often with quite a lot of color in the ink, it was true tone, identical with the tone in photographic prints. Even though this ink layer was of only one value (below the point at which halftone dots began to appear and modulate the lighter tones), its smoothness gave a photographic "look" to the reproductions that was terrific.

The second benefit of the tritone is harder to describe, and I must diverge a bit to explain it. The short version is that the tritone allowed all the work done in the negatives and presswork to be somewhat sloppy, yet to be correctable at the end. Here's what I mean by that.

Anyone who makes physical objects knows that they never turn out exactly as envisioned. This is true of all art, but also of all types of manufacturing. No matter how clear the maker's preconception, or how precise the design used, the thing finally produced is never exactly predictable in all its details. In art this indefiniteness is creative; the artist gradually surrenders his or her vision to the thing being made, and the divergence between initial idea and final product is a place of possibility. For the industrial manufacturer, on the other hand, the discrepancy between plan and execution is a tremendous problem. Historically the problem was met by hand-fitting all parts of any complex construction to each other. A great step was taken in the nineteenth century, when the invention of interchangeable parts produced a different solution. Design parameters were established that assumed that no part in any complex device would be made directly to fit the other pieces to which it was connected. Instead the idea of "tolerance" was devised: parts were made to fit a design within such-and-such a tolerance. For a machined part this tolerance might be described as plus or minus so many thousandths of an inch. The finished device was built up of pieces that were never fitted to each other in advance but were designed to function without that precision. Virtually all modern manufacturing is based upon the idea that parts must fit an external design, often in the form of a blueprint, rather than fit perfectly into the complex entity that they go to make up. We can go so far as to say that modern manufacturing is based upon the principle of no manufactured parts ever having to fit each other "properly." I have always suspected that the legendary "lemon"—the device that never works as planned—comes about when many of the tolerances in its manufacture, by chance, happen to fall on the same side of the measure.

For the artist this notion of pieces that don't really fit is anathema. When we make a picture we demand, above all, that every part is perfectly related to every other, and executed so that it fits. In printing a book, however, we are manufacturing something, using industrial systems and spending a great deal of someone's money. This reality has led to a great conservatism in the printing trades. A reproduction tends to be gray, because this almost guarantees that all the picture's detail will be visible. If a beautiful white sky is part of a picture, it too usually turns out gray in the reproduction, since this creates a clear rectangular edge, saving the printer from being faulted for "dropping out" that part of the picture.

Before the invention of the computer, the exposure and development of halftone negatives was a haphazard affair. No matter how hard the photographer tried to control things—exposure times, developer temperature, developer agitation—no halftone negative ever turned out exactly as planned. Because I was an artist, and one who made objects in many different materials, this came as no surprise. It was also clear to me that the conceptual notion of the blueprint could not be applied to the printing negatives (or plating or presswork) of book manufacture. Another solution had to be developed.

On press, Lee and I (and the other friends with whom I worked) always had to instruct the pressman in the final adjustments that had to be made before the run started. After a few years of this I realized that the system we were evolving was designed so that no step of the reproduction needed to be done in a precisely correct manner until the very last one. I invented the tritone to make this possible. The negatives we were printing with were not exactly correct, and we weren't carrying out our job according to some notion of tolerances, but we were building up pictures on the press in a succession of stages, each of which could be corrected by the one that followed. If the black in the first impression wasn't adequate, for example, we could run the dark-gray second impression a bit heavier for that picture and correct it; if the lightest values in the reproduction were weak, on the final, light-gray impression we could correct the top end only, without needing a heavier ink film that would darken the rest of the picture. The tritone perfectly suited the notion that each discrete element of the production could be sloppily done, and the only steps that had to be done exactly correctly happened at the end. This ending was the moment on press, when final adjustments could be made to drag all the earlier errors back into some relation that produced a good print.

The first tritones I made, some in research mode, some in early books such as *Flowers and Trees*, were printed on single-color presses. If an ink layer is printed and then dried before the next impression is put down, the printer can build up a very different image than can be done if the printing is "wet-on-wet," in a multicolor press. Lee and I had produced all his early books on single-color presses, using duotones and tritones printed "dry trap," as the printers used to call it. When I finally figured out the tritone in a dependable form, after *Flowers and Trees*, and after MoMA's Atget books, Lee and I decided to print on a multicolor press, designed for color printing, and to give up the old practice of dry-trap printing. All the books that followed—*Cray at Chippewa Falls* (1987), *Like a One-Eyed Cat* (1989), *Nudes* (1991)—were done on four- or five-color presses.

Printing multi-impression reproductions—duotones, tritones, or four-color process—on the older single-color presses was a terrifying procedure. There was never enough money around to press-proof an entire book, so we would often choose six or eight pictures and do a proof of them before making the final halftone negatives. When the day came to print the book, the black plate, usually the first one printed, was run up and made ready, and then we had to print the entire run for that form without knowing what the finished reproductions would look like with the next color printed on top. In the early books with Lee the black printer was often quite radical in its tonality, and the single black impression didn't look at all like the finished plate. I remember many times when Lee would look at the sheet, which bore no resemblance to his pictures, and take my word for it that everything would be alright the next day, once the gray impression was put on top. If things were incorrect then, all the paper for the run of that form, and all the labor on press, would have to be discarded. Close friendships can be built while doing multipass printing on single-color presses.

We printed the later tritone books on multicolor presses at Franklin Graphics, a superb printing company in Providence, Rhode Island. They had two large Heidelberg color presses, of four and five colors each. Lee and I had a great time experiencing the pleasures of these large presses. The machines had been built to print successively the four layers of ink necessary for color reproductions, but we were putting various shades of gray ink into the printing units instead. The tritone required only three cylinders—for black, dark gray, and light gray—and we jumped on the possibilities of the fourth unit, which idled unused. Right at the start we put varnish into that unit—the last one printed—and a plate that put down a solid layer on the picture area only (not on the surrounding margins). The tritone with varnish made the best reproductions we had ever seen, and Lee and I actually got to the stage where we expected our books to be beautiful, instead of living in blind terror that they would be disasters.

I did, however, manage to have one disaster still coming up, and that was *The Jazz People of New Orleans* (1992), the first book of Lee's I produced using digitally derived film. When we printed *Cray at Chippewa Falls* at Franklin Graphics there was a new department in the company, deeply sapping its financial assets, that used computers to produce film for color reproductions. My hand-developed negatives would obviously become obsolete if the digital monster, hovering in its temperature-controlled room behind glass doors, ever got its act together. And in fact the story of my involvement with Lee's books draws to a close with the development of computer technologies.

The general run of printing throughout the world took a great step upward, though, when digital tools were refined, and the computer was irresistible to me. I managed to purchase a large, and already old, Crossfield scanner and started to use it to produce my own photographs, which I was then making with acrylic paint. An odd combination of digital and analog, the scanner produced halftone film with analog screens, using a laser driven by digital data as an exposure source. I was an unabashed—and stupid—advocate of the computer, and decided to do Lee's next book with the Crossfield. The film that resulted was simply terrible, and to make matters worse, it was printed overseas. My friend and partner Thomas Palmer supervised the job, and he and Lee suffered mightily on press; it is a testimony to their friendship that our relationship survived this book. I did one other book—equally a disaster—with the Crossfield, then put it in a dumpster, where it belonged in the first place.

I made no more books for Lee after *Jazz People*. My name appears in the back of some, credited with the halftones, but the introduction of the computer allowed me to have some degree of involvement while someone else actually did the work. It is a terrible by-product of old age and success that we often get credit for work done by others, and can never quite set the record straight and give credit where credit is due. In any case I had given up the life of the artist/printer and was becoming increasingly involved in my work in the School of Art at Yale University. By the mid-'90s I had given up printing altogether, and the grand run of books by Friedlander after that were done almost entirely by Thomas, who had set up his own shop in Newport. The computer, and its data and film-generating peripherals, gradually became refined and dependable, and hand-developed halftone film disappeared from the world. I can't speak in detail about the books that followed, but would like to wrap up this essay by describing the manner in which Lee's books have been made using the new technologies. To this day, Lee's approach is not quite like anyone else's, and the originality and freshness of his books run counter to the glossy and brilliant printing that makes so many contemporary books boring to look at.

Before the computer, a reproduction was made by photographing the original through a halftone screen, and then exposing the resulting screened negative to a printing plate. The plate was placed on the press cylinder, inked up, and printed on the paper. The halftone negative had to be the exact size of the reproduction, since the exposure to the plate was made with film and plate in contact with each other (as opposed to exposing with an enlarger). A tremendous number of variables attended this process, and the final dots printed on the press had only a rough relationship to the ideal ones that might have been planned for the reproduction. Making the film was complex, but the printer also faced terrific difficulties with the plating procedure. The opaque dots in the negative, sharp and clear when viewed with a magnifying glass, were actually soft and indistinct at their edges. When the plates were exposed, a slight variation in the exposure time could result in a large difference in the printed image.

The biggest single change wrought by digital technology in printing was the gradual elimination of this host of variables. We think of the computer as revolutionary because of the freedom it gives its user in manipulating the *content* of pictures. Noses can be straightened, warts removed, dark shadows opened up, and all sorts of other manipulations carried out. These new possibilities are undeniable, but far more significant is the ability of digital tools to do the same job we have always been engaged in but to do it better. Digital tools allowed the overall quality of picture printing to improve immensely, and they did this by introducing a system that gave printers greatly extended control over the variables that exist in every stage of the process.

When Lee does a book today he begins by creating a set of prints specifically for reproduction. This has always been his practice, but many books made by others use a widely varying group of originals— some old, some new, some big, some small, some analog, some digital. Lee hands Thomas Palmer this set of consistent prints, and Thomas then scans them using a digital scanning back mounted on a 4-by-5-inch camera. The camera lens introduces some variation, because the overall brightness of the different pictures varies from one to another, producing different degrees of camera flare. After scanning, then, Thomas tunes the digital files so that the shadow, mid-tone, and highlight values are consistent, and he saves this set of master gray-scale files to be used as the basis of the reproductions.

This set of master files has a consistency that never existed in any stage of the reproduction process in the years before the introduction of the computer. Film-based halftone negatives, even made with the highest degree of care, varied one from the other, and, once made, they were not changeable. The old errors—a bit of added density here, a slightly underdeveloped highlight there—would magnify themselves as each step of the printing process was advanced. The computer's master file, made to exacting standards, has none of these hidden problems; what's more, if it does, they can be corrected later on.

The master file is next passed through a tone-adjusting curve—something we can think of as a filter, which alters the tonal steps in the file—and each adjusted file is renamed as a new copy. If Thomas is making a duotone, the master file is adjusted twice, and renamed to produce two different gray-scale files. One becomes the black printer and the other the gray. As recently as two years ago these files would have been used to produce film negatives, using an expensive device called a film recorder. Such negatives possessed a hard-edged dot, which could be plated with terrific consistency. Today the files are instead assembled into a large master file (representing the full press sheet, which might have as many as eight pages of the finished book to a side), and this large file is exposed to a printing plate directly, without the intermediate film step. The variations in the old film/plate system are eliminated, and the printer has the added ability to tune the exposure of the plate with preset controls, adjusting for paper and press conditions within the shop.

This new system has revolutionized printing, and Lee has jumped onto the bandwagon with great delight. The old tritone, which allowed us to control the variables by a sequence of adjustments culminating with the third impression on press, has disappeared, because the new digital duotone is better. Lee has shifted the process of his bookmaking to this simpler and cheaper method, and has used the savings to direct the printing of his books to presses here in the United States, rather than overseas, where lower labor costs have pushed virtually all publishers.

Lee has also bucked the trend toward coated paper, producing two great books within the last couple of years that use the multicolor press to print beautifully on a soft uncoated sheet. One huge downside of the computer revolution has been to establish coated paper as the norm for illustrated books. I clearly remember the day when Lee, Leslie Katz, and I grappled with the task of comparing reproductions on coated and uncoated paper: the coated sheet was superior by any rational standard, yet we all felt that the uncoated paper was the right choice. The printing industry, book designers, and publishers have all faced this choice in one way or another, and almost without exception they have made the easy choice of printing on coated paper.

Stems, Lee's wild book of still-life photographs from 2003, was printed in two passes on an old two-color press, and it looks like no other book made today. He followed this with some small and intensely printed duotone books on coated paper, and then came along with his newest creation, *Sticks & Stones* (2004), done as a duotone book, with varnish mixed into the second color (a necessity because of the two-color press), and printed on a matte semicoated paper.

This last book is really Friedlander's greatest work to date. The pictures record his inquisitive mind and eye cramming themselves into every corner of the American architectural landscape. They are extraordinary, and make us wonder why all the other photographers are so boring. The printing, done with great skill by Meridian Printing, Rhode Island, from Thomas's remarkable files, gives us a tonal landscape to revel in that perfectly matches the wild and personal one of the photographer's mind and eye. No one has ever so perfectly understood—and executed—such a complex visual treat, and done it all in the ancient and changeable realm of printing as it is being recast as a digital practice.

---

1.   It is impossible to discuss the printing techniques of Lee's books without making it sound as though I was inventing fine offset printing as the books came along. It is important to understand that during the '60s and '70s many people were working on the challenges of reproducing photographs, and many of them were achieving innovative fine printing. Sidney Rapoport, in New York, had invented a system of duotone printing that was capable of terrific results. Dave Gardner, in San Francisco, and Bob Savinni, at electronically produced halftones came along. I was just one of many working on the tremendously difficult task of replicating silver in ink, and the reader must realize that the history I recount is of necessity a one-sided one.

I met Richard "Chip" Benson for the first time in the fall of 1998, soon after I became director of the Yale University Art Gallery (YUAG). As dean of the Yale School of Art, he secured an academic position for me as an adjunct professor in photography at Yale, one I gratefully accepted. Chip thus greeted me warmly, and knowing that one of my major charges was to oversee a full renovation of the gallery's historic buildings, took me on a tour of the former, long-vacant Jewish Community Center on Chapel Street that Yale had purchased. He was already hard at work planning its renovation and expansion in collaboration with Deborah Berke, then an adjunct professor of architecture (and as of this writing, the Yale School of Architecture's first woman dean). That day, I grasped right away that my new colleague wanted to be helpful and that we were going to become fast friends.

A week later I invited Chip to visit me in the print room of the YUAG to survey its photographic holdings. He showed up with a photograph of his own making, placed it on the viewing table, and began vigorously rubbing the surface of the print with his hand. He then proclaimed provocatively: "I believe in wearing images out." I soon discerned that what he really meant was that he wanted his students to come and view the YUAG collection as often as possible, much in the way he constantly shared his personal library and his own collection of photography, cameras, and printing ephemera with them at the drop of a hat.

As the greatest printer of photographic books in the world, Chip also wanted students in each MFA photography class to learn how to organize, edit, and print a book of their work together at the end of their program. This endeavor enabled them to go on press and learn how to get the best printing results possible for their collective work as a cohort. He also invited every class to his home in Newport, where his beloved wife Barbara hosted them for a lobster fest. Students also saw how the Benson family lived and how Chip spent considerable time in his machine shop making steam engines, clocks, and telescopes. He was a self-described "gear head" in addition to being a remarkable photographer.

Chip also constantly advanced his knowledge of photographic processes. When he felt that the early cascade of digital photography was not meeting his high standards for visual acuity, he chose to actively and fervently explore computer software, scanners, and digital printing equipment. He did so until he was finally able to present digital prints of his making that were indiscernible from the masterly platinum prints in the special, limited edition of his first book *Lay This Laurel*, published in 1973 with the Eakins Press Foundation. And as Chip advanced his own knowledge of the rapidly expanding digital landscape, he also founded, staffed, and equipped the Digital Media Center for the Arts at Yale. Both undergraduate and graduate students were given twenty-four-hour card access to take classes and produce creative work there. Chip accomplished this and much more with the strong intellectual and financial support of Yale alumnus Allan Chasanoff, with whom Chip and I became close friends overtime. When *The Printed Picture*, another landmark book of Chip's, was published in 2008, the world was essentially offered a full view of how and what Chip taught at Yale. Published by Peter Galassi for MoMA, the book fully documented a major exhibition Chip presented in the museum's photography department galleries. Each Tuesday when MoMA was closed, Chip gave guided tours of his exhibition; these sessions were videotaped, thanks to Chasanoff's generous support. As a result, the inimitable lessons Chip once offered at Yale are now freely available on both MoMA's and YUAG's websites.

Readers wishing to gain a fuller grasp of Richard Benson's remarkable legacy can visit a seminar room named for him in Yale's Wurtele Study Center. It contains a full complement of all the major books Chip published; more than six hundred of his photographs and others he printed for the likes of Walker Evans, Paul Strand, and James Van Der Zee; and a large trove of his ephemera. Visitors can also freely access many important video interviews featuring Benson and Chasanoff.

Michele Abeles has held solo exhibitions and presentations at the Whitney Museum of American Art, New York; Karpidas Collection, Dallas; Sadie Coles HQ, London; and 47 Canal, New York. Her work was included in the Museum of Modern Art's 2012 *New Photography* series.

Marion Belanger is a Guggenheim Fellowship recipient and honoree for the 2017 Shpilman International Prize for Excellence in Photography. Her work has been published in the books *Everglades: Outside and Within* (2009) and *Rift/Fault* (2016). Belanger teaches at the Hartford Art School and Wesleyan University, both in Connecticut.

Barbara Benson is a music teacher who taught privately as well as within the Connecticut public school system. She was a partner and collaborator with Richard Benson; they were married for fifty-one years.

Dawoud Bey's numerous honors include a MacArthur Fellowship, Guggenheim Fellowship, and National Endowment for the Arts Fellowships. A major career retrospective of his work, *An American Project*, was co-organized by the Whitney Museum of American Art and the San Francisco Museum of Modern Art (2020–22). Bey is professor of art and a former Distinguished College Artist at Columbia College Chicago. His books include *Class Pictures* (Aperture, 2007), *Seeing Deeply* (2018), and *Street Portraits* (2021).

Andrew Borowiec has received a Guggenheim Fellowship, National Endowment for the Arts Fellowship, Ohio Arts Council Fellowship, and Cleveland Arts Prize. He is the author of *Along the Ohio* (2000), *Cleveland: The Flats, the Mill, and the Hills* (2008), and *Wheeling, West Virginia* (2018), among others. He taught photography for three decades at the University of Akron and was named a Distinguished Professor of Art in 2009.

Lois Conner is recipient of a Guggenheim Fellowship, New York State Council on the Arts Fellowship, and National Endowment for the Arts Fellowship. Publications of her work include *China* (2000), *Beijing: Contemporary and Imperial* (2014), and *Lotus Leaves* (2018). Conner has held teaching positions at Yale School of Art, Princeton University, and Sarah Lawrence College.

Matthew Connors's first book, *Fire in Cairo* (2015), was awarded the 2016 International Center of Photography Infinity Award for Artist's Book. Since 2004, he has been a professor in the photography department at the Massachusetts College of Art and Design in Boston.

Tim Davis has published several monographs of his work, including *My Life in Politics* (Aperture, 2006), *The New Antiquity* (2010), and *I'm Looking Through You* (Aperture, 2021). He is recipient of a Joseph H. Hazen Rome Prize and Leopold Godowsky Jr. Color Photography Award and a longtime faculty member at Bard College, Annandale-on-Hudson, New York.

Benjamin Donaldson is recipient of the Hungarian Multicultural Center residency and a Connecticut state arts grant. Donaldson is a senior critic at Yale School of Art, previously serving on the faculty of the School of Visual Arts, International Center of Photography, and Hunter College, New York.

Dru Donovan is recipient of a John Gutmann Photography Fellowship and Guggenheim Fellowship. In addition to *Lifting Water* (2011), part of a monographic publication series, her work has been featured in *Aperture*, *Blind Spot*, and *Picture Magazine*. She is an assistant professor of art at Lewis & Clark College in Portland, Oregon.

Martina Droth is deputy director and chief curator of the Yale Center for British Art, and chair of the Association of Research Institutes in Art History. She is the curator of the exhibition *Bill Brandt | Henry Moore* (2020) and coeditor with Paul Messier of the accompanying book.

Shannon Ebner is an artist who lives and works in Brooklyn. She has held solo exhibitions at the Institute of Contemporary Art, Miami, and MoMA PS1, New York, among others. Her publications include *The Sun as Error* (2009), *STRIKE* (2015), and *A Public Character* (2016). She is chairperson of photography at Pratt Institute.

Lucas Foglia has exhibited his work at institutions and festivals such as Place du Palais Royal, Paris; Museum of Contemporary Photography, Chicago; and Les Rencontres d'Arles, France. He has published four books of his work: *A Natural Order* (2012), *Frontcountry* (2014), *Human Nature* (2017), and *Summer After* (2021).

Peter Galassi is a scholar, curator, writer, and recipient of a Guggenheim Fellowship. He was chief curator of photography at the Museum of Modern Art, New York, from 1991 to 2011. During that time, he curated more than forty exhibitions, including *The Pleasures and Terrors of Domestic Pleasure* (1991), *Friedlander* (2005), and *Henri Cartier-Bresson: The Modern Century* (2010).

John Gambell is a graphic designer and the Yale University Printer. From 1977 to 1979, he worked on a range of photographic printing projects under the direction of Richard Benson, and later opened his own design studio. He has been teaching graphic design at the Yale School of Art since 1983 and was appointed senior critic in 1998.

Jon Goodman is a veteran printer of photogravure since 1976. In addition to his own work, he has produced prints and portfolios in photogravure of the works of Dorothea Lange, Edward Steichen, Alfred Stieglitz, Paul Strand, and others—reviving a medium not commonly used since the 1940s.

Bryan Graf has exhibited his work at Atlanta Contemporary; George Eastman Museum, Rochester, New York; and Institute of Contemporary Art, Portland, Maine. He is recipient of a Pollock-Krasner Foundation grant. His books include *Wildlife Analysis* (2013), *Moving Across the Interior* (2014), *Prismatic Tracks* (2014), and *Debris of the Days* (2017).

Gail Albert Halaban's work has featured in numerous group and single-person shows, including a solo exhibition at the George Eastman Museum in Rochester, New York. Her books include *Out My Window* (2012), *Paris Views* (Aperture, 2014) and *Italian Views* (Aperture, 2019). She teaches photography and visual thinking to students and physicians at Columbia University Irving Medical Center.

Gary Haller, an educator for over fifty years, is the Henry Prentiss Becton Professor Emeritus of Engineering and Applied Science at Yale University. He also holds joint appointments in the Departments of Chemical Engineering and Chemistry, as well as serving as director of the Henry Koerner Center for Emeritus Faculty at Yale University.

Heyward Hart founded and operates the photographic and prepress studio Technikal Support in South Pasadena, California. He received the Yale School of Art's Richard Benson Prize in 2011.

Robert J. Hennessey is a photographer and printer specializing in making separations for illustrated book reproduction. Some of the books he has worked on are *Roy DeCarava: A Retrospective* (1996), *Alfred Stieglitz: The Key Set* (2002), and *Diane Arbus: Revelations* (2003), among other titles featuring the work of artists such as Robert Adams, Nan Goldin, Emmet Gowin, Sally Mann, Richard Misrach, Paul Strand, and Garry Winogrand.

Peter Kayafas is director of the Eakins Press Foundation in New York. He is recipient of a Guggenheim Fellowship, and publications of his own photography include *The Merry Cemetery of Sapanta* (2007), *O Public Road! Photographs of America* (2009), and *The Way West* (2020). Since 2000, he has taught photography at Pratt Institute in Brooklyn.

Lisa Kereszi has published three monographs of her work: *Fantasies* (2008), *Fun and Games* (2009), and *Joe's Junk Yard* (2012). In addition to teaching at the Hartford Art School, she is senior critic in photography at Yale School of Art, where she also serves as director of undergraduate studies.

Justin Kimball is recipient of a Guggenheim Fellowship and Aaron Siskind Individual Photographer's Fellowship. His work has been published in the monographs *Where We Find Ourselves* (2006), *Pieces of String* (2012), and *Elegy* (2017). Kimball is the Conway Professor in New Media at Amherst College in Massachusetts.

David La Spina is a regular contributor to the *New York Times Magazine*. He cofounded the independent press Roman Nvmerals and works closely with artists to produce small-run publications.

John Lehr has exhibited his work at the Walker Art Center, Minneapolis; Carnegie Museum of Art, Pittsburgh; and Museum of Modern Art, New York. His first monograph, *The Island Position*, was published in 2019. Lehr is an associate professor of photography at Pratt Institute in Brooklyn.

Susan Lipper has published her work in the trilogy of books comprised of *Grapevine* (1994), *trip* (1999), and *Domesticated Land* (2018). She is recipient of a National Endowment for the Arts Fellowship, New York Foundation for the Arts Fellowship, and Guggenheim Fellowship.

Salvatore Lopes has exhibited his work at the Art Institute of Chicago, San Francisco Museum of Modern Art, and International Center of Photography. Over his long career as a platinum and silver printer, he has printed images by many photographers, including Ruth Bernhard, Robert Mapplethorpe, Mary Ellen Mark, Paul Strand, and Carrie Mae Weems.

Peter MacGill is a gallerist and art historian. A former director of Light Gallery, he cofounded Pace/MacGill Gallery, where he oversaw the photography program for thirty-seven years. In 2019, MacGill left the gallery to forge a partnership with Godfrey Dadich Partners to develop streaming content to tell the story of photography.

Tanya Marcuse is a Guggenheim Fellowship recipient. Her books include *Undergarments and Armor* (2005), *Wax Bodies* (2012), *Fruitless/Fallen/Woven* (2019), and *Ink* (2021). She teaches photography at Bard College, Annandale-on-Hudson, New York.

Lesley A. Martin is creative director of Aperture and cofounder of the Paris Photo–Aperture Foundation PhotoBook Awards. She has served as a visiting critic at Yale School of Art since 2016.

Miko McGinty has been designing art books since 1993. She founded and directs her own graphic design firm in Brooklyn as principal designer. McGinty has worked with a range of artists, museums, and publishers on publications and exhibitions, including the Art Institute of Chicago; Yale University Art Gallery; Asia Society, the Studio Museum, and Whitney Museum of American Art, New York. She is a lecturer at MIT, Cambridge, Massachusetts, where she teaches book design.

Sue Medlicott has overseen the production of countless publications of art and photography by artists, publishers, galleries, and museums for over three decades. In 2016, she cofounded the Production Department, a full-service print production team for art organizations, artists, and designers.

Sarah Meister is executive director of Aperture, following more than twenty-five years at the Museum of Modern Art, New York, where she curated numerous exhibitions, including *Fotoclubismo: Brazilian Modernist Photography, 1946–1964* (2021), *Dorothea Lange: Words & Pictures* (2020), and *Making Space: Women Artists and Postwar Abstraction* (cocurator, 2017).

Paul Messier is the Pritzker Director of the Lens Media Lab at Yale's Institute for the Preservation of Cultural Heritage. The LML is dedicated to the material history of photography with a current focus on black-and-white photography of the twentieth century. His Boston-based conservation practice serves institutions and collectors worldwide.

Andrea Modica is a Guggenheim Fellowship recipient and a Fulbright Scholar. Several monographs of her work have been published, including *Minor League* (1993), *Treadwell* (1996), *Lentini* (2019), *As We Wait* (2020), and *January 1* (2020). She teaches at Drexel University in Philadelphia.

Matthew Monteith is recipient of two Fulbright Research Fellowships, a Pollock-Krasner Foundation fellowship, and an Abigail Cohen Rome Prize in Photography. His work has been published in *Czech Eden* (Aperture, 2007) and many magazines, including *GQ*, the *New York Times Magazine*, *Interview*, *W*, and *Dwell*. He is department chair and associate professor of photography at the Massachusetts College of Art and Design in Boston.

Abelardo Morell has published several books of his work, including *A Camera in a Room* (1995), *A Book of Books* (2002), *Camera Obscura* (2004), *Abelardo Morell* (2005), *Tent-Camera* (2018), and *Flowers for Lisa* (2018). Morell is recipient of a Guggenheim Fellowship and the International Center of Photography Infinity Award in Art. He was professor at the Massachusetts College of Art and Design in Boston from 1983 to 2010 and also served as chair of the department for many years.

Arthur Ou has shown his work widely in group exhibitions in Los Angeles, New York, Chicago, London, Vancouver, Paris, Berlin, and Beijing. His writing has been published in the *New York Times*, *Aperture*, *Blind Spot*, *Art in America*, *Brooklyn Rail*, and *Camera Austria*. He is associate professor of photography in the School of Art, Media, and Technology at Parsons the New School for Design.

Thomas Palmer is a photographer, printer, and separator specializing in preparing color and black-and-white images for offset reproduction. He has worked on numerous publications by artists such as Ansel Adams, Robert Adams, Walker Evans, Lee Friedlander, Helen Levitt, and Paul Strand. From 2011 to 2015, Palmer served as a visiting critic in photography at Yale School of Art.

Tod Papageorge is recipient of two Guggenheim Fellowships and two National Endowment for the Arts Fellowships, and was shortlisted for the Deutsche Börse Photography Foundation Prize in 2009. In 1979, he founded the Department of Photography at Yale School of Art, where he served as the Walker Evans Professor of Photography and as director of graduate studies in photography until 2011. In addition to a collection of essays *Core Curriculum* (Aperture, 2011), he has published books of his photographic works, including *Passing Through Eden* (2007), *American Sports, 1970* (Aperture, 2009), and *Dr. Blankman's New York* (2018).

Ted Partin has exhibited his work in New York, Paris, Düsseldorf, and Tokyo. In 2010, he held his first solo museum exhibition, *Eyes Look Through You*, at the Kunstmuseen Krefeld/Museum Haus Esters in Krefeld, Germany. Partin is a lecturer in photography at Yale School of Art.

Bradley Peters was recipient of the Richard Benson Prize for excellence in photography in 2008. In addition to receiving frequent commissions and lecturing at schools such as Concordia University, University of Nebraska-Lincoln, and Yale University, he has had work appear in publications such as *Image Makers, Image Takers* (2007).

John Pilson has exhibited his photo and video work at Hamburger Kunsthalle, Germany; the Venice Biennale; Guggenheim Museum, Museum of Modern Art, and MoMA PS1, New York. He is the author of the monograph *Interregna* (2006) and founder of *Picture Magazine*. In addition to having taught at Bard College, Annandale-on-Hudson, New York, Pilson has served on the faculty of Yale School of Art since 2001 and is currently senior critic in photography.

Kristine Potter published her first monograph *Manifest* and received a Guggenheim Fellowship, both in 2018. In 2019, she was named recipient of the Grand Prix Image Vevey for 2019 and 2020. Potter is an assistant professor of photography at Middle Tennessee State University in Murfreesboro.

Caitlin Teal Price has exhibited widely, including at Fotografiska, Stockholm; Bernarducci Meisel Gallery, New York; and National Portrait Gallery, Washington, DC. Her images have appeared in periodicals such as the *New Yorker*, the *New York Times*, and *TIME*, and her first monograph *Stranger Lives* was published in 2016.

Sergio Purtell taught photography until the mid-1980s before starting his New York–based studio Black and White on White, specializing in printing works by photographers such as LaToya Ruby Frazier, Wendy Ewald, Ralph Gibson, Gauri Gill, Deana Lawson, An-My Lê, and Tod Papageorge. The first book of his own work, *Love's Labour*, was published in 2020.

Jock Reynolds was Henry J. Heinz II Director of the Yale University Art Gallery from 1998 to 2018. He also previously served as executive director of the Washington Project for the Arts and director of the Addison Gallery of American Art. As an artist, he frequently collaborates with his wife Suzanne Hellmuth. He is recipient of two National Endowment for the Arts Visual Artists Fellowships, a Fulbright fellowship, and multiple National Endowment for the Arts awards.

John Robinson is the founder of GHP Media, a printing press, mailing, and fulfillment company based in West Haven, Connecticut. In addition to running the commercial printing company, he has worked with artists such as Jim Goldberg, Helen Levitt, Duane Michals, Edward Tufte, and Donovan Wylie to print their books. Robinson also produces the annual catalogue for the MFA students in photography at Yale School of Art, a tradition developed in collaboration with Richard Benson.

Jeff L. Rosenheim is curator in charge of the Department of Photographs at the Metropolitan Museum of Art, New York. He is the author or coauthor of over twenty books on Diane Arbus, Walker Evans, Robert Frank, Paul Graham, Stephen Shore, and others. Rosenheim has lectured at Columbia University, Institute of Fine Arts at New York University, Cooper Union, and Bard College.

Sasha Rudensky is recipient of an Aaron Siskind Individual Photographer's Fellowship and Leica Camera/ Jim Marshall Photo Scholarship. She is a regular contributor to the *New York Times Magazine* and has published her work in *Aperture*, *Artforum*, the *Guardian*, and *Der Spiegel*. She is an associate professor of art at Wesleyan University, where she is also head of the photography program.

Gary Schneider began his career as a printer working with artists such as Richard Avedon, Peter Hujar, Lisette Model, and David Wojnarowicz—as commemorated in the Schneider/Erdman Printer's Proof Collection at Harvard Art Museums. His own work has been recognized via a National Endowment for the Arts Fellowship and a Guggenheim Fellowship, and his publications include *Nudes* (Aperture, 2005), *Handbook: South African Artists* (2015), and *Salters Cottages* (2019).

David Benjamin Sherry currently lives and works in Santa Fe, New Mexico. His work has been featured in group exhibitions at MoMA PS1, New York; George Eastman Museum, Rochester, New York; and Museum of Fine Arts, Boston. Publications of his work include *It's Time* (2010), *Earth Changes* (2015), *American Monuments* (2019), and *Pink Genesis* (Aperture, 2021). In 2020, Sherry joined Yale School of Art as a visiting critic.

Steve Smith is recipient of a Guggenheim Fellowship and Kittredge grant. His publications include *The Weather and a Place to Live: Photographs of the Suburban West* (2005) and *Your Mountain Is Waiting* (2020). He is a longtime professor of photography at the Rhode Island School of Design in Providence.

Mark Steinmetz is a Guggenheim Fellowship recipient and has taught photography at Yale School of Art, Harvard University, and Sarah Lawrence College. He has published over twenty books of his photographs, including *South Central* (2007), *South East* (2008), *Greater Atlanta* (2009), *Angel City West* (2016–19), *South Trilogy* (2021), and *Berlin Pictures* (2021).

Sarah Stolfa is founder and director of TILT Institute for the Contemporary Image in Philadelphia (formerly the Philadelphia Photo Arts Center). Her photographs were published in the monograph *The Regulars* (2009). She is a lecturer at Stuart Weitzman School of Design at the University of Pennsylvania.

Ka-Man Tse has exhibited her work in Hong Kong, as well as in group exhibitions at the Brooklyn Museum, Tate Museum in London, and Leslie-Lohman Museum in New York. She is recipient of a Robert Giard Fellowship and Aaron Siskind Individual Photographer's Fellowship. Tse is director of the BFA photography program at Parsons School of Design in New York.

James Welling has published over thirty books and catalogues of his work, including *Light Sources* (1996), *Flowers* (2007), *Glass House* (2010), *James Welling: Monograph* (Aperture, 2013), and *Choreograph* (Aperture, 2020). Welling was head of the photography area in the Department of Art at University of California, Los Angeles, from 1995 to 2016, and since 2012 has served as professor and lecturer at Princeton University in New Jersey.

Jeff Whetstone is recipient of a North Carolina Arts Council Artist Fellowship and Guggenheim Fellowship. He is a professor and head of photography at Princeton University in New Jersey, where he also serves as director of the Program in Visual Arts.

A book such as this is the product of a genuinely collective effort. Our heartfelt thanks and appreciation for everyone who responded enthusiastically and generously to our request to participate, and our apologies in advance for those who did not make it into the sweep of our calls for participation. Coeditor and designer Miko McGinty has described the project as a visually centered reimagining of a Festschrift, a book form used in academic circles to honor a scholar, typically filled with writings related to the work of the scholar and often the work of doctoral students who directly extend the legacy of the scholar. She and her studio, most notably designer Rebecca Sylvers, were instrumental in finding the right physical form for the project and as well as its editorial shaping. Sarah Stolfa served as an invaluable sounding board and collaborator, and translated the contents of this book into an exhibition that launched at the TILT Institute for the Contemporary Image in Philadelphia and was on view from September 21, 2021, through January 8, 2022.

John Pilson also helped inform the overall approach and framing of the project. Amelia Lang spent countless hours in conversation with the featured contributors, helping to expertly hone many of the anecdotes that appear in this book. Thanks, too, to Peter Kayafas for his loan of books to photograph; and to Barbara Benson for her generous encouragement and for sharing her partner with us.

Finally, this project would not exist without the inspiration of Elizabeth Kahane, one of the many friends and photographers influenced by Richard Benson, who pays forward his generosity by making this book possible. Many thanks to her lead, and to the generosity of Aperture's trustees, in particular Dawoud Bey, Kate Cordsen, and Cathy Kaplan, as well as to the additional generosity of Minnie Cushing Coleman, the Doran Family Foundation, Jeff Hirsch, Carol LeWitt, Suzanne Hellmuth, Jock Reynolds, and the White Cedar Fund.

—Lesley A. Martin

Page 19, Michele Abeles: courtesy the artist and 47 Canal, New York; page 23, James Van Der Zee portfolio: Portland Museum of Art, Maine, Promised Gift of the Judy Glickman Lauder Collection, image courtesy Luc Demers; page 33, press release for *Tina Modotti*: digital image © Museum of Modern Art / Licensed by SCALA / Art Resource, New York; page 51, Shannon Ebner: courtesy the artist, Altman Siegel Gallery (San Francisco), kaufmann repetto (Milan and New York), and Sadie Coles HQ (London); page 57, Paul Strand: © Paul Strand Archive / Aperture Foundation, Inc.; page 67, *English Drawings and Watercolors, 1550–1850*: courtesy Robert J. Hennessey; page 79, Carl Van Vechten: image © Van Vechten Trust, gravure © Eakins Press Foundation; page 107, bound press sheets for *Seeing Things*: courtesy Sue Medlicott; page 109, Sarah Meister: digital image © Museum of Modern Art, New York; pages 110 and 111, *The Printed Picture* installation view: digital image © Museum of Modern Art / Licensed by SCALA / Art Resource, New York, photograph by Jonathan Muzikar; page 113, Bill Brandt: courtesy Hyman Collection, London, photography by Richard Caspole and Robert Hixon, © Bill Brandt / Bill Brandt Archive Ltd; pages 121 and 122–23, Abelardo Morell: courtesy Edwynn Houk Gallery, New York; page 150, *The Printed Picture*: courtesy Miko McGinty Inc.; pages 151 and 152–53, *The Printed Picture* press sheets: courtesy John Robinson; pages 156 and 157, *Home Work*: courtesy Jeff L. Rosenheim; pages 188–89, Dawoud Bey: courtesy Yale University Art Gallery, gift of the artist; pages 29, 30–31, 68, 69, 70–71, 75, 76, 96–97, 99, 101, 161, 162–63, 197, 201, and 213: photography by Daniel Salemi.